SoulStroller

experiencing the weight,
whispers,
& wings of the world

Kayce Stevens Hughlett

Virginia

Published in the United States by WriteLife Publishing
(imprint of Boutique of Quality Books Publishing Company)
www.writelife.com

978-1-60808-201-8 (p)
978-1-60808-202-5 (e)

Library of Congress Control Number: 2018952765

Book design by Robin Krauss, www.bookformatters.com
Cover design by Marla Thompson, www.edgeofwater.com

First editor: Olivia Swenson
Second editor: Pearlie Tan

Praise for SoulStroller and
Kayce Stevens Hughlett

"If you are longing for adventure, Kayce will spark you to book a flight, if you are skeptical of magic, she will turn your heart, and if you are tired of worrying what others think, Kayce will gently take your hand and lead you to a place of peace with yourself and inspire boldness.

"This book is a delight, full of heartfelt stories of courage, love, and loss, brimming with tenderness and vulnerability, dappled with humor, you will keep reading because you want to know how she unfolds and in the process you will experience your own unfolding as well. From bliss to grit and back again, this story feels true because it is so much like true life. And like all good storytelling, it offers you the gift of your life back through a new lens."

—Christine Valters Paintner, PhD,
author of eleven books including
The Soul of a Pilgrim: Eight Practices for the Journey Within

"Hughlett finds her voice in the most unexpected places—amidst the grief of life's challenges, in spaces of letting go, in strengthening through presence."

—Pixie Lighthorse, author of the bestselling book
Prayers of Honoring Voice and the 2018 release of
Prayers of Honoring Grief

Other Books by Kayce Stevens Hughlett

Blue, a novel

As I Lay Pondering: daily invitations to live a transformed life

"I see a time of Seven Generations when all the colors of mankind will gather under the Sacred Tree of Life and the whole earth will become One Circle again."

—Crazy Horse

This journey is dedicated to the generations who have come before me and all those who will follow after.
With hope and gratitude.

Table of Contents

PART SEVEN

PART EIGHT

Shall We Stroll?

SoulStroller (*n.*) A person who is present to life in all its intricate details, who listens to the voice of his or her heart and pays attention with all the senses. A SoulStroller sees connections to past and future while living in the abundance of now. She's willing to take risks and forge her personal pathway, knowing it is inevitable that getting lost and going it alone will be part of the journey. This is how she will be found.

One step, one moment, one heartbeat at a time, a SoulStroller inches, leaps, and soars forward and backward into the fullest version of her true self. Guided by intuition and Spirit, the SoulStroller takes her own hand and strolls through the streets of life—content, curious, compassionate, complete, and filled with gratitude.

A Note from the Author

"Sometimes you must travel far to discover what is near."

—Uri Shulevitz

When I began writing *SoulStroller: experiencing the weight, whispers, & wings of the world*, the working title was *An Accidental Pilgrim*. I thought the overarching story was about my travels—Paris, Egypt, Ireland—and how I'd stumbled into them. Simple enough. I was going to share with readers the places I'd traveled and introduce them to the world through my eyes. Then I began to notice there was no way my inner journey was going to stay out of the narrative.

My story of writing *about* journeys became its own adventure.

In 2013, dear friend and fellow Parisiophile Sharon Richards and I christened the concept of SoulStrolling®. Like this book, our SoulStrolling® business wove its way into being through the stories in our individual lives. Sharon visited Paris for the first time when she was fresh out of college. One moonlit evening she stood atop the Eiffel Tower and whispered, "I'll be back." She's

When we are intentional about our travel, both the travel and the intentions have a way of changing us.

been traveling to the City of Light on a regular basis for more than thirty years. I traveled to Paris for the first time in 2008 and the city wove its magic around my heart too. France is now the most oft-stamped destination in my passport. In his book *The Art of Pilgrimage*, one of our favorite authors, Phil Cousineau, invites readers to "take your soul for a stroll." This became our mission and SoulStrolling® was born!

Through SoulStrolling®, Sharon and I offer adventures for individuals who express a passion to explore extraordinary places, who want to take their personal journeys to new levels, and who seek gentle guidance along the way. SoulStrolling® is a practice of discovering the holiness and wonder in everyday life.

A SoulStroller is a person who chooses to step into the unknown with great intention. To hop on planes to foreign destinations or explore oft-trod neighborhoods with new eyes. To strap on a parachute, take a death-defying leap, and drift into a perfect, soundless stratosphere. To embrace what it means to be inspired, immobile, and immoveable. Action with no visible response. Words without sound. A SoulStroller heeds whispers from the past or present and moves toward the future.

In a very early draft of this book, three of my great aunties hopped into my suitcase and asked to come along for the stroll. My deceased father and young adult son showed up in a recurring dream that I first experienced when I was a girl growing up in Oklahoma. The generations—both living and past—moved seamlessly forward and backward through my thoughts and words as I wrote and slept. They clamored to be heard like sounds on a Sayulita street:

> *Beep, beep, beep. Back up.*
> *Zoom. Yip. Zoom. Forward ho!*
> *Breathe. Flow. Whisper. Listen.*
> *This is how we heal.*

I kept writing page after page, consulting with mentors, attending writing classes and weekly groups. I meditated, prayed, and listened to nature. I scoured my journals and found stories I'd written in the past that spoke to me in the present. It wasn't until I was deep into the writing that I realized this was a story about voice and healing and so much more than descriptions of the places where I'd walked. It was my personal tale of learning to speak up for myself and finding comfort when I was alone. That and more. This story reaches forward and backward and all around me like the spray of the ocean crashing onto volcanic rocks that hold secrets ancient as the heavens. My hope is that it will reach into your life too.

There is no word, adjective, or sound for what it feels like to have all of this—my travels, my great aunts, the rules I despise, and more—wrapped up inside me, pressing to fly out. Words stick in my throat. I hold the tension of weight and wings, grounded and open, love and fear. A mysterious muse calls me to write about voice then leaves me speechless. I long for my words to flow like a river, to wash over each one of us like holy water in Bali or the baptismal font in Notre Dame, to feel the lift of every wing that has held me throughout this incredible journey. Spirit. Yahweh. Mysterious Unknown.

The theme of wings surfaced in Ireland when feathers lined my pathway. They were there on the Camargue in France when I rose from a stallion's saddle to become Pegasus lifting toward the moon in a setting raspberry sun. Hot air balloons waved Sharon and me into a tiny hamlet after a long day's journey, like sphere-shaped feathers dancing in the wind. Pink flamingos sang ça va, ça va on the Mediterranean coast and resplendent peacocks sat with me and read my novel *Blue* in the Bois du Bologne. Wings on t-shirts. Owls in storefronts. Bees, dragonflies, and crows. Birds whispering from palm fronds and barren oak trees, wrapping their silky feathers around the seasons of my life. White birds in Balinese rice fields and parrots racing across a Sayulita sky. Roosters crowing in the middle of the night. Chachalacas making a racket and butterflies as whispery as eyelash kisses.

Weight, whispers, and wings. The stuff of my life.

I had no wings when I dreamed I rolled down a red rock plateau inside a garbage can. I choked on the feathers that others tried to stuff down my throat. I picked wet plumes out of golden pools of rain and wrapped them with twine to make my own magic wand. I declared with great trepidation that I was a wizard, a white witch, a wondrous being in a human—a very human—body.

There are not enough words to describe where I've been or who I'm becoming. I have a hunch the same might be true for you. There is no descriptor for the peace that comes when all the inner and outer chatter ceases and the words and meaning come of their own accord and float to my side.

Author and retreat leader Joan Anderson once said, "There is no arriving, ever. It is all a continual becoming." No wonder it has taken me decades to arrive. There is no arrival. There is only fluidity of time and a continual blossoming. And still I know that I am here now. I am here now. More whole than when I began this story. Wiser. Stronger.

A bumblebee dives into the orange tendrils by my side, swift and fleeting like the time of which I speak. She whispers, "Be. Simply be. Time is not something to master. It is something to befriend and revere. Befriend the years of your becoming, for they are great and true."

True. Truth. Trust. I must trust that I am meant to write these stories of wise bees and laughing ancestors. What better person to speak of ethereal beings than a shy accountant from Oklahoma? For if I can believe in the extraordinary, then anything is possible.

SoulStroller has been written in ways similar to how I travel— loose and fluid, like watching the waves roll out and waiting for what the tide brings in. I once warned a cabin mate to be wary of following me home through the woods as I tend to go off the beaten path. I am an explorer. I find tremendous value in getting lost and finding my way again. In fact, I believe that yielding to the act of being lost, whether it be in my hometown or on foreign soil, is a pivotal building block of who I am today.

An urgent desire fuels me to write more about magic and the ineffable. Alongside the desire, fear arises. What if this is all bunk? What if I carry a healing voice within me and no one listens? What if the secrets I hold cannot be adequately named? Is my lifelong loneliness a product of this fear that I will be misunderstood? What if my words hold the key to unlocking individual truths? It's scary to declare that I hold the secret of bees and butterflies. Do I hold back because I'm afraid to say aloud that I have touched the Great Divine?

How can I speak if I am still the silent one, the lonely girl, the forgotten child who is not important? I linger on my early initiation into loneliness that came one evening in 1962. A tiny princess in a taffeta dress, abandoned in the silence. The weight of alone hanging around my slender neck like a dark talisman. Alone. Always alone. Not important. Always alone. A white butterfly swoops over my head and I swear she is flipping me the finger with her translucent wing. I hear her whisper, "You are not alone. You, my dear, are a wild goddess of the earth. It's time to share the stories of stones, and wings, and magic with the world!"

The Universe conspires on my behalf to continue to heal my pain and bring song to my voice. I know now that I am never alone as long as there is sky and earth, wind, fire, and water. I must remember to flow like water, to burn brightly as the flame that lights my way, and to ground myself in the earth, to roll around in the red clay of my Oklahoma childhood until the dirt and I become one. Only then can I wash myself clean in the oceanic font that is filled with tears of joy and sorrow. "Alone" is the story I needed to make peace with to grow, to heal, to know that I have everything I need in this life.

I had to be silenced before I could learn the power of my voice.

The act of SoulStrolling® begins when something deep inside—a longing, desire, or dream—whispers Come along and your heart or feet respond Yes! Though sometimes, the greatest journey begins with a definitive Hell no!

Most people think of life-changing moments as the day they fell in love or got married, the birth of a child or death of a parent. But what about those moments that come out of left field and smack you down to the ground, bloody your face, or break a limb? When you pull yourself back up, you aren't the same person as when you fell. You don't know how or why or exactly what change the moment has incited, but you know things are different. You are different. You rarely want to relive those moments, because they're *that* kind. The hard kind. The painful kind. The oh-God-why-me kind. But you also know that without that moment, you wouldn't be who you are today.

When my moment arrived, I would have described myself as a brown-eyed Oklahoma good girl who had misplaced her autonomy in daughterhood, wifehood, and motherhood, a dreamer who disregarded her ability to see clearly because she had been looking through everyone else's lenses, and a free spirit who'd given away her soul to the uncompromising conventions of society. I would have described myself that way, except I was also clueless, voiceless, and wordless.

SoulStroller is filled with yes-and-no moments from my life— delightful, disastrous, delicious—but the crystallization began with one smack-down moment when I knew my life would never be the same. Perhaps you've already had your moment. I wouldn't wish those times on anyone, but I wouldn't turn away from mine either, because that moment . . . Well, I'm immensely grateful for it. And perhaps, after reading this book, you might be a measure more grateful for your moment too. How wonderful would that be?

Cheers to SoulStrolling® and to your glorious life!

Kayce S. Hughlett

PART ONE

Way Back When

"Beginnings are sudden, but also insidious. They creep up on you sideways, they keep to the shadows, they lurk unrecognized. Then, later, they spring."

—Margaret Atwood

CHAPTER ONE

Life as I knew it... Gone

"You may not have signed up for a hero's journey, but the second you fell down, got your butt kicked, suffered a disappointment, screwed up, or felt your heart break, it started."

—Brené Brown

Labor Day Weekend, 2003

There is an eeriness in the atmosphere and the sky turns a putrid shade of grayish green moments before a tornado hits. On Labor Day weekend in 2003, the signs of impending doom were less obvious than gray-green skies, but they were there. Deep inside my bones, a niggling unease told me our family walked a fine line between tranquil domesticity and despair. I could feel the twister coming but hoped it would lift back into the sky before striking.

"Who wants to go see *Finding Nemo*?" I asked. It was Saturday morning. Our family of four sat scattered around the kitchen and dining room eating breakfast and catching up on email and current events. It was rare that we were all awake and in one place at the same time.

"Me! Me! Me!" Ten-year-old Janey bounced up and down. "Can I get popcorn?"

"Sure, honey. Movie sounds good to me." My husband Bill looked up from his Blackberry.

"Do I have to go? Sounds lame," Jonathon groaned over his Cheerios.

"It'll be fun," I urged. "We haven't done anything together in a long time and summer's almost over."

"Yeah. I know. I'd rather go to Bumbershoot with my friends," Jonathon pressed.

"We already had this discussion," Bill replied. "No Bumbershoot. You're too young to go alone."

"Daaad." Jonathon made that phlegm-clearing noise, perfected by teenagers everywhere to show disgust as only they can.

I don't remember the inciting conversation or even if there was one, but on that Saturday evening in early September 2003 after we'd gone as a family to see *Finding Nemo* at the Bay Theater, Jonathon walked out of the house and didn't come back. Our beautiful boy with my smile and my father's lean build disappeared.

The hours that followed Jonathon's disappearance were a blur. We called every friend we could think of, but he'd jettisoned his old crowd and the new list was elusive. The hours dragged on. We were panicked maniacs, calling anyone we could think of until we finally called 911 and a kind, somewhat patronizing police officer showed up at our front door.

"These things usually resolve themselves quickly," Officer Bounds assured us. I could feel the subtext: *Overreacting parents, here we go.*

It was odd to see the police woman sitting at our dining room table, poised with her note pad. She reminded me of a young Sharon Gless from *Cagney and Lacey*—feminine, all business, and dressed in navy blue chinos and a white button-up shirt. "Any friend's house he might be at?"

"We've tried them all," Bill answered.

"Okay. What was he wearing when he left?" The questions were incessant, but they felt like our only lifeline to getting Jonathon back. "Eye color? Hair length? Hair color? Height? Weight? Any distinguishing marks?" We answered as best we could.

"All right, Mr. and Mrs. Hughlett. Since he's only fourteen, we can put out a missing person/runaway report and keep an eye out for him. Please let us know if you hear anything."

She left her card on the table along with a copy of the incident report.

"Is Jonathon coming back?" Janey peeked around the staircase where she'd been hovering.

"Of course he is, honey," I assured her with a confidence I didn't feel.

Officer Bounds walked out the front door and moments later Bill headed out the back to begin a late-night driving vigil. It was futile, but necessary. We had to do something. I stayed home with Janey and tried to get some sleep, but mainly I stared at the coved bedroom ceiling. Bill came home around 2:30 a.m., and the two of us tossed and turned together. Our silence was heavy with thoughts of the direst kind. *He's gone. Dead. In a ditch somewhere. Kidnapped. Stabbed. Shot. Lost. Scared. Alone.* There was nothing we could do or say to comfort each other. Exhaustion finally won and we nodded off, only to awaken at daybreak overcome by a sense of guilt that we could sleep while our son was missing.

After a full weekend of hide and seek between Jonathon and us, the *pièce de résistance* came when Bill called from Harborview Medical Center.

"Um, honey, um . . . I don't know how to say this . . ." His voice creaked on the line like a garbled recording. "They've done a blood draw and an intake screening for drugs." He paused and I heard him sob. "The nurse says he needs in-patient treatment *now*." That sentence stretched out over thirty seconds or more.

I could hear my husband talking through the phone line, but his words weren't connecting with my brain.

"Wha-what?" I gasped, breath vacating my lungs and threatening to never return. A mass settled inside my throat while I struggled to inhale. Twilight filtered in through the windows of the living room where I stood. Photos of Bill, Jonathon, Janey, and me smiled down from every angle. I pushed the phone away from my ear as if it were a venomous snake. My arms felt like twenty-pound weights were tied to each wrist, and my legs gave way as though someone had kicked me behind the knees. Curry, our golden retriever, circled me on the Oriental rug, panting in confusion.

Our beautiful, boundary-pushing Jonathon was fourteen years old—full of life, full of confusion, and apparently full of drugs.

Time stopped until anger took hold. *How could this be? What the fuck? No! No! No! It's got to be a mistake!* I was furious. Terrified. Lost. Searching. Grasping for answers. *How did this happen? Why couldn't I protect him? How could I keep him safe?* Nothing had prepared me for this, not even my own experimentation with alcohol and pot that I secretly indulged in as a teenager. The borders of my love and understanding were being stretched to their very limits.

The boundaries that adults set for me when I was a child flared in my mind. *Do things right. Follow the rules. Stay inside the lines and everything will turn out fine.* I once heard that fine was an acronym for fucked up, insecure, neurotic, and exhausted. F.I.N.E. Well, here we were. Everything was fine.

Somehow, I made it to Harborview on that Labor Day evening to meet with Bill, a doctor, and a social worker. Before the night was over, Jonathon had agreed to enter his first in-patient treatment center.

Tired. Bone tired. Weary. Worried. Then and now. Digging up the bones like a grave digger, resurrecting the story of that summer of 2003. I feel the exhaustion of that time, the exhaustion and worry more than the details. The worry I couldn't name, was afraid to name, am still wary to name. The underbelly, undercurrent, the river that runs beneath our stories like the one in Hades. I see it. A river of hell. The one with gaping mouths and peeling flesh and floating bones. A life out of control. A child gone. A mother, wife, and woman, alone with her thoughts.

CHAPTER 2

Follow the Rules

"Maybe, in spite of everything and because of everything, you are miraculously, perfectly whole."

—Bakara Wintner

January 1962

"Mommy, I don't feel so good."

"What? No. You're fine." My mother reaches her painted fingernails (Avon's latest winter shade) toward the bottom of my taffeta dress and fluffs the tulle petticoat into a larger circle. "You were flat on one side. That's better. Now stand up straight."

I'm in kindergarten and my sister, Dianna, is getting married. It's the evening of the rehearsal dinner or some equally important affair. Our household is in a flurry and I've spent all afternoon having my hair brushed and teased by a woman dressed in a bubblegum-colored smock. Her fingertips are brown with nicotine stains and every time she leans down to whisper in my ear to say how pretty I am, I nearly gag from the smell of stale coffee and cigarettes. Now my hair looks like a tiny helmet formed with Aquanet spray. I'm wearing a black velveteen vest that covers my chest like a soft plate of armor. A tiny girl dressed for show, but the attire doesn't protect my fragile soul from the acerbic tone flowing from my mother's lips, which match her nail polish.

"This'll have to do." She tries to adjust a stiff curl next to my right cheek. The curl resists.

I squeak out the words one more time. "But I don't feel good."

"Goodness gracious, Kayce. I don't have time for this. It's a big day. You should enjoy it. Now, let's go." She tugs at my hand, but I don't move. "What?" She throws me the look.

I feel my heart withering underneath the velvet bolero and my throat closes up inside my dry mouth. My pink-glossed lips tighten into a grimace and I feel my two front teeth wobble under the pressure. My tiny body wavers and when I think I might fall on the floor, my mother scoops me up and lays me on my sister's four poster bed. A deep sigh escapes her lips. "We'll be back later," she says and turns away, closing the door without a backward glance.

I grew up in Bethany, Oklahoma, a land of red earthen clay trimmed with miles of golden fields and dotted by man-made lakes and oil derricks. Oklahoma is a far cry from the evergreen landscape of Seattle where I now reside. In Oklahoma, blistering humidity leaves a sheen of moisture across your skin through the summer, which begins in April and can carry on until November when storms, brutal with black ice, become sport for those brave enough to dare driving on it. I have a healthy respect for black ice.

Born the second daughter and third child to Daisy Ernestine (an Avon lady) and John David Stevens (a mechanic and truck driver), I was raised to follow rules and be polite while doing so. I was constantly corrected about appropriate use of grammar—always say please and thank you, never say "ain't." My crooked posture was a source of constant criticism from my mother and other teachers. I attended etiquette school to become more ladylike and soaked up beauty pageant culture, although I never qualified to compete. I wore corrective shoes, had plastic surgery for a lop-sided lip at age thirteen, and frequented beauty parlors from the age of five. But inside my well-groomed exterior beat the heart of a street fighter, a "firecracker" as my son once called me.

As my mind scans through the stories of my early childhood, I can hear my mother speaking as though I were still six years old. "Kayce's our shy girl. She doesn't talk much." I ingested that line like a dark witch's potion. I tucked the potential firecracker into my back pocket with the fuse on a slow burn. Instead of lighting up my world, I chose to believe that as long as I followed everyone else's rules and stayed within the lines, life would turn out right, no matter what the situation.

Inside the silence and all of the rules, I learned that asking for what I wanted or being my true self often led to disaster—someone got hurt, disappointed, or felt ashamed. One of my earliest memories is standing in my crib with outstretched arms. I'm about two years old. I can see the anguish on my face and hear my own wailing cry. I need someone to comfort me. Perhaps I've had a bad dream or my diaper is full. It doesn't really matter. In my mind, I see my young mother nursing a black eye and for a moment I wonder if my father was to blame, but in a flash of certainty I know the answer is no. I was the one responsible. I feel it in my bones.

I remember that Mother was on her way to get me that night when she misjudged the angle of the doorway in her grogginess and hit the doorframe with her upper cheek. In the chaos that ensued—mild cursing, tears, an icepack—I was forgotten, left standing alone, and my mother was the injured party.

There was always a downside to being me. I'd be having a glorious time one moment and the next minute criticism or self-doubt would bring the joy-making to a halt. Kindergarten was the one magical place in my childhood memories. Skipping around the block to Mrs. Peck's school was a grand adventure. I had a sparkling wand of ribbons and stars and loved to wake the other children up after naptime on our floor mats. I felt like a fairy princess.

On my walks to and from Mrs. Peck's, dandelion wishes called my name and stray kittens became my best friends. If I was feeling especially naughty, I'd scan the block to make sure no one was looking, then scuff my saddle Oxfords on the pavement. The white leather reminded me of the heavy corrective shoes I had to wear at nighttime. Sleeping in the torturous contraption was supposed to correct my toes that turned in at an unacceptable angle. They had a thick metal bar attached to the soles with the toes turned outward. It's hard to SoulStroll when your feet are tethered together.

A SoulStroller has feet free to wander.

Another story surfaces. I'm six years old and it's September in Mrs. Collins's first grade class. I have to pee. I glance at the black-and-white clock over the door and hope it's close to dismissal time. No such luck. Bulletin boards with neat displays of Dick and Jane readers are arranged around the room, and a row of twelve-inch-high alphabet letters sits beneath the florescent lighting panels. I inch my right hand into the air like a soldier offering a flag of surrender. The teacher doesn't see me although I swear we make eye contact. I curl inward and feel the underside of my plaid wool skirt stick to the seat and form an itchy nest around my thighs. My Oxford shoes create a muted tap dance on the black-and-white tiled floor as I shimmy side to side, holding my breath and trying to be quiet.

See me. Don't see me. See me. Don't see me. My feet wiggle side to side and my left hand slides beneath my skirt, putting pressure on the white cotton panties that cover the v of my crotch. It's wet, damp. I'm losing the battle to hold the flow back. I hope my classmates don't notice the sudden whoosh.

For a moment relief fills my sixty-pound body until I look down and see the putrid yellow ring at my feet. I try to make myself as small as possible and concentrate on keeping the crayons within the lines of my coloring sheet. I seek perfection on the page in front of me even though I know the wrong I've committed won't go unnoticed.

After my classmates pour out of the room like bumbling puppies, Mrs. Collins stares at the puddle in disdain, clucks something under her breath, then turns away to call my mother, whose own embarrassment is evident in her face when she comes to get me.

In fourth grade my mother, father, best friend, and I went to a lake resort for a long weekend. My friend and I felt the freedom of running around the complex on our own, giggling as we pushed every elevator button before climbing out and scuttling poolside to sip Coca-Cola. The most present memory of that time, however, was when I later found a photo of my friend and me on the diving board. When my mother saw it, she commented on my chunky thighs and roundish belly, then insinuated how it was too bad I wasn't more petite like my friend. I was ten years old.

When we were thirteen, that same friend used her small hands to write in my journal about an incident that I was too ashamed to pen for myself. One day a boy from our class stopped by my house after football practice. My parents were out and when he realized this, he said something lame like "I'm tired." Before I understood what was happening, we were laying on my bed. His attention was sweet and confusing. I'd only kissed one boy before, during a spin-the-bottle game at a sixth-grade party. The boy on my bed kissed me with dry, closed lips and then without prelude, slipped his sweaty hand under my blouse and proceeded to fondle my bra-covered breasts. A dull roar rose in my ears, laced with my mother's words: *Good girls don't.* I'm not sure if she ever finished that sentence, but it spoke volumes on its own. Tears formed in the corners of my eyes, and I lay on my bed like the giant Raggedy

Ann doll in the corner of my room and waited for the time to be over. Once again, my words failed me.

Good girls don't was the mantra of my hometown in the '60s and '70s. While women's liberation was happening around the country, the preachers, teachers, and parents of Bethany, Oklahoma, were making sure that young ladies behaved in a respectable manner. My mother's sex talk consisted of our hometown mantra, plus her sage advice not to sit on boys' laps, "because they can't handle it." Girls were divided into three classes of sexual prowess: those who did it, those who didn't, and those who probably did but kept it very well hidden. I fell solidly into the middle group until I was in college, when heavy petting mixed with alcohol and low-grade marijuana tipped me over the edge into a "girl who did it."

In August 1976, I married the boy who'd been my first sexual partner and who brought me flowers when my father died in a trucking accident eleven months earlier. I was nineteen years old. My sister and mother tried to talk me out of getting married at such a young age, but for once, I swore I knew what was best for me. They didn't know I'd broken the sacred good-girls-don't rule, and I was certain that if they did know, they'd agree this was the best course of action.

Dressed in a full-length white gown and veil, preparing to walk down the aisle, my inner voice screamed *Run!* Instead of listening, I pasted a smile on my face and put one foot in front of the other. Like Scarlett O'Hara in *Gone with the Wind*, I determined I would figure things out later. Standing at the end of the aisle, I couldn't even consider disappointing that church full of people. Money had been spent and expectations set, plus my vocal chords were weak. They had no practice speaking true desires.

Around the time of our first anniversary, I decided it was time to break free from the young marriage. We liked each other, but our love was tepid. I went so far as to rent a small room near the university campus where I was working and my husband was finishing school. Then I told my mother about my plans. Even though she'd tried to talk me out of the union, she was adamantly opposed to divorce.

"No one in our family has ever been divorced," she reminded me. Keeping up appearances was a huge part of our family culture. "The first year is always hard. You'll get used to it," she said. So I stayed. When my husband finished college and began working full time, I left my administrative job and went back to school to finish my accounting degree. About a year after I began working in Tulsa, Oklahoma, my husband and I finally agreed that it didn't make sense to stay together. We amicably divorced six and a half years after we married.

One divorce, a second marriage, and thirteen years after I'd walked down the aisle and heard the prompt to *run*, Jonathon was born in May 1989. Little did I know my firstborn child would be one of my greatest teachers, and that he would induct me into a world where breaking and creating rules was the norm rather than the exception. Without understanding why or how, he would be instrumental in helping me realize that it was time to live my own life and toss off the chains of perfection and piety I'd been obeying for so many years.

CHAPTER 3

Beautiful Boy

"Perhaps it takes courage to raise children."

—John Steinbeck

Neither Bill nor I ever claimed to be perfect parents, but we'd always done the best we could, driven by love and a modicum of Christian fear. As adults we can tout our parenting skills, lack thereof, or claim nature versus nurture in measuring our successes and failures, but I believe children come into this world with their own personalities and agendas, ready to conquer their world. Jonathon's disappearance and subsequent admission to Harborview was not the first time he had done something that was difficult for us to understand. Our 6 lb. 13 oz. baby boy came into this world with the foremost mission to stretch boundaries and challenge us, his parents, to follow him into uncharted territory, whether or not we were ready to go there.

One evening in 1992 when I was six months pregnant with Janey, I was trying to get dinner on the table before Bill got home from work. Jonathon went onto the back porch and pushed the gas grill against the screen door, trapping me inside the house. He looked me in the eye, pulled down his pants, and pooped all over the back porch. He was three years old.

In that moment, my sense of humor was stretched into non-existence. I hightailed it out the front door, stormed around our corner lot, came in through the back gate, looked at the mess on the porch, and burst into tears. Was God laughing at this childish display or shaking his head in judgment? Was Jonathon relaying a deeper message or merely stretching his independence? The only thing I felt at the time was that I was a failure as a mother. Even the pediatrician shook her head when I relayed the incident to her later. She had no words of compassion or encouragement. I was on my own without a manual to figure out this new chapter of raising and being a human.

Looking back, I realize I wasn't prepared for this bundle of creativity. I was busy memorizing parenting plans and organizing carpools and fundraisers. Jonathon was a child who needed freedom as much as, if not more so, than he needed a plan. Bursting with innate talent, he created realistic artistic renderings from the time he could hold a pencil, made fabulous costumes out of masking tape and Legos, and spent hours enamored by bumblebees he would capture in a jar, then let go at the end of the day.

In the sixth grade, Jonathon was fed up with the plan we'd created, so he flipped the bird, gave the finger, whatever you want to call it, to his favorite teacher at the small private school that experts had recommended would be a "solid, structured fit" for him. His action caused an uproar, fueled by comments like "behavior unbecoming a good Christian boy." I was mortified, confused, and exhausted.

Standing in the shower one morning shortly after the incident, I heard an audible whisper: *Bring him home.* The message both shocked and terrified me, but I also felt a deep sense of peace inside my soul. After much discussion, Bill and I agreed it was the best decision for all, so we pulled our son out of school, and I joined the ranks of homeschooling moms.

Homeschooling Jonathon was a journey in itself. While Bill and

I knew it was the right course of action at the time, I was a novice in the world of lesson plans and middle school education. It's easier to remember what I learned during those eighteen months than what course work Jonathon and I covered. In the writing of this book, however, I remembered how we studied ancient Egypt and the land of the pharaohs where I would travel a few years later. We also studied Michelangelo's masterpieces and Vincent Van Gogh's world as an artist that came to life for me when I eventually visited France and Italy. Future SoulStrolling memories were forming while I homeschooled my son.

In addition to lessons on art and history, I affirmed that Jonathon had his own unique way of taking in information that looked nothing like mine or many of his peers. He absorbed stories best by having them read to him rather than reading them himself. Words on the page frustrated him. He preferred drawing to writing, so it became my pleasure to read stories aloud to him while he lay on the sofa with his head in my lap. He taught me that paying attention doesn't always mean sitting at attention and making eye contact.

Written tests stymied him, but I knew he was learning because he could remember and discuss concepts and topics we'd studied days before with great accuracy. He wasn't a traditional student, and unlike his mother who had sucked it up and obeyed the rules, he was bursting to break free and making it known. He yearned to be a normal kid, not a sheltered child, and made it his personal mission to attend public school. Bill and I agreed to give it a try if Jonathon finished his curriculum by a set date in the springtime, which he did. For the final quarter of his seventh grade school year, we enrolled him in Seattle Public Schools.

Letting go of the reins was necessary, but looking back, I can't help but wonder how things might have been different if we'd made another choice. By the time school was out in June, we'd been summoned to the principal's office more than once, and Jonathon was banned from an end of year school trip "for his personal safety." According to the principal, he'd made an enemy of another kid and been threatened with bodily harm. The school thought it best if he stayed home that day. The public school experiment had failed. We were at our wits' end both parenting- and education-wise, so Jonathon spent his eighth grade year at a wilderness program outside of Black Mountain, North Carolina.

After he returned home almost a year later, our roller coaster existence continued. Jonathon stretched the boundaries. We tightened curfews and house rules. He broke them. The cycle spiraled until that weekend in 2003 when his childhood came to an abrupt halt and the world as I knew it shattered. I was left, once again, with the task of making a new plan and trying to figure out how to reassemble the pieces of our broken family.

CHAPTER 4

Entering the Desert

"The desert is a place of deep encounter, not superficial escape. The ultimate paradox of the desert is that to find ourselves in it, we have to relinquish everything we think we know about ourselves."

—Christine Valters Paintner

November 2003

Three months and two treatment programs after Jonathon's overdose on Labor Day weekend, I found myself alone on a road in Mexico driving to check out yet another therapeutic boarding school for our son. This one was in Kino Bay, a small fishing village on the mainland, nestled between rugged coastal mountains and the Sea of Cortez. It lies sixty miles due west of Hermosillo, the capital of Sonora. Bill's vacation time had been exhausted with other visits to treatment centers, and my part-time accounting job allowed more flexibility. Therefore, I became the designated parent to visit this school that could be the next step for Jonathon on his road to recovery.

Until then, my experience with travel had always been in the company of others. I was well into my fifth decade by the time I acquired my first passport. Before that, travel consisted of visits to see family around the United States: Oklahoma City, Houston, San Diego, New York City. Bill, the kids, and I spent our scarce weeks of vacation each year sleeping in relatives' guest rooms or buying package deals to destinations like Disneyland and Cabo San Lucas. We followed the roles our parents had modeled before us.

As far as Mexico went, I'd only visited border towns like Tijuana or Matamoros, plus one rowdy pre-marriage vacation to Cancun. My knowledge of the Spanish language was limited to *Hola* and *Me llamo Kayce*—not very helpful when I had to negotiate car rental contracts and road signs.

After a jarring layover in Las Vegas where slot machines spat out quarters and half dollars and machines unrelentingly chanted "Wheel . . . of . . . Fortune!" (which my brain transcribed into "Bad . . . Bad . . . Mother!"), I arrived in Hermosillo. I felt like I might throw up when the rental car agent escorted me to the compact, canary yellow vehicle with a horizontal crack across the windshield. It was hideous and foreign, just like my situation. Breath caught in my chest and throat, and my sweaty hands shook as I placed the key in the ignition. If I'd known about mirroring and metaphor at the time, I could have told you the crack in the windshield was a reflection of my broken life and the shattered expectations of what I thought life was supposed to look like.

I was convinced the car was a wind-up toy, and if it was in fact a real vehicle, I'd probably just signed papers agreeing that it was unsafe to drive and suspected of being stolen. I had serious doubts about whether it would make it the sixty miles to Kino Bay. I wasn't sure I even wanted to arrive, but my body kicked into autopilot. Numbly, I kept my foot on the gas pedal, one mile after another.

The previous driver had cranked the radio to its highest decibels, and nothing in me registered that I had the power to turn it down. As I left the airport, the tinny stereo screamed unrecognizable lyrics at me while I headed west along the narrow two-lane "highway." The surreal nature of the situation clutched at my insides, like my own hands gripping the ragged steering wheel. I was in a desolate landscape, racing against the sunset to reach a place I had never been and didn't really want to go. I was miles away from any life as a mother (or woman) that I could ever have imagined.

I wanted to scream. I wanted to quit. I wanted to drive off the edge of the earth and make the madness of my world stop. *What the hell am I doing here? How can this be right? Why am I here all alone?* My mind raged to the beat of the blaring radio. The miles ticked off, each one seeming like a hundred. Time folded and warped like it had that day in our living room when Bill called from Harborview. I wasn't sure whether I could pick myself up this time. I felt like Jesus on the cross. *My God, my God, why have you forsaken me?*

As I rounded a bend in the pot-holed road, the quality of the atmosphere shifted and my heart rate slowed. As if a magician had pulled an active volcano from his knapsack and tossed it across a canvas of sky, pure unadulterated beauty spread out in one of the most breathtaking sights I have ever witnessed.

In front of me stood a vast saguaro cactus field in silhouette, like worshippers with uplifted arms raised toward the heavens, backlit in beauty, singing to the sky, powerful and majestic. The wild vista held me spellbound, wrapped in those mighty arms, like being safe in a mother's gentle caress.

Even though I had been warned over and over to reach Kino Bay before sunset (and darkness was coming fast), I couldn't resist pulling to the side of the purported perilous road. As the car slowed, the head-banging music drifted into the background and the darkening sky burst into wild shades of fire and azure. Cloud-like tendrils reached toward the heavens. The fingers of God waved in the breeze and an incredible sense of peace and hope washed over me. I knew I was no longer alone.

Like the desert fathers and mothers who fled to the wilderness in search of solace, I had reached a personal place of deep encounter, and there was nothing superficial about my escape. Looking back, I know that this was the paradox of beginning to find myself while at the same time relinquishing life as I had known it. I was crossing a border both physically and spiritually. There would be no turning back. Only moving forward. The journey was mine to live. This path was made to follow.

March 2004

"How long have you been writing?" I can still hear Alix's voice as if we spoke yesterday. She was another mother I'd been paired with to do our Twelve Step work during the parents' weekend in Kino Bay, five months after my first visit in the beat-up yellow car.

"I don't write" came my reply.

Midway through our long day of training, Wally, the teacher and leader of our parents' class on co-dependency (modeled after the Twelve Steps of Alcoholics Anonymous), invited each of us to find a quiet place to practice step number eleven: meditation.

Meditate on command? Are you kidding me? The voice inside my head groaned at the man with a fringe of reddish brown hair circling his crown. He reminded me of a gentle medieval monk. Still, being the conformist, I picked up my paper and pen and headed outside into the warm Sonoran air.

I longed for respite at the beach, but it was too far for me to get there and back in the short time we had for the exercise. Instead, I chose a place next to the rectangular swimming pool of the modest motel and settled in with my pad and pen. I'd never meditated before and wondered how it might be like prayer. Actually, I wondered if meditation might be acting against the laws of prayer as I knew them. My conservative Judeo-Christian upbringing was firmly implanted, and fear remained a major patriarch in my life. What if this meditation thing was against God's plan? What if lightning struck? What if I opened the doors to the unknown? What if?

Wally had given us simple instructions: *Be still and notice what arises. Take notes if you like.* It sounded harmless enough.

Sitting beside the pool, I closed my eyes, settled my back against a concrete pillar, and stretched my legs out in front of me on the retaining wall. I took one deep breath and then another. My shoulders softened and my bones warmed in the sunshine. It may have been the first time I'd relaxed in weeks. I felt like a cat curling up for a nap—that is, until the words began to flow with a force I'd never before experienced. It was like taking dictation and my hand could barely keep up with the pace.

Follow your dreams.

Figure out what they are.

Do them with Bill.

Seek guidance from others.

Follow Me.

Quiet your heart. Be still.

Tune the naysayers out.

Hear the birds.

Be still my soul.

Love your son. Love him well. Forgive him.

Relax. Feel the breeze. Feel the moment.

Pray.

Do the work.

Feel the wind. The wind blows hard. The wind is blowing your family in a new direction. Guide the sails through Me.

Forget about Seattle. Seize the day.

Step out of your comfort zone. Forget about comfort. You are still young.

Save the children. You have a gift.

Let them encourage you. God, I'm scared! *I will be with you.*

Be still and listen.

You are an encourager. It is your spiritual gift.

Help the families with your gift.

Tears streamed down my face and blurred the ink on the page.

Lord, please stop! It's too much. Too much.

And then my pen ran out of ink, but not before one last whisper.

It's okay. You can stop now. This is only the beginning.

With wobbly knees and trembling hands, I stood up and made my way to the bathroom. When I looked in the mirror, my reflection seemed somehow different. I splashed water on my face and looked again at the unfamiliar woman staring back at me. Like the story in the Bible of Moses coming down from the mountain, I was glowing. Had I just heard God? I was having a hard time catching my breath and wandered toward the snack table to grab a Diet Coke—something, anything familiar.

Wally opened a tiny window that day and my hungering soul flew through it. The still, small voice that I'd allowed to be replaced by booming voices of culture, society, and boasting preachers raised her vibration through my open hand and declared above the rest, *This is only the beginning.*

Mysterious seeds of personal power were planted by the pool that afternoon. I had come to another fork in my journey. Two choices spread before me. I could let the overwhelming events of my past and present carry me further along the road of despair and complacency. Or I could acknowledge the miracle of that moment in the sun and carry my tender spark forward onto a mysterious and unknown path.

It felt like my authentic voice was asking me to write, a practice I'd given up in fourth grade because of overzealous teachers wielding red pens who told me my words were imperfect. *Ignore or step forward? Flee or fly? Bury the words or write more?* Writing, as it turned out, chose me.

Shortly after I returned home from that parents' weekend in Kino Bay, I received a package in the mail from Alix, the woman who'd asked how long I'd been writing. The gift was a slightly worn copy of Julia Cameron's *The Artist's Way*. I devoured it like the sky swallowing the sound of church bells. It was pure magic. I began to take myself on Cameron-prescribed "artist dates"—days set aside for my personal creative encouragement—and I started naming the darkness in my life on the pages of my journal. I wrote about dreams and disappointments, where I'd been, and who I longed to become. I considered how I could take my struggles with motherhood and turn them into something that could benefit others. I wrestled with the balance between doing for others and healing myself. I longed for the place those two actions might intersect. During this time, the option of graduate school arose via another miraculous path and by June 2004, I was enrolled in classes and working on a master's degree in counseling psychology.

For decades, I'd let the voices of the naysayers be the loudest in my world. When did I forget to trust my own voice that had always been there? I could hear it in the wind and see it in the sky, but there was a part of me that said, "Don't listen," and I complied.

My mind tried to tell me that my life's true story was lost. An internal encourager said, "Start writing" and the story wound its way back to me . . . as if by magic.

CHAPTER 5

Voice, Call, & Kittens

"Not all explicable things are true. Not all truths are explicable."

—Jan-Phillip Sendker

Voice and call are intimately intermingled concepts. For me, the call feels bigger than voice, and while still internal, its qualities seem less within my control. The call is expansive and epic, like a ship named *Destiny* or the foreshadow to a shift in our spiritual center of gravity. It reeks of transformation and invitation into the unknown. With the call comes a request, but it is our inner or outer voice that has the ability to refuse or accept. Voice, while sometimes difficult to articulate, is within our personal control. It carries its own power.

For decades, I refused the call to strengthen my own spirituality. Each time I heard my intuition speak, I turned it off like a drippy water spigot. It happened as a child when I soaked up Bible stories blindly and didn't ask the questions that were on my tongue, like how could a loving God send more than half the world's population to hell simply because they'd never heard of Jesus Christ? Or how come God was a man, and why was Eve punished when Adam ate the apple, too? And how were all those children and races populated from two people? Where did all the colors come from? My voice should have had the power to ask those questions, but I'd been taught to not question my elders, and I had come to believe my mother's line that I was the shy, silent one with nothing of value to say. As long as my mom, dad, teacher, sister, brother, grandmother, grandfather, aunt, uncle, or anyone older than I had a plan for me, then it was my job to comply with it.

I may have squeaked out a few of my questions in Sunday school until the teacher patted me on the head and said something patronizing like "That's just the way it is, sweetheart. God can do everything." I couldn't fully dismiss this God who they preached about, but the pat answers were unsatisfying to my young self. Even with all my unanswered questions, I clung to the belief that a being greater than I existed in our Universe. I'd always felt the presence of something ineffable, even when the "facts" never quite made sense. Still, I turned to other human beings most often for wisdom and guidance.

When I was in high school and exploring majors for college, I had a conversation with my older brother and his wife. My role in the family had always been "the baby." My sister was "the pretty one," and my brother was "the smart one." It made sense, therefore, to ask his advice. I didn't really understand what college credits or majors meant, but since my choice—according to my parents—was to either go to college (which they would pay for) or go to work, college sounded like an appealing option.

My brother and his wife suggested I major in something easy, like "fashion merchandising" (their words, not mine). Their suggestion of an easy major made me feel like I wasn't smart enough for anything challenging even though I'd graduated in the top 10 percent of my huge high school class. My scholarly status hadn't been cause for celebration. Getting high grades was one more thing that good girls did.

My choices in life (and thereby my voice) continued to rely heavily on others, so I took my sibling's advice and began the semester in the home economics department at Oklahoma State University. I hated it. The teachers told us what was appropriate to wear to class if we wanted to succeed, and I was becoming tired of people telling me what to and what not to do. I was away from home for the first time and ready to test my wings. When the dean said no jeans allowed in class (and this was 1974, people!), I sought out a guidance counselor to look for a new major. My parents were supportive but emphasized they would not pay for a sociology or psychology degree, even though psychology had been my favorite class during my first semester. They would only support something "practical and useful."

By second semester, I was in the school of business working toward an accounting degree even though it nearly bored me to tears. By the end of my sophomore year, my father had died and I was in love and in mourning (even though I couldn't acknowledge the latter). My grades dropped and one of my accounting teachers assured me that I would never cut it as an accountant. So, I quit school and got married. It seemed reasonable at the time.

Two years later I re-enrolled at Tulsa University and proved that professor wrong by achieving high marks and getting hired by an international accounting firm. The work still didn't excite me, but the pay was good, and it was certainly practical and useful. I might have been moving in a direction that wasn't my passion, but I was inching toward doing it my way.

SoulStrollers are aware and act intentionally, following their true inner voice.

Several years later, married for the second time with a growing family of my own, I still leaned heavily on other people's opinions. I resisted the internal nudges to change the course of my own family life when I let others tell me how to raise my children, where we should go to church, where the kids should be in school, which books were appropriate to read, and what rules to revere to stay in accordance with the word of God.

As I went about my journey with little self-awareness or intention, the weight of the refusals to claim my own voice grew within me.

December 2004

The sun was fading in the December sky of Kino Bay where Bill, Janey, and I had traveled to spend Christmas with Jonathon, who was completing his fourteenth month in the therapeutic boarding school there. On our drive west from Hermosillo, there was no blazing cactus field to welcome us like I had experienced before, only a stucco residence, a handful of teenage boys in khaki pants and navy polo shirts, and a few house counselors. It could have been a frat house at a US college, except the boys were younger and not necessarily there by choice.

As we stood in the entryway, two boys passed by, their wrists tied together.

"What's that about?" I asked Jonathon. He shrugged.

"They were having a hard time getting along," answered one of the counselors. "We thought maybe a little togetherness might help resolve their issues."

Jonathon rolled his eyes and said, "I'm hungry. What's for dinner?"

Upon our arrival, some of the other parents told us about a great taco stand in Old Kino, the village on the other side of town where the locals lived, as opposed to Kino Bay, which was filled with expatriates and newer construction. Old Kino sounded like an adventure, a way to break the ice and reacquaint our family after several months apart.

Settling into the rental car, we drove the three miles to the other side of town. We were happy to be together *and* it felt like any errant word could shatter the pseudo-calm. After a few minutes, we arrived at the crossroads we'd been given (there were no street numbers or signs) and entered "the restaurant" through a faded wooden gate. On the patio, half a dozen picnic tables were arranged around the backyard of someone's home. An oversized outdoor oven emitted puffs of gray smoke like a wild steam engine. A thirty-something woman in a white cotton top and floral skirt motioned toward a square table with four plastic white chairs and a blue-and-white checked tablecloth. Bill sat to my right, Janey to my left, and Jonathon across from me, his green eyes brighter than they'd been the last time we saw him.

"Would you like something to drink?" the woman asked.

"Jarritos. Orange," Jonathon answered.

"Me too."

"Me three."

"Me four."

She nodded, then turned and walked into the house. I could see part of a kitchen and an overstuffed floral sofa next to it, bathed in the flickering light of a television screen. At the table, we scanned the creased paper menu she left behind. It offered basically one item: *carne asada*. We laughed. Would you like the carne asada platter or the carne asada tacos? Good thing we were all carnivores.

While we waited for our food beneath the bare white lightbulbs strung across the patio, something soft brushed my ankle and scurried out of sight.

"Oh!" I startled before seeing Jonathon's face brighten.

"Mom! Mom, look! Kittens!" he exclaimed, diving out of his seat, long fingers stretching to pet them.

Three tabby kittens, maybe nine weeks old, tumbled across the stone patio. One peeked out from behind a tattered cupboard while the other two disappeared beneath another table. The joyful child inside me lurched forward to join my son, but before I could lift out of my seat, an invisible glass wall slammed in front of me. Instead of responding to the carefree tug to leap and play alongside Jonathon, I heard a voice that sounded vaguely like mine say, "No! Don't touch them. They're dirty."

Clutching the Jarritos in my hand, I saw my blue-eyed husband nod to affirm my negative response. An image of myself at twelve years old flashed through my mind, and I heard my mother telling me not to pet stray kittens because they were dirty. The naysayers pushed an invisible button and the glass wall rolled up between my longing to pet the furry creatures and the word that came out of my mouth: No. I shook my head again and lowered my eyes in what I now know was shame, but not before seeing the damage written on Jonathon's face. Still, I felt helpless to do anything different.

Becoming self-aware is essential for a SoulStroller even when it's messy or challenging.

I'm so sorry, sweet boy. I didn't know any better.

By this time, I was a first-year graduate student studying counseling psychology, and I was becoming aware of the impact of the cultural and familial messages that filled my psyche. It had been a rough couple of semesters as I learned that family dynamics didn't have precise outcomes like columns of debits and credits. The tidy structures I'd always relied on were shifting, and while I knew becoming more self-aware was essential for both me and my family, the work was messy and at times excruciating.

All I wanted to do in that moment was feel soft kitten fur beneath my fingers, to experience the joy of being a child, and to laugh with my children. Instead, I shut everything down with the shake of my head.

I could make my husband out to be the bad guy in this scenario by saying he was the one who made me say no, but that would be the easy way out and he wasn't the bad guy. He was merely a person sitting at the table doing what he thought was best at the time. It had been me—not Bill or my mother—who had said no. I was responsible for my own choices and in that moment, I chose to listen to old scenarios instead of acknowledging my internal longings. I wondered if there was any inkling of my own voice left. My son knew what I was refusing, even before I did. He understood that those kittens were the harbinger to a call that represented all the times I'd said no when I really wanted to say yes.

Sitting there with my son who didn't feel like he could trust me, a husband I felt like I couldn't trust, and a daughter wondering what had just happened, I wanted to crawl under the table and disappear. Even with decades of good-girl, get-it-right messages to keep me company, I had never felt so alone in my life.

CHAPTER 6

The Silence of Going Solo

"To dig deeper into the self, to go underground, is some-times necessary, but so is the other route of getting out of yourself, into the larger world, into the openness in which you need not clutch your story and your troubles so tightly to your chest."

—Rebecca Solnit

In those early years of self-discovery, between the time a social worker recommended drug and alcohol treatment for Jonathon and the summer of 2006 when I completed my degree in counseling psychology, our family was immersed in the therapeutic world. We attended group family sessions, personal counseling appointments, and experiential workshops where we pounded mattresses to release pent-up emotions and spent days in isolation to confront our deepest fears. I discovered there was nothing like a deserted island to highlight the profound abandonment and loneliness issues that haunted me.

Three days into a week-long workshop in Texas in June 2005, the facilitators awoke the six female participants before daybreak, told us to pack a modicum of items that didn't include cell phones or other electronics, loaded us into a small life raft, then ferried us out to a small island in the middle of Lake Texoma, a lake I'd frequented as a child.

I stood on the beach with my supplies—water, tarp, sleeping bag, journal—and watched the jet ski and empty raft shrink into the distance. My inner chatter was incessant from the moment I set foot on the sand. *You're a fool. What the hell are you doing here? You'll never get this right. You're alone. Always alone. Never important.* The mantra of alone taunted me as I stared out at the lake and realized I'd been left to figure things out on my own. *They've left you here, you know. You'll never get anything right. You won't survive.* If I was alone, then why were there so many voices yammering inside my head?

Less than a mile from shore and the comfort of a warm bed, I might as well have been sitting on a volcanic speck in the middle of the Pacific Ocean. The sound of racing jet skis and motorboats punctuated the summer air. We had each been given a cordoned patch of land—perhaps fifty feet square—to call home for I didn't know how long. A hundred feet to the south of my campsite, I could see the edge of my friend Lisa's tarp if I tried, and directly to the north, I caught a glimpse of Laura's white blouse. Our site boundaries were marked with fluorescent orange tape, and we were expressly forbidden from crossing them with our feet or our words. A brush-filled incline with scrubby plants rose to the east with wide open water in the west. I stood on the sand, wrapped in a rare moment of silence that drowned out the chattering voices in my mind—until they began again.

Loser. Wimp. Fraud. You're not important. It's all a trick. They've left you here. You'll starve to death or die from the headache that's no doubt a brain aneurysm waiting to burst.

I wanted to scream, but that wasn't ladylike. Instead I struggled to attach my tarp to the strongest of the spindly bushes but the damned plant bent and refused to hold the weight of my tarp. I failed, then whipped my head to the left and the right, certain that the others were spying on me and laughing their heads off at my expense.

Why didn't I eat dinner last night? There was no food in my small knapsack, no nourishment in my mind. Only the nattering of a thousand years of conditioning. *Be perfect. Get this right. This is a test and you're failing. Have failed. Will always fail. You're a horrible mother. A horrid, wicked failure of a woman. You can't even provide shelter for yourself, much less anyone else. Your son. Your daughter. Your husband. They're not here now. It's only you, babe.*

Only me.

It turns out that I was a formidable ally and advocate for myself. Despite the near manic talk in my head and my incessant need to always get things right, those qualities ended up being exactly what I needed on that deserted island. I needed silence and time away from my daily life to hear what that chatter was really telling me. I needed to dig in and explore what I was actually afraid of so I could face those fears head on instead of watching them lash out sideways.

After wallowing in my "poor me" attitude for a while, I finally found a twig strong enough to hold my tarp so I could have a square foot of shade. I plopped onto the ground and opened the packet given to me by the facilitators. Homework.

Great. Sarcasm reared her ugly head. *Yay! Something to do so I don't have to think about the heat and the fact that I have no food.* Good girls are proficient at homework.

I struggle to convey all that transpired on that island in about thirty-six hours. Minutes passed like slow syrup as I lay under the shadow of my tarp with sweat pouring down my back. Biting flies. Sweltering heat. A pounding headache that wouldn't let up. Ambient island sounds. Distant laughter from playing children and beer-drinking adults. Hunger. Panic that I would starve. Knowledge that there was no way that could happen.

I raged at the audacity that I'd actually paid money to be

there. I dug into my homework, complying with the rules and putting words to my greatest fears. I followed the instructions and completed the requisite worksheets with their probing questions.

My FEAR . . .

How has this FEAR controlled my life?

How does holding on to this FEAR keep me from LOVE?

If I changed my mind about this FEAR, what would I believe?

If I changed my mind about this FEAR, how would that affect my life?

I filled out one sheet after another. Three in the morning. Three in the afternoon. Three in the evening. Throughout the day I watched the fears loosen their hold on my mind, and then I grabbed them back like a toxic lifeline. *What if I'm wrong? Could I really turn into my mother? Lose my mind? I am a lonesome loser. No one loves me. My God, my God why have you forsaken me?*

I wrote like a maniac, sweat pouring down my face and spine. I raged that I had no choice. I was stuck, persecuted, put upon. I blamed the facilitators for tricking me and leaving me there. I cursed my son for getting me into that outrageous situation in the first place. I whined about my mother and her sarcastic ways. I cried because my father left me. I wondered why my husband— who'd done this same workshop two weeks before—hadn't warned me about this part.

I crawled out from underneath the oppressive heat of the plastic tarp that drooped ten inches from my face. I put down my pen and stared at the water. A breeze wafted across my sweaty skin like a whisper. I thought about my fears and miracles that suggest things *can* change. I wondered what evidence I had that miracles *never* happen. I had none. No evidence except for my shitty attitude. I pondered the fear of nothing miraculous happening on the island. I considered how my striving to find something meaningful kept me from experiencing the beauty around me. If I changed my mind about making things happen, what might I believe?

Hot, sweaty, cranky, hungry, stinky, and pissed off at the world, I stared at the water and considered going in to cool off. Then I talked myself out of it because I didn't have a towel. It was a hundred degrees and I was worried about a frickin' towel? I tried again to get angry at the facilitators because they didn't tell me to bring one. I couldn't muster the energy. It wasn't their fault. I was a big girl. I could make my own decisions. I walked to the water and dug my toes into the moist sand and pebbles. Cool relief moved through my feet, up my legs, and into my attitude. I took another step and then one more until the water rose to my knees. It felt like butterfly kisses and angel wings.

A flash of worry about wet clothes screeched through my mind. I waved it away like a pesky fly, bent my knees, and plopped down into the lake. A giggle, the first in what felt like years, escaped my lips. My fears began to wash away. *Who cares what others think? My clothes will dry! This is heaven.* A school of inch-long silvery fish swirled around my toes. More giggles escaped my lips. *Oh sweet Jesus. This is a miracle!*

I played in the water until my fingers resembled prunes. I climbed onto the sand, changed into an oversized t-shirt, and let my clothes dry in the sun. An ant chomped on my big toe. My bladder shouted that I needed to pee. The afternoon heat and my monkey mind began to absorb any sanity I had gained in the water.

I'm a slow learner. Lessons need to be repeated over and over to loosen the grasp of stubborn and ingrained patterns of thinking and behavior. I began shutting down. This was not the spiritual awakening I'd hoped for. I was covered in sand and flies kept biting my bare skin. My head still hurt, my stomach was empty, and I couldn't fathom that I had chosen to be there. I was counting on my life being different, but why the incessant torture? Surely, I could do without it—or could I?

Day turned into evening and the setting sun lowered in the summer sky. Two fishing boats pulled up close to shore and bass music blasted from a stereo. I wondered what the boaters might think about the six solitary women lined up along the shore. I imagined they thought we were all nuts, but I didn't care. A little bit crazy is okay by me. I calmed as the temperature dropped. The flies lessened their bites, but I kept expecting the mosquitoes to come out once the sun went behind the horizon. I became absorbed in the textures of the sun, round like a ball, crimson, strong, and stunning. I caught a glimpse of one of the women down the beach, watching the men in the boats. I was comforted by her presence.

I pondered my fears. I wasn't afraid of sleeping alone on the sand. It felt safe. What if we had to spend another whole day solo? After moving past the lethargic and out-of-control feelings of the midday heat, I'd loved sitting in the water and watching the fish jump all around me. I noticed a diving bird pick a small perch out of the water and three stunning white cranes standing in the shallows. I realized that I feared the light would fade before I finished writing in my journal. The enormity of the statement lodged in my chest. I feared I would lose my light. I turned the notion over in my mind. I thought of my daughter and prayed the light didn't fade from her eyes. I worried that Jonathon's light might never re-ignite. I breathed into the discomfort. I stopped, paused, and perhaps I prayed. Prayer felt different on the island than it did a day or two before. The cicadas began to sing. The sun dipped into the water. I turned away from my fears, crawled into my sleeping bag, and drifted into an exhausted slumber.

Journal entry: June 24, 2005

It's a calm, still morning and the sky is beginning to turn pink. Birds are chirping. The waves gently lap against the shore. A boat motor hums in the distance. The bugs are starting to stir, but haven't begun to bite. My headache is gone, my water tastes like a cup of fresh-brewed coffee, and last night God spoke to me. "I will fill your cup. I will fill it with belly laughs." I heard these words as I lay on my back staring at the Big Dipper in a starlit sky.

I've been to hell and back. Yesterday. With Jonathon. In my overall life. Still, I awaken and hear the words, "I will never leave you nor forsake you." They sound like God and they sound like a wiser version of me as they continue. "I am there in your darkest moments even when you refuse to acknowledge me. I will never leave nor forsake you. I am your choice. Choose me. Choose life. Choose love." A slight breeze rustles my hair, the world's blessing that this is real.

My journey is far from over, but I know I can travel the road and travel it well. To hell and back. I can always come back to this place in my mind that is oh so sweet. Remember the heat, the pain, the hunger, and the small miracles. Do I want to go through it again today? Hell no! Could I? Absolutely. I would survive. It might be painful—just as pieces and days of my life are painful—but I would survive and possibly even thrive.

This was truly a desert time. Hot. Barren. Excruciating. Yesterday was painful, yes, but I had to do it. Alone. I couldn't think my way out of this one. I had to feel it, to stay on the island, to wallow in the pain, and watch myself come out on the other side like the sun rising through the trees. Right now it is serene and beautiful, but later it could be my enemy, hot and scorching. I'd love to spend another night out here, and I know that the cool night wouldn't be the same without the searing daytime. We need both. The bitter and the sweet. Hot and cool. When we've gone to hell and seen it, felt it, lived it, life is so much sweeter when it settles down.

Like the moon and sun, we need the gradations of both fear and love. The fears keep me running and reaching for life lest I ever take it for granted. It is a swing of the pendulum where love is on the other side. I may never know how far a situation will go toward darkness before it makes a turn toward change. The only choice I have is in my own response. Will I covet and grovel in pain, fear, and self-pity like I did yesterday or will I patiently wait and trust that love, like the cool of night, will eventually come?

Today is different. Things look and feel different. Same beach. Same site. Still, I found a place in the shade and every now and then a cool breeze blows across my journal. I'm down to my last sips of fresh water, but I'm trusting that more will come and if it doesn't there is a whole lake for me to drink from. Fears? I feel like I could handle anything.

Peace lives inside me. I choose life. I choose love. I want this feeling to last forever.

But nothing lasts forever.

Take Your Soul for a Stroll

SOULSTROLL

It's hard to SoulStroll when your feet are tethered together.

S is for surrender, solitude, silence, and SoulStrolling®. Solo experiences. Skipping. Savoring. Simplicity. Setting intentions.

It represents surrendering to solitude and your own sense of wonder. Seeing the wisdom in silence. Setting aside time to make it happen.

As a child I loved skipping around the block to Mrs. Peck's kindergarten without censorship or control from anyone else. As I grew older, I forgot what it was like to wield a wand of feathers and stars or to speak up for myself, even though both came naturally to me when I was very young. What have you forgotten?

For years I fought the idea of being alone and saw it as a bad thing. I believed everyone else held the answers to *my* life. It was in surrendering to solitude and surrounding myself in silence that I began to discover the core of who I am, what my own wise voice sounds like, and what it feels like to fill my soul.

Practice SoulStrolling®

- Find a place where you won't be interrupted. Set a timer for five minutes to be silent and do nothing but breathe. Practice this. Repeat. Extend the time when available.

- Make your own list of twenty or so items of what S means to you. Then go back through the list and circle the items that make you giggle, feel lighter, or yearn for something within.

- Set an intention to find time for silence each day plus practice one of the items from your list.

PART TWO

Illumination in the City of Light

Paris 2008

"A walk about Paris will provide lessons in history, beauty, and in the point of Life."

—Thomas Jefferson

CHAPTER 7

Paris Perhaps?

"Twenty years from now you will be more disappointed by the things you didn't do than by the ones you did do. So throw off the bowlines. Sail away from the safe harbor. Catch the trade winds in your sails. Explore. Dream. Discover."

—Mark Twain

January 2008

Three years after the desert island experience, Paris illumined herself as a welcome balm for my soul that was still finding its way in the world. Bill was experiencing fulfillment in the venture capital world, and I was establishing my career as a psychotherapist and practicum facilitator at the graduate school I'd attended. Jonathon was out of therapeutic boarding school and approaching eighteen, the time when we would no longer be legally liable for his actions—actions that continued to stretch our limits. Janey was exploring her own independence in high school and holding her first job as a courtesy clerk at the local Fred Meyer. I needed space to spread my wings, space away from the day-to-day details of family life and work.

One never knows when or how we will receive the call to travel, but once I began to listen, I discovered that true knowing springs out of deep listening. Some moments, perfect in their own right, invite us to stay close to home and others tug at our heartstrings and we know it's time to hit the road.

I can still see that gloomy, gray morning in Seattle when my Paris adventures began. My family had given up going to church on Sunday mornings—actually we'd pretty much given it up all together. Bill was downstairs drinking coffee and reading. The teenagers were dead to the world in their beds since it was before noon. I was snuggled under the covers sipping my own latte and glancing through my favorite blogs while our golden retriever, Curry, lay on the floor beside me.

That morning, I'd learned via email that the group of women I was planning to travel to Mexico with for a kayaking trip in February had disbanded. Disappointment kicked around inside my chest, but possibility lingered in the background. After all, I had time scheduled off from work, plus money set aside to travel. I was ready for an adventure, but my pals didn't want to play. I'd say I was crushed, but something exciting was bubbling up inside. Instead of wallowing in the disappointment, a voracious curiosity took over and my longings began to sprout tiny wings.

A few years before, I would have dismissed this curiosity as foolish and crushed the budding wings, put the laptop away, and resigned myself to stay home as others would probably expect of me. Instead I paused, closed my eyes, and listened to the voice that was speaking from inside me. This trip was my choice. I could go to Mexico without my friends. When I listened more closely, however, I realized that kayaking in Mexico wasn't my deepest desire.

Taking a sip of coffee, I turned to another blog and—*wham!* There it was, the Mark Twain quote that propelled my life in a wild new direction. *Explore. Dream. Discover.* I knew that I was going somewhere even if I had to go by myself.

Closing my eyes in my new form of prayer that involved listening more than pleading, I asked the question: *Where would I go if I could go anywhere in the world?*

It was such an ordinary moment. An outsider looking in would've seen a middle-aged woman of medium height and size, shoulder length brown hair with a hint of beauty shop red, Life is Good pjs, and sleep still in her eyes, sitting in the middle of a pine four-poster bed with an Apple laptop perched on a pillow. They would've seen her lips move slightly to form a single word. *Paris.*

If my life had been a movie production, this would've been the moment the music swelled. My insides flipped then flopped, and I did a happy dance while waving wild arms saying, *Yes! Yes! Yes! Pick Paris. Pick Paris. Pick Paris!*

And then the practical naysayer chimed in, *Oh hell no. You don't even speak French.*

Mais oui, countered the happy revelers. *We took French in high school. We've got this.*

Sitting in my bedroom, I began to explore what it might look like to visit Paris. In less than four weeks' time. Alone. I had never been outside of North America except to London. And alone? The word itself was the bane of my existence.

Paris is the stuff of movies and romance. Growing up I was enchanted with falling in love and fairytales. In its own way, Paris is a real-life fairytale. Women look chic and men are well-groomed and charming. The buildings, statues, and gardens offer a visceral impression of castles and dream worlds.

For centuries, writers and romantics have been drawn to Paris. I count myself among them. Paris has been home to rebels (*Les Miserables*), mystics (Joan d'Arc), and artists too numerous to name. She is the originator of *les flâneurs*, stately strollers who walk merely for the pleasure of it. The City of Light is designed for walking with her wide boulevards and intimate parks. She is gorgeous and orderly. Winding and wild. Serene and spiritual.

I had been drawn to this idea of Paris for many years, but somehow it never managed to make it onto our family itinerary. My husband wasn't crazy about the idea of going to France. He'd visited there as a child and preferred exploring places closer to home and hanging out with family and friends, but Paris had always been on my short list. How could I let two wonderfully open weeks, set aside for pure enjoyment, go to waste?

I began with the familiar and checked airfares to London. Janey and I had visited five years earlier, and I'd heard there was a tunnel from London to Paris, so I decided to explore flights to Heathrow. It felt safer. I could land where English was the primary language and then set off to Paris. Step by step. But the travel gods—those brave little imps—were having none of that. The strategy to get from London to Paris seemed confusing and out of reach. I almost gave up the whole trip, chalking it up to foolishness. Curiosity tinged with tenacity, however, would not give up.

Just for fun, I decided to check airfares to Paris and discovered they were less expensive than London. In fact, I could go on frequent flyer miles for a total cost of about $75. I got all goose-bumpy—truth bumps, I call them—and knew something bigger than I was at work.

The brave side of me said *Go for it!* as did my wonderful and supportive husband who still had no interest in going to France. The insecure side of me said things like *Are you crazy? You only have two years of high school French. Where would you stay? What would you do? You don't even know which side of the Seine the Eiffel Tower is on!*

And then I remembered brave women like Elizabeth Gilbert (*Eat, Pray, Love*), Alice Steinbach (*Without Reservations*), and Anne Morrow Lindbergh (*Gift from the Sea*) and realized this could be an amazing adventure. *My* amazing adventure.

The not-so-brave voice was unrelenting and piped back up. *Are you sure? I mean, really sure?*

So, I did what any self-respecting, crazy-out-of-her-mind vacillator would do—I put a ticket on hold. This gave me two weeks to make my decision and a mere four weeks to plan an overseas trip. I was sailing away from my safe harbor, and I could feel my inner sails filling up.

My inner poet squealed, *Yes, yes, yes!*

My practical side answered, *I need to put dinner in the crock pot.*

CHAPTER 8

Bienvenue á Paris

"To awaken quite alone in a strange town is one of the pleasantest sensations in the world. You are surrounded by adventure. You have no idea of what is in store for you, but you will, if you are wise and know the art of travel, let yourself go on the stream of the unknown and accept whatever comes in the spirit in which the gods may offer it."

—Freya Stark

February 2008

Beginning with another author's words is a form of stepping into their shoes and tracing their footsteps from one's own perspective. When I recorded Freya Stark's words in my journal as I prepared to go on my first trip to Paris, I'd never awoken in a strange land alone. Sure, I'd been on solo business trips to Williston, North Dakota, and Kansas City, Kansas, places unique in their own way. But there was something effusive about knowing I would be waking up in France with no one but myself to rely upon.

"God has special gifts for those who travel alone." A trusted friend who's spent much time traveling on her own shared those words with me before my departure. I tucked the sentiment in my pocket, full of hope.

On the way to the airport, my breath caught in my throat and I felt giddy. Not sure whether I was going to cry or burst out laughing. As Bill and I topped Phinney Ridge near our home, the Cascades spread out before us. My insides giggled, *I'm going to Paris! Paris, France. Me . . . by myself!* The spirit of the kindergarten girl who skipped around the block, carefree and alive, was back!

The airport was uncharacteristically mellow and eerily quiet, in comparison to my pounding heart. I bought a Starbucks latte to keep me company and a turkey bagel for later. In a few short minutes, I'd checked in, collected my boarding pass, dropped off my baggage, and purchased euros. I was certain I paid too much for them at Travelex, but I felt better knowing I already had the correct currency before arriving in Paris.

With euros worth almost 40 percent more than the dollar, my money would go fast if I wasn't careful. My accountant brain piped up, admonishing that I'd have to stick to a budget for each day. How much was a museum pass? The bus ticket to my apartment? Would I walk the final mile from the Arc de Triomphe to Rue Cler or take a taxi when I arrived? My mind calmed as I focused on details I could manage. I made a list and looked up maps and answers in the Rick Steves guidebook. I would decide when I got there.

The traveling mercies began when I scored an emergency exit row seat with extra leg room to New York. A swell of gratitude filled me and I hoped my luck would not run out too quickly. The flight was smooth from Seattle to JFK, and I loved the exit row seat with no one in the middle seat. It was almost as luxurious as tucking into first class—without the champagne and personal service, of course. We landed at gate 34 and would leave for Paris from 37. Traveling mercies, yes.

At JFK, there were people waiting to board who spoke French, who *were* French. Again, I felt giddy. I scanned the floor and saw lots of tennis shoes. *I thought the French were more stylish*, said a silly voice in my head. The people surrounding me looked like normal people. I laughed to myself, realizing how weird I sounded. Weird and wired. Naive and novice. The excitement was almost more than I could contain as I surveyed my fellow travelers in the lounge.

Did I need to show my passport for this flight? My only other international flight was pre-9/11. It would make sense to check our passports now. I was frightened that someone was going to speak to me in French. I was scared of using my Rick Steves guidebook and looking like I didn't know what I was doing or where I was going. The magnitude of this trip was starting to feel very real. The sensation shifted from giddiness and bona fide fear stepped forward. I needed to quit being scared. Isn't that what this trip was about?

While I waited, I read some of my book, Hemingway's *A Moveable Feast*, trying to convince myself that reading about French culture disguised in literature was a chic way to stay under the radar. I considered whether I could simply wander around for the week without speaking. That way no one would figure out I was an idiot. In the moment, I wished I could be kinder to myself, but my defenses were kicking up big time and panic was weighing in.

Wait. What was that I heard? The flight attendants were speaking English. Maybe everything was going to be okay after all.

Je suis arrivée. I have arrived.

Who ever heard of a plane arriving an hour early? Well, my first flight to Paris did. It was a seamless crossing except for a few bumps over Greenland. I chose to nap through dinner because sleep seemed like the balm I needed to soothe my over-stimulated self.

It was 7:30 a.m. and drizzling in Paris when I arrived, much as it was when I left Seattle. After hours of research on how to get from Charles de Gaulle Airport into the city center, I decided to take the Air France bus. I'm not a particularly extravagant traveler. I don't like paying for things like taxis that somehow seem excessive, especially when there are other reasonable options.

After deplaning and exiting customs, I cautiously left the airport building in search of the Air France buses. A kind porter walked me to the correct one after I squeaked out, "Arc de Triomphe?" Lightheartedness took over when it sunk in that my destination was a historical site I'd only theretofore seen on television newsreels. I handed my fare to the driver and a fellow passenger, a gracious English-speaking man, confirmed I was on the correct bus.

Once we arrived at the Arc de Triomphe, the same kind man asked if I knew where I was going. I'm sure he could tell by the blank look on my face that my answer was questionable. *No. Yes. Sort of.* "I just need to catch my bearings," I responded. With an assuring nod, he tipped his hat and I found myself standing alone in the large, spoke-like intersection of Place Charles de Gaulle where the Arc de Triomphe holds court in the center. Twelve avenues spin out from the center of the wheel. Twelve! I inhaled, exhaled, and opened my map. Fortunately, the woman at the travel store near my Seattle home had recommended an excellent one and my bearings were caught, at least for the moment.

Taking my time, I circled the Arc de Triomphe until I found Avenue Marceau and began the mile walk toward my apartment in the 7th arrondissement near the Rue Cler market. Along the way, I found a payphone and dialed Aurore, my apartment hostess, to see when my studio would be ready. In 2008, cell phones were limited for international travel, and phone booths were still the norm. The graces of the day continued and my apartment was ready for my arrival.

There's a level of anticipation when entering a new space for the first time, especially when you know that space will be your home for the next week or so. In that moment, I was filled with excitement and exhaustion from the eighteen-hour journey. I had high, romantic expectations of what this studio in the center of Paris had in store for me. The rental company had promised that it would be perfect, and the photos online showed a tasteful space with a golden glow. One thing I would learn on this trip is that Parisian apartments are folded in everywhere, behind gorgeous gated doors and not-so-grand passageways. They nestle under rooftop eaves and some even possess private caves dedicated to fine wine storage. My reserved studio happened to be tucked behind a navy blue door between an electronics shop and a boutique hotel.

As Aurore and I entered the first passageway, my expectations dropped a measure or two. The courtyard was small and non-descript. It was a pale gray shaft of a passageway with buildings on every side and a patch of dull sky five or six stories up. Next we crossed the threshold that led into my specific hallway. The two of us could barely fit in the space at the same time. I was dizzied by the economy of size, the labyrinth of keys, and the memorized passcodes one must navigate when residing in Paris.

My inner sanctum on this trip was a one-room studio (two, if you count the bathroom). My initial reaction (or dare I say, letdown?) was in response to how compact it was along with its timeworn edges. Unlike our hundred-year-old home in Seattle that had been remodeled to look fresh and new, this building was restored in its own shabby chic style that I would quickly (although not immediately) come to adore.

The kitchen was sparse, but a welcome basket sat on the counter filled with water, juice, and tea for now, plus a bottle of French wine for later. The bed looked like something out of a fairy tale with draping gauze arranged as a headboard and fluffy cream-colored pillows atop a matching duvet.

Two petite chairs cuddled next to a small round table, and a white secretary's desk was the perfect companion for my laptop. A low dresser rested at the foot of the bed with a small TV and an assortment of DVDs ready for my entertainment pleasure. I took it all in through bleary eyes and fell in love with the barren stone wall that ran alongside the cozy bed.

With keys in hand and Aurore's phone number for backup, I bid her farewell, peeled off my clothes, crawled under the covers, and fell asleep to the sound of my new neighbors pacing overhead. Two hours later, I awoke to the quacking of my alarm. It was midday in Paris, time to wash my face, put my contacts back in, and let the Parisian adventure begin.

CHAPTER 9

Sustenance & Statues

"To live is to venture beyond ourselves to taste the sweetness of the unknown."

—Sr. Joan Chittister

February 2008

I stood next to the outdoor menu at Café du Marché on Rue Cler and surveyed it as though I could actually read French. My brown eyes, fuzzy with jet lag, moved from side to side, up and down, to see what other diners were eating. "I should have changed my clothes," I muttered under my breath. After my nap, I put back on the clothes that I traveled in and suddenly felt like a country bumpkin surrounded by svelte Parisians. Brown and maroon Timberline trail shoes peeked from beneath matching brown corduroy pants. The sea of chic black around me made me want to dive beneath the nearest red-checked tablecloth.

What was I thinking? Who was that person who thought coming to Paris on her own was a good idea?

Journal entry: February 28, 2008

I can see this will take persistence and willpower. I am so hungry and everything is so strange. Dogs barking in the street. I sit at Café du Marché on Rue Cler. It is raining. I am starving. Feeling a bit lost. Very tired and not wanting to waste a minute. The young man next to me looks like my nephew and I feel old right now. I smile as though I am not stupid, ordering a Caesar salad that has arrived and looks like no Caesar I've ever seen. It's a very rich salad, some of it unidentifiable. I ordered the only thing on the menu I recognized and it was not what I thought.

I go back and forth between worrying what others will think of me and realizing that no one is paying attention to me at all.

Occasionally I wonder how I resisted the urge to scurry back to my tiny apartment after that first painful lunch. I remember sitting there in my corduroy pants and clunky shoes feeling like an alien in my own skin. I had landed in Paris yet hadn't quite arrived. Everyone else looked relaxed and comfortable, but I know from experience that what we see is not always the case.

I wonder how it felt to be a sojourner in older times, when all you carried were the clothes on your back, the shoes on your feet, and a small pouch of currency. There were certainly no worries about whether or not one's shoes were stylish. Shoes were simply shoes. Food was food, and travelers were grateful to have their bellies filled with whatever was served. Expectations were low or non-existent.

We expect so much in our day-to-day lives. Instant this and automatic that. While I didn't expect anyone at the restaurant to speak English or strike up a conversation with me, I did count on my Caesar salad to be familiar. What I found out later (as I perused my guidebook) was that I'd managed to order their house salad complete with duck pâté and a few other ingredients that challenged my jet-lagged tummy. Lost in translation . . . sometimes that is the traveler's way.

After surviving my first meal alone in Paris, I challenged myself to stay outside and walk through the neighborhoods surrounding my apartment. Bordered on the east by Parc du Champ-de-Mars that hosts the Eiffel Tower, Esplanade des Invalides with its golden domes and Napoleon's tomb to the west, and the flowing river Seine to my north, I found myself in a stroller's paradise.

With map in hand, I headed toward *la Tour Eiffel*. My first glimpse of the international landmark had come earlier in the day as I pulled my rolling suitcase behind me in the misty morning and rounded a corner off Avenue Marceau. *La dame de fer.* The iron lady. Her elegance is clearly that of a graceful and self-assured woman, all air and iron. Her gray legs, almost indiscernible in the fog, rose above ground into the matching sky. Even in the monochromatic morning, her magnificence twinkled and I swear she winked at me from across the Seine.

The Eiffel Tower is something I never tire of seeing. Whether in person or pictures, illuminated at night or half seen on a misty day, close up, far away, she mesmerizes me. A friend of mine calls the Washington Monument her "symbol of becoming." She told me that during a transitional period in her life, she often traveled to Washington, DC, and noticed that when she arrived in the city, she immediately felt more like herself. The Monument was her signal to lay down her masks and step more fully into herself. When I heard her words, something resonated in my soul, and I wondered if the Eiffel Tower was my own symbol of becoming.

Serendipitously, it was in the Tower's shadow that I fell in love with my first statue. One of the many things I didn't know about myself on that first trip to Paris was my affinity for falling in love with statues. Statues are steadfast, loyal, and solid, and they ask nothing in return from us, except perhaps that we linger and pay attention to what they might have to say if they could speak aloud.

The statue of a mother and child is part of an installation called *Monument des Droits de l'Homme* (the human rights monument). In my limited research, I haven't been able to uncover a detailed description of the woman and don't know who she officially is. This leaves my imagination free to run amok as I ponder the wildness and serenity I see in her.

She holds a large branchlike talisman in her hand and is draped like a Greek goddess. Next to her is a naked male child, four or five years old, reaching for something in the distance. At their feet lie two masks and some pomegranates, including one broken open with its juicy seeds spilling out. She reminds me of the myth of Demeter and her daughter, Persephone. Persephone is kidnapped by Hades and taken to the underworld. When Persephone unwittingly swallows pomegranate seeds, the act ensures that she will return to the underworld for a part of each year. Every time I stand at the foot of this statue of mother and child, I feel my own humanity. I wonder about my own underworld where loneliness trails me like a dark shadow and how this loneliness lives alongside the golden woman I am becoming.

During my first meeting with the statue, I paused and snapped a few photos, not even noticing the two Egyptian obelisks and a bronze man draped in a toga that completed the installation. Only this piece mesmerized me. She became a symbol for my own journey—wild and serene, broken open, laying down masks.

Several times during my wanderings in Paris, I asked myself: *What the heck are you doing here?* When nothing seemed familiar, I resisted the urge to dive into the neighborhood Starbucks even though there was one right around the corner on Rue Saint-Dominique.

The impulse reminded me of the time my daughter and I traveled to London when she was ten. After a couple days of British breakfasts and damp weather, Janey implored, "Mommy, please, I need something familiar." She begged me to choose Starbucks instead of the hotel buffet filled with stewed tomatoes, blood pudding, and other unrecognizable delicacies. It was an excellent suggestion and from that day until the end of our trip, we began each morning with an American latte for me, steamed milk with raspberry syrup for her, and two scones. Once fortified, we were better prepared to face any unfamiliar situations tossed our way.

My first day in Paris was an endurance test to stay the course through jet lag, strange surroundings, and opinionated inner chatter. It was my first lesson in the beauty of traveling solo. There was no one else to answer to, and I was responsible only for myself. Travelers more experienced than I recommended that I stay awake until the evening to help combat jet lag, so my "self" was determined to stay awake until bedtime. I did this by walking.

After standing at the foot of the Eiffel Tower and encountering my first statue, I strolled across one of Paris's many bridges, Pont de l'Alma, toward the chic Right Bank. It is in Place de l'Alma that the perpetual flame burns at Princess Diana's shrine, marking the site where she died in a car crash in 1997. It was surreal to be in that place I'd heard about one Sunday morning a decade before. I paused for a brief moment and sent a prayer into the heavens for spirited Diana. Onward, my feet carried me past the Grand Palais and the Petite Palais, glass structures built in 1900 for the World's Fair. I crossed the ornate Alexandre III bridge with its golden sculptures and walked back past Esplanade des Invalides. Like a tenacious pilgrim, I put one foot in front of another and pulled out my map whenever I felt discombobulated or at a loss for which direction to go.

The precious neighborhood near Rue Cler market was filled with delightful surprises like the hidden Temple Saint-Jean on

Rue de Grenelle and riotous blooming flowers in garden boxes that adorned a weathered Tudor house. Bicycles leaned against the grocery store on Rue Cler and pre-teen boys demonstrated their swagger with raised chins and designer t-shirts like boys in any country around the world.

When evening approached, it was time to assemble my first Parisian picnic. As travel guru Rick Steves says, "If you wish to learn the fine art of living Parisian-style, Rue Cler provides an excellent classroom. And if you want to assemble the ultimate French picnic, there's no better place." The particulars of negotiating the meal hang fuzzy in my mind like the pale gray cast in the air that day. I came home with a few simple items to brighten the cozy studio and make it mine. A small potted cyclamen in shades of ruby and fuchsia. An authentic quiche Lorraine from Maison Auvray along with my first French pastry, *tartelette framboise*. Baguette. Cheese. Strawberries and fresh yogurt. Simple fair for an anything-but-simple adventure.

CHAPTER 10

Leap Day

"To travel is to take a journey into yourself."

—Danny Kaye

February 2008

It's fitting that the year I first went to Paris was a leap year and I gained an extra day, since I lost one flying east. Leap Year. My leap of faith into the unknown. I didn't realize how brave I needed to be until I began wandering the city.

How lucky am I? How scared and excited?

A fair amount of fear is expected when embarking on a grand adventure. Waking after my first night's sleep in Paris, I took a deep breath. A friend I had met through the world of blogging, Tess, would arrive the next day. *How do I let her in?* I didn't recall my apartment number and hadn't asked Aurore which of the multiple buzzers to press. So many details to uncover. *Where will we go for lunch?* Saint-Germain-des-Prés and Café du Monde popped into my mind. I imagined lingering in the shadows of Hemingway and other famous Americans in Paris.

I thought about the weather, because what traveler doesn't take that into consideration? I hoped it wouldn't rain all day and considered whether I'd need to add an umbrella to my budgeted list of items to purchase.

I had oriented myself with the neighborhood the day before, and as I gazed at the cyclamen next to the bed through sleepy eyes, I pondered where I'd have coffee to begin my day. Coffee is an essential ritual in Paris and one in which I was excited to partake. My studio apartment was perfect, but I longed for a scenic view instead of the scruffy courtyard outside my shuttered windows. A room with a view . . . now that sounds Parisian!

The clock read 4:45 a.m. My inner voice sang, *I can do anything*! *No musts. No have-to's.* Only the call of my heart's desire awaited me.

My practical traveler piped up. *I want to get some bus passes and a museum pass.* My mind started clicking through the items and my budget and I moved between the tension of wanting a plan and not getting caught up in details. I told myself this might be my only trip to Paris. Another voice inside me laughed because she knew that wasn't true.

A naysayer to my solo trip told me that Paris "*must* be shared." Her words sounded reasonable, so I decided to blog about my trip and invited the world to share it with me. It proved to be a satisfying way to journey as I began or ended each day conversing with my online friends. Finishing my blog post for the morning, I snapped a few pictures around the apartment, checked my bag for provisions (euros, journal, map, key) and ventured outside for day two, where anything could happen.

By 6:00 a.m. I was ready to get going. If I hurried, I'd be able to see the sun rise, although I had no idea whether or not it would rise over the Seine, three blocks from my apartment. Yes, I am directionally challenged.

Early in the morning, Paris awakens like a sultry woman stretching her limbs, sleep caught in her eyes. Before anything was open, I wandered toward the Seine and noticed that *Les Égouts de Paris* (the sewer tour) was close by. Visions of *Phantom of the Opera* mingled in my mind alongside the sense of scavenging rats and putrid smells. The air was fresh and the sky was tender pink, but it seemed like another overcast day was on the way. The temperature felt warm and humidity hung in the air. I was having trouble regulating my own body temperature. Jet lag? Nerves? Menopause? God forbid!

My thoughts were a jumbled mess.

Café de l'Université sits at the corner of Rue Malar and Rue de l'Université, less than a quarter mile from my apartment. Upon entering the café, I sensed that I'd entered a traditional French neighborhood haunt rather than mega tourist land. This was my hope, to immerse myself in Paris instead of ticking off sightseeing sites one after another. This is what distinguishes a SoulStroller from a tourist—an ability and desire to slow down and become part of the culture rather than insisting the culture acclimate to him or her.

SoulStrollers have the ability and desire to integrate into a foreign culture.

I made my first attempt to order *café à la français* that began with a drawn out "uhhh." Even though I tried to ask for decaf and the man behind the bar nodded in understanding, I'm certain it didn't translate. I knew I'd probably have caffeine withdrawals when I returned home, but I decided I'd rather adapt to the culturally caffeinated way and sip tiny cups of espresso than complain or compare it to what we had back home.

The buzz of espresso coursed through my body as I scanned the café through veiled eyes and wondered about a woman at the next table reading *A Thousand Splendid Suns* in English. Was she an American on vacation? Did she wonder if I was French? Oh how

I wished I could turn off the wild faucet of thoughts that gushed through my mind.

The fear of looking foolish crawled up my spine and even though I knew it wouldn't happen, I imagined everyone in the café standing up and pointing accusatory fingers at me. *C'est une Américaine. Elle est folle.* (That's an American. She's crazy.) Glancing around, I decided no one was paying any attention to me and it was safe to pull out my guidebook. My stomach rumbled. This café was what they called a *tabac*, known for selling public transit tickets, postage stamps, and cigarettes. While the espresso is commendable, there isn't much food available. I wasn't ready to venture any further, so I settled on a cheese and tomato sandwich and munched away while I wrote in my journal that stuck to the table.

It was quiet in the café. The language around me sounded like a poem, but my ears strained to hear English. There was a couple on the street and the man was saying, "Yea, yea, yea," but I think this translation is universal. I realized I'd been slipping into Spanish (which I know even less than French) with words like *sí* and *gracias*. I sounded like a fool and wondered if people thought I was a Spanish woman traveling instead of an American. Silly me. They did not think of me at all.

The strangeness of these unfamiliar surroundings was making itself known and I realized the immensity of deciding to travel alone instead of with a larger group. I reminded myself that I had chosen this journey. I prayed that with the challenges, unimaginable gifts might come. Each moment was its own exploration. A coming and becoming.

Stepping outside the *tabac*, I felt more French in my black slacks and European flats compared to the previous day's brown tones and hiking shoes. The more stylish footwear invited me to slow down. To stroll. To be intentional in my steps.

The City of Paris was born on the Île de la Cité, and the site where the Notre Dame cathedral now resides was once a place where Gallic and Roman gods were worshipped. Her history is rich with stories of destruction and repair . . . like mine. It's no wonder I felt a kinship from the moment I first laid eyes on her through dappled gray clouds and blue sky.

Inside, the cathedral can only be described as holy. Within her walls there is a silence so sweet that it envelops even the most cynical of believers. Rose-colored glass glimmers with two-euro candles that send prayers into the rafters, out the mouths of gargoyles, and onto the banks of the swollen Seine.

Standing inside the church, there was a lump in my throat that felt representative of the stories of the millions of people that had gone before me into this oh-so-holy place. Centuries of Christian tradition reside there. Our Lady is filled with floor-to-ceiling stained glass windows, gentle chanting music, and thousands of illuminated candles. I could only imagine what it was like to come to mass there.

I was drawn to stay in the silence, even with crowds of people milling around. Most of the visitors were respectful and subdued, but there was an occasional blurt of someone who either couldn't contain themselves or had no concept of where they stood.

The light was dim and my penmanship scrawled across the visitor's book page at odd angles. I wrote prayers for my friends and family. I missed them *and* was delighted to be on the pilgrimage alone. It was in that moment that I knew I would return and bring others with me. The music filled my senses and kept me rooted to my seat. Several times, I attempted to rise from the pew but was called by Something Greater to stay planted where I was. Gratitude and thanks for the moment filled me with endless amens.

After receiving my bounty of awe and wonder from Our Lady, I left and crossed Pont Saint-Louis to the island of the same name. Before coming to Paris, I didn't understand that two islands sit in the middle of the Seine—Île de la Cité, which hosts Notre Dame, and the smaller Île Saint-Louis, a residential area known for its restaurants and famous for being the home of Berthillion, touted as the best ice cream in the world.

Île Saint-Louis is a charming piece of land. In my search for Berthillion ice cream, I discovered many shops closed during the French version of siesta. The wind picked up and made it too cold for ice cream, so instead I found a scarf and jewelry shop that drew me in with fabulous turquoise colors that decorated the exquisite window display.

The twenty-something shopkeeper was attentive and spoke excellent English, so I ended up buying a turquoise silk scarf and matching earrings, thus blowing my budget for the day. A loose budget it was, and who can resist buying a signature scarf in Paris? Whenever I don either of those gifts, I'm transported back to that exquisite afternoon on Île Saint-Louis. Gifts of the moment translating into gratitude for a time past.

I made up for the splurge by spending £1.90 on a delicious *l'aubergine et fromage tartine* (a roasted eggplant and cheese sandwich resembling flatbread or pizza). Years later, I still dream about that delicacy I savored by the Seine on Île Saint-Louis. It was a perfect picnic with my feet hanging over the river bank and sunshine on my shoulders. Since that time, I've searched high and low to replicate that simple meal without success. Evidently, it was a taste and a memory for that time.

Paris weather is a lot like Seattle—except, of course, it's Paris. The sun teased me with a peek-a-boo dance all day long. Now you see me. Now you don't. I wandered back to Île de la Cite, crossed over to the right bank on Pont Neuf, the oldest bridge in Paris, and waited for the number 69 bus to take me back down the Seine toward my apartment.

At home in Seattle, I know which areas of town are sketchy or safe, where homeless people are likely to live on the street, and which corners support panhandlers. It's easy for me to remain insulated from the world of poverty, either by turning away or staying cocooned inside my car. It's not a trait I'm proud of, and being in the City of Light brought some of my idiosyncrasies out of the shadows.

Near the bus stop, there were a group of people dressed in ragged clothes and drinking out of paper bags. I'd seen two other individuals with crippled feet turned inward, supported by double crutches. My instincts flickered on medium alert, tinged with guilt for my privilege and choice. In that moment, I could either engage or turn away. My internal pulse softened in a way it hadn't at home and I decided to stay.

A man sat next to me on the bench and unwittingly kicked over his brown-papered bottle that made a clunk on the pavement. A woman thought this hysterical and a stream of words rushed from her mouth. Joking ensued along the bench. While the levity was unmistakable, the language was still a mystery to me. I wondered if her joke was crude and mean. Or did she show light-heartedness for her fellow man? Without a solid answer, I sat and absorbed the scene and felt a smile cross my own lips.

When I started this Parisian journey, I didn't understand it would be a pilgrimage of sorts. Looking back, I understand it was SoulStrolling in its infancy. A pilgrim or SoulStroller differs from a tourist or casual traveler because of their intention or desire. Tourists operate with to-do lists and

To SoulStroll means to travel by the heart instead of agendas and to-do lists.

destination goals. Pilgrims proceed as if on a quest. They travel by their heart.

It's our response in moments like those at the bus stop, when our humanity bumps up against the culture we're visiting, that distinguishes a pilgrim from a tourist. A tourist might harrumph in disgust and complain about their vacation being marred. A SoulStroller carries those images home and allows them to percolate and deepen. Even though she may walk away, she walks away changed by the encounter in ways she may never understand.

On the bus ride home, we passed the Père Lachaise Cemetery and the courtyard of the Louvre. Of the two landmarks, Père Lachaise was the one that beckoned me to return. I can't put words to why this was, but I felt a tug to go back and walk through the winding gravestones. Perhaps a piece of my own personal history lay there among Colette, Oscar Wilde, and Edith Piaf.

Exiting the bus in my neighborhood, I purchased a *quiche fromage* from a bakery on Rue de Grenelle that was filled with locals on their way home from work. After walking by the Eiffel Tower to see her dancing in the night sky and feeling the pull of the swirling carousels, but saying no to the ride, I tucked myself into my apartment to sip sweet wine and enjoy my quiche in solitude.

It was a day filled with contrasts. Rain and sunshine. Beauty and depravity. Strength and tenderness. The city was starting to come alive for me through both shadow and light. Twice in one evening I was mistaken for a French person, once while standing in line at the bakery and another when a couple asked me for directions. There was something soothing about feeling like I was becoming an integral part of this city that I was falling in love with. My inner SoulStroller who carries confidence and speaks her mind was emerging and merging with the luscious landscape. Closing my eyes and pulling the golden comforter around me, I offered a prayer—*merci*—and slipped into a grateful slumber.

CHAPTER 11

Meeting Tess

"In a certain sense, to gaze into the face of the other is to gaze into the depth and entirety of their life."

—John O'Donohue

March 2008

Never in my wildest dreams had I imagined a foreign trip where my principal traveling companions would be virtual peeps from around the world. While in Paris, I discovered a soothing rhythm of venturing out on my own during the day, then coming home tired and satisfied in the evening to share my adventures with friends in cyberspace. With a nine-hour time difference to the West Coast, my schedule was topsy-turvy with my friends in the United States. It was fun to awaken each day and see what comments awaited me.

On the third day of my trip, my friend Tess from England came to join me for a long weekend. There was a satisfying symmetry to her visit, because it was on her blog that I read the Mark Twain quote that spurred me to "throw off the bowlines" and book this first trip to Paris. I also found an added sense of pleasure that it was her first time in the City of Light even though she'd lived across the channel for half a century. Serendipity had invited each of us to take a risk and step into new horizons.

The morning Tess arrived was a picture-perfect Paris day—sun shining, flowers blooming, birds singing. Can you hear the soundtrack? I was anxious and excited to greet her in person. Our meeting was similar to a blind date. My palms were sweaty and my pulse raced at the thought of seeing her face-to-face and hearing her speak for the first time. We'd only communicated through the internet. I'd never heard her voice, nor she mine. While I waited for her to arrive via Eurostar, I went for a walk in my neighborhood.

Everywhere I looked, I saw red. Not angry red, but deep, solid, soothing red. Red ceramic planters glistened outside the local fire station. A crimson bike sat chained outside a closed door. The painting of the woman in a red hat and dress from Île Saint-Louis danced into my consciousness. Bright geraniums waved from window boxes. Like them, I was beginning to blossom as I wandered through those Saturday morning streets.

Years later, when I looked back on this time, I made the connection between the crimson color and the sturdy essence of the root chakra associated with that magnificent hue. I was grounding myself but I didn't know it. By physically moving and allowing nature to guide me, I was arriving more deeply into myself. Such is the way of the SoulStroller. We learn while we walk. We get to new destinations, internally and externally, by going and slowing.

SoulStrollers learn while they walk, reaching new destinations by going and slowing.

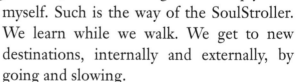

And then Tess arrived. After hugs and laughter and raves of "I can't believe we're really here!", we stowed Tess's luggage in my apartment and walked down the street for a cup of coffee. It was in my newly discovered shop on Rue Saint-Dominique—a place where the server patiently spoke French with me and served coffee in china cups—that Tess and I met an expatriate from Canada named Madame Martine and her male poodle, Ginger.

Madame Martine shifted fluently between English and French while she chatted, explaining that she'd been sitting at the same table for more than fifteen years, most of them with Ginger. The tables in the café were chrome and laminate, and the pastry cases reminded me of the bakery on Route 66 in Oklahoma where I went with my mother as a child, except the French cases were filled with croissants and handmade chocolates instead of gingerbread cookies and angel food cake. If I'd been offered one of those gingerbread cookies on that morning in France, I wonder if I would have picked out the raisin eyes and buttons like I had as a child.

Our coffee arrived in elegant china cups with a steaming carafe of milk. I was comforted by both the cup and the age-spotted hands that served it. Ginger, curled at our feet, perked up at the activity. His once-red coat had faded along with his eyesight. He didn't seem at all bothered by his feminine name even though Madame Martine insisted on calling him "confused." He was content to lay on the floor beside us and share croissant crumbs amidst the morning chatter. He was an excellent muse for being present to the surroundings and not worrying about what others might think. His stubby tail thumped with pleasure as I scratched him behind the ears, said *au revoir*, and left the café with Tess for our day's adventures.

Museums are a personal thing. I thought I hated them until I walked through one on my own when I was pregnant with Janey and discovered it wasn't the museum that I disliked, but rather the assumption that I needed to follow someone else's rhythm. Fortunately, Tess and I agreed on that philosophy so we parted ways at the entrance of the Musée d'Orsay and set a time to meet and share our favorite sights.

Art was disregarded in my growing-up years. I had been

confined to studying the color wheel in elementary school, with strict instructions to keep my crayon colors inside the prescribed lines someone else drew. Great art was deemed irrelevant and actually not that great at all. My exposure to the masters like Monet or Renoir was limited, so it was an awakening experience to stroll through the second largest museum in Paris and notice what works called my name. Because call my name they did. I swear Van Gogh's *Girl with Parasol* winked to call me over for a visit. Another moment I heard a six-year-old boy shout in his sweet British accent, "Grandmama, it's the *Blue Dancers*," before turning to see Edgar Degas's breathtaking works. I nearly swooned, they were so magnificent.

Walking with intention through Musée d'Orsay, I learned that I'm an impressionist girl, drawn to dancers, soft light, and free-spirited women. Claude Monet's works called to me, the Giverny scenes in particular. Ever since I'd seen his room-sized water lilies in New York City when I was in my thirties, I'd longed to wrap myself in those giant canvases and roll around in the colors, absorbing all the blues, greens, and golds into my whole being. Alas, sitting on a bench and soaking them in through every pore was the next best thing. Sculptures and impressionist works filled my senses as I strolled through the second half of the museum after a break for tea and *fromages* with Tess. By the time we were ready to leave, I was bursting with sensory overload and my lungs begged for fresh air.

Back out in the crisp spring day, Tess and I strolled along the right bank then crossed back over to Rue Saint-Dominique on the left where we shared another coffee and the requisite pastry. Once back at my apartment, we pulled out our guidebooks and began plotting and planning the remainder of our afternoon and evening only to find that many restaurants were closed that night and most markets, too. Would we starve? *Mais non!* The Rue Cler market saved us with a wonderful quiche, a salad to share, and a fine bottle of wine.

I felt so French that evening, sitting in my *petite* flat with the ancient stone wall, having engaged conversation with a new friend before heading toward the Seine and the *bateaux-mouches* for an evening cruise. Arm in arm, Tess and I stood on the deck of the boat, oohing and aahing at the Eiffel Tower and the lights on the Seine, all the while giggling like schoolgirls. Every few minutes, we squeezed each other and whispered, "We're really here." A sudden rainstorm sent us scurrying inside the boat but didn't dampen our spirits or the grins on our faces.

Many trips later, I still arrive and giggle, "I am here now."

Just past midnight on our last night together, we parted at the foot of the Eiffel Tower like heroines in an art film. Our journey to the observation deck of the Tower in the midnight mist had instilled me with Tess's bravery as she overcame a fear of heights to ride the elevator with me and stand above the City of Light surveying the twinkling beauty from bird's eye views.

She and I were no longer one-dimensional photos on a computer screen, but flesh-and-blood friends with stories to tell and more dreams to manifest. Together we'd opened doors to new vistas in art, friendship, and travel simply because we had chosen to say *yes* when Spirit issued an invitation to come.

The Eiffel Tower, all legs and iron and glistening light, stood guard over us while Tess turned toward her hotel in the west and I strolled eastward to Rue Malar. Glancing over my shoulder, tears of gratitude filled my eyes. *Until we meet again, my friend*, I whispered into the night.

CHAPTER 12

Absorbing Paris

*"Paris is to be absorbed in through the pores . . . sensing
it and feeling it rather than seeing and doing. When you
sit at that cafe with that glass of French wine and write
in your journal (or on your maps and guidebooks!) raise
a glass to yourself for giving yourself this amazing gift!"*

—Kate Iredale

March 2008

My intuitive friend Kate sent me those glorious words before I left
for Paris, and as my trip came to an end, I pondered how Paris had
been absorbed into my pores. My time with Tess had been filled
with museum excursions and metro adventures. I could still feel the
press and smell of harried locals and wide-eyed tourists searching
for their destination. Hope tinged with tiredness rested inside my
bones. Sacre Coeur, the white cathedral atop a hill, glistened in the
soft twilight of my mind and painted the evening on my soul like
the artists filling their canvases in the village square. The day after
Tess left was a continuance of the magical times we'd experienced
together. Walking alone again, everything fell into place and time
poured on with new delights around every corner. With practice,

I was becoming more adept at syncing with my personal rhythms, stepping into the way of deep listening, and answering the whispers that called from inside and out.

While I was in Paris, I learned a colleague in Seattle had died from a brain aneurysm. She was thirty-one years old. I didn't know her all that well, but I knew her to be a special young woman, and her passing touched me deeply, so much so that my first visit the day I found out was to Notre Dame again, to sit in remembrance and light a candle for a life lost too soon. Allyson's passing reminded me to take nothing for granted, to embrace my good health, and remember the angels that move between earthly and ethereal realms. After my time in the chapel, I climbed to the top of the tower where the gargoyles held court over the city. I stood in the crisp, sunny day overlooking the panoramic view of Paris, allowing the fresh air to fill my pores and soothe my sorrow.

Shakespeare & Company, the infamous English bookstore near Notre Dame, was the next stop on my morning stroll. Legends such as Hemingway, James Joyce, George Bernard Shaw, and Gertrude Stein went to Shakespeare & Company to get their fill of English-language books while they were in Paris. It was refreshing to see titles I could read without translation and the accommodating sales clerk gave me the superb recommendation of nearby Café Panis.

The restaurant across the street from Notre Dame was bustling with activity when I entered. I settled into a table near the center of the room. After a few moments, a tall waiter in a formal tuxedo approached.

"*Bonjour, madame.*"

"*Bonjour.*"

"Are you alone today?"

"*Oui.*" I nodded.

"Ah, well then. This will not do. A woman as lovely as yourself cannot be stuck back here. You must have a view as beautiful as you."

A flush rose on my cheeks.

The waiter gestured for me to rise, then picked up the menu and carafe of water and escorted me to a table for two by the window with a view of the Seine and a corner of Notre Dame.

"This is much better, *non?*"

I smiled and settled in my seat with the stature of a queen.

"Champagne, *madame?*"

"*Bien sûr, merci.*"

Journal entry: March 5, 2008

Today I am pinching myself. Everything is so delicious . . . so French . . . sitting in Café Panis at Rue LaGrange across from Notre Dame. It is still cold, but the sun is shining. My kir champagne was just poured and I shall toast to myself. I am beautiful, brave, and in Paris!

Fortified by *kir royal au champagne Montgivroux et soupe a l'oignon gratinee* (champagne with raspberry liqueur and French onion soup), I peppered my path to Saint-Séverin chapel with several stops at petite shops in the winding Latin Quarter. My steps felt fluid as I navigated the cobblestone alleyways and entered the establishments with a greeting of *Bonjour* and exited with *Au revoir et merci.* Later I took my favorite bus 69 to Père Lachaise Cemetery where I answered the call that had come earlier in the week. There I meandered through the ancient tombstones and visited the likes of Colette and Jim Morrison. Crumbling stones and faded bouquets sprinkled the pathways as I searched for my family surnames, Stevens and Moore, without success. Nevertheless, my spirits weren't dampened and I continue to be certain that I am indeed part French.

Returning on the bus, I exited near the Louvre but decided I didn't have the energy to tackle the massive museum. Instead, I opted to visit the spectacular Monet water lilies at Musée de l'Orangerie. In the museum, there are two rooms formed like an infinity symbol, each curved wall draped in Monet's works. The experience is an immersion in the outdoors while still being inside. There are no adequate words to describe the experience. I simply offer: *Go! See it for yourself. If the tiniest hint of a call is there, you won't regret it.*

Leaving Musée de l'Orangerie and the Tuileries Garden where it resides, I walked up the Right Bank toward the Avenue des Champs-Élysées, chasing a glorious sunset over the Seine and ended at the place I'd begun the week, the Arc de Triomphe. This time the monument was bathed in an evening glow instead of morning mist. It was an apt finale for my last night in the City of Light.

"Breathe deeply," said Aurore the next morning as we finished going over the details of my departure. She could sense my fragility about saying goodbye to Paris. Tears filled my eyes as I hugged her and waved *au revoir* before she left me on my own for my last hours in the city.

My first steps out of the studio found my local café closed. *Quelle horreur!* I thought it must be closed on Fridays and found that I couldn't bring myself to enter another café. I walked with heavy steps to say goodbye to the Eiffel Tower from the first place I saw it at Pont de l'Alma. The morning was dove gray like when I first arrived, though not as wet. Still, I felt the moisture in Paris's eyes and mine as I stood on the bridge and watched people heading to work. I'd like to believe I didn't stand out as *l'Américaine*, because this city had come to feel like home.

I returned to my apartment for a brief stop and resigned myself to going to Starbucks down the street. I wasn't willing to risk having a bad cup of coffee at a new café; instead, I was going to forego my resolve by resorting to the old standard of familiar. But Paris is a place of magic where dreams, both large and small, really do come true. When I neared the end of Rue Malar, I saw a morning miracle. The nighttime bars had been removed from my favorite spot at the corner of Rue Saint-Dominique and *voilà!* they were open for business.

The bell above the door tinkled as I entered and began my French patter with Madame Barista.

"*Comment allez-vous?*"

"*Bien et vous?*"

"*Trés bien.*" Attempting to mask my sadness, I ordered my breakfast. "*Je voudrais un grand café au lait et un croissant, s'il vous plaît.*" (My conversation a far cry from the stumbling "Uhhh" of a week before.)

One last time, my coffee arrived in its elegant china cup, the espresso served first followed by a small pitcher of warm milk. The croissant tasted like heaven, buttery, fresh, and warm.

With a final *au revoir*, I left the shop, where one more surprise awaited me. Madame Martine and Ginger were coming up the street toward me.

"*Bonjour, madame, et au revoir.* I'm leaving Paris today. It was a pleasure meeting you. I'm very sad to leave."

"Oh, *mais non.* Do not be sad for leaving. Paris will always be here waiting for you." Madame Martine touched my arm in reply.

"It's in here," I said, placing my hand over the center of my chest.

She nodded. "See you again. You will be back. Same place," and she pointed to our favorite café.

More than eight years later, I ran into Madame Martine on the sidewalk of Rue Amélie in the 7th arrondissement. She had another old dog, a mix this time instead of a poodle, that she'd rescued from an abusive owner. The deep lines around her mouth soared upward when I reintroduced myself and said I'd known Ginger.

Together, we bemoaned the remodel of our favorite coffee shop where the new owners had replaced china cups with nondescript mugs and the laminate tables had been exchanged for harsh lines and cold fixtures.

Later that same trip, I ran into Madame Martine a second time. She shared how the luster of Paris was fading for her. She spoke of walls marked by graffiti, homeless people on too many corners, parks that were less than pristine, and young people who showed no respect. Things had changed.

The third time I came upon her, I pretended not to see. It was difficult, but her bitterness felt contagious. She was no longer the convivial hostess I'd met over china cups and croissants. Madame Martine felt more like our remodeled café—harsh and cold. I silently prayed for her well-being and peace, then crossed the street and continued my stroll in what was still my City of Light.

Nothing will ever compare to that first trip to Paris. It was exactly what I needed to do for myself at that moment in time. As I walked through Rue Cler, slowly breathing in the morning, I knew that I was a different person than the one who arrived eight days before. I was more of me. It was like I found a piece of myself that had been tucked away.

I strolled once more through the market. The locals had their two-wheeled shopping carts filled with baguettes and fresh produce, and the dogs were out *en masse* in their well-mannered Parisian way. It was drizzly and threatened to rain, but the sky never opened. I visited the streets that were foreign to me a week before and now felt like home. I snapped a few more photos of market stalls and pastries and enjoyed the graciously aging women, walking arm in arm wearing knee-length skirts and Ferragamo shoes. When we were together, Tess commented that "The older women are not invisible here." *Mais oui*. I think perhaps I would love to grow old in France with a friend to link arms, a dog by my side, and sensible, stylish shoes.

When I turned the corner to go back to my apartment and retrieve my bags, I saw the taxi already waiting for me. Like my flight into Charles de Gaulle, the car was early. Time was trying to right itself and rush me back toward Pacific Standard Time. I wasn't ready to go *and* I missed my family and my own golden dog.

The driver opened the door to his Mercedes and loaded my luggage in the trunk. He was polite but not talkative, and I wondered if he, too, sensed my need for quiet reverie on this final drive through Paris.

The trip to the airport played out like a scene from a movie where the heroine surveys the landscape with conflicted emotions. I was going home. I was also leaving home. New clothes stretched my suitcase and fresh stories filled my journal. There would be a lot to unpack in the time that stretched before me. The car stereo swelled with a Pavarotti aria as we toured the Right Bank past Hermès and the other couture houses. Finally, the car turned onto the Champs-Élysées and we circled the Arc de Triomphe one final time.

Au revoir, Paris. Je t'aime!

CHAPTER 13

A Gift Each Day

"Paris is always a good idea."
—Audrey Hepburn

In those transitional years from full-time mom to citizen of the world, I stumbled along, seeking my personal path and noting new ways to discern which turns in the road were of my own choosing and which were blind footsteps following someone else. I longed to discover and claim the places and ways of life that made *my* heart soar. I was ready to put voice to the songs I'd been too frightened to sing. A persistent tug whispered that Paris had been a glorious place to begin.

Paris is elegance, beauty, and light. She is articulate and mysterious, gorgeous in her flamboyance, serene in her subtlety. The City of Light. A seductress with tree-lined streets that twist and curve and invite me to join their intrigue. She speaks to me in a language I can't quite conjugate; nevertheless, I hear her in the longing of my soul. Her voice makes sense to me even when I don't fully comprehend. Still, in the quiet moments when I allow myself to simply be, I feel her whisper, *Je comprends.* I know.

Writing and reflecting on my first trip to Paris became a sacred journey in and of itself. It gave me an opportunity to ponder and share

> **To be a SoulStroller is to welcome and engage with the places in the world that make one's soul come alive.**

what I continue to learn about my growing practice of SoulStrolling. To be a SoulStroller is to welcome and engage with the places in the world that make one's soul come alive, to pay attention to the whispers that speak through cobblestones and acknowledge winks of sunlight in trees and seas.

Paris is that place for me.

I know for many (myself included), traveling to Paris is a luxury and isn't the stuff of everyday life. And as I ponder why my musings return there again and again, it isn't the extravagance that captures my attention.

It's something more powerful, and, in many ways, quite simple. Paris is the place where I learned to distinguish the rhythms of my own life.

Paris is an edge for me. I don't speak the language well, but I'm trying and I become more comfortable each time I visit. I continue to put myself into situations that challenge me, like exploring new neighborhoods, eating in chic restaurants alone, and shopping in markets and boutiques where I must rely on others to help me.

It is in such contrasts and connections that Paris has been and continues to be a gracious and wise teacher, helping me become aware of my own rhythms and responses, and how to interact with the world on a larger platform. She teaches me lessons in her streets and cafés and then invites me to bring what I've learned back home to share with my family and others.

It was in booking my first trip to Paris on that Sunday morning in January 2008 that I took an indescribable leap of faith and stepped into the great unknown as a solo sojourner. On that lone journey, I discovered what it was like to have only myself to answer to. When I was hungry, I ate . . . whatever I wanted. When I was tired, I paused . . . for as long as I desired. If I wanted to walk, I did.

If the muse invited me to stand in front of a single painting for an hour or a day, it was okay. I got to make up the rules for my life. And that is what I brought home with me: the rules for my life and permission to follow its rhythms.

A SoulStroller enters each day on her own two feet with a heart willing to let the world fall in. She steps in with intention and full of wonder and curiosity about who she will encounter and how they might engage.

SoulStrollers create their own rules and rhythms and take life at whatever speed feels right in that moment.

Much of the time in ordinary life, we enter our days with thoughts clouded by what we think we should be doing or worrying about how others may judge us rather than how we can serve them. We live in fear rather than opening our hearts to love. We keep our authentic selves hidden behind have-to's and shoulds. As I've learned to discern my own rhythm, I've been able to shed the shoulds and bring a better self to the world.

There are all sorts of rules I've set up in my thinking brain. Thank goodness I began traveling before the shoulds swallowed me alive. It is through curiosity and travel that I've cracked open my rigid thinking. Travel has helped me break those shoulds. What if my body says it's in a different time zone than what the clock registers? Can that be okay? Can I go with that flow? In my logical mind, I determine that sleep comes in seven or eight-hour blocks between 10 p.m. and 6

A SoulStroller enters each day with curiosity and openness, willing to let the world fall in.

a.m. Writing is done early in the day, after meditation and with a warm cup of coffee. I'm not supposed to look at email or open up other doors of distraction before diving into my craft.

When I traveled to Paris that first time, I experienced the absolute freedom of doing what called to me in each moment. If I couldn't sleep in the middle of the night, I turned on the light and engaged in something pleasurable like watching a movie or writing a blog post, or having a snack. I didn't lay in bed for hours fighting reality. If I was awake, I embraced it. It was a soulful existence and when I think about it, I see it was an existence that actually blended quite well with the world. I was happy and so were the people I encountered throughout my day. What more could a person ask for? Why not embrace those rhythms every day? Why not here? Why not now?

Paris is a fabulous metaphor for the cloudiness that can hide an individual from his or her authentic self. In Paris, the skies are often gray and overcast. But even on the darkest day, something magical happens as the afternoon turns toward night. Light appears everywhere and we witness the brilliance hidden behind all those clouds! Beginning at dusk each night, the lights of the Eiffel Tower twinkle for a few brilliant moments each hour on the hour. It is a sight I never tire of witnessing and one that fills me with hope and joy.

Traveling has taught me to make the most of each day. There is a multitude of beauty waiting at every turn. I can't imagine there's ever any state of being called "seeing it all," especially with eyes open to the newness that is everywhere. And then the question comes: how do I bring home what I've learned?

I returned home to Seattle after nine days away and was immediately immersed in the realities of home life. I learned that Janey was angry with me because I hadn't invited her along for the trip. She didn't take into account the fact that she vehemently protested anytime I suggested she part from her friends for more than a few hours. Plus, she had school to attend. Jonathon was struggling with his sobriety again and was scheduled to enter yet another treatment center less than twenty-four hours after I landed. Bill was delighted to have me home to help manage our daily activities, and classes at the school where I helped facilitate training groups for new therapists would resume on the Monday after my arrival on Friday evening. The swift immersion swirled around my body along with jet lag, and I wondered if anyone could see the changes that I felt so deep inside me.

Time passed. Life came rushing. I missed Paris. My worries felt smaller there. I could wake up and let the wind blow me where it would. At home, I awoke from dreams of the Musée d'Orsay, Tess, the grandmother with her British grandson, and Degas's *Blue Dancers*. The urge to return to Paris rose in my chest. The City of Light and I were not finished with each other.

I was dreaming in French, but I understood that soon the trip would start to fade. In our bedroom at home, Bill slept peacefully beside me. Our golden retriever clamored for attention. Janey continued to grumble at me from beneath her hooded sweatshirt, and I wondered if something was legitimately wrong or if it was simply "normal" teenage angst. Jonathon was in treatment for the nth time. Lord, help us all. There was no such thing as control or predicting the future. Could I hold onto the changes I'd felt in Paris or would they be absorbed into the daily grind of life?

Take Your Soul for a Stroll

sOULSTROLL

A pilgrim or SoulStroller differs from a tourist or casual traveler because of their intention or desire. Tourists operate with to-do lists and destination goals. Pilgrims proceed as if on a quest. They travel by their heart.

O is for owning and embracing personal desires. Opening to the world. Stepping Out of comfort zones. Embracing Opportunities. Operating from the place that is life-giving rather than life-draining.

It would have been easy for me to question my motives of leaving home to travel to Paris in 2008, but something inside whispered: *Own this. Do this. This is important.* I didn't realize it at the time, but this was my opportunity to step into a larger world. To explore my rhythms on my terms. To stretch my ideas of what it felt like to be authentically me.

When I was hungry, I ate. When I was tired, I slept. I visited the sights that I wanted to see. I didn't follow a list of prescribed shoulds from other people. I opened my heart to myself and in return I opened it more widely to the world. What would it look like to embrace your world as if on a valiant quest instead of getting caught up in familial and cultural agendas? What if you embraced others as you yourself want to be acknowledged and welcomed? What if you tried it one tiny step at a time?

Practice SoulStrolling®

- Remember tip #1: Set aside time to get grounded, do "nothing" and then begin to imagine your heart opening first toward yourself, then loved ones, next strangers, and finally people you don't know or with whom you have differences. Breathe into the expansion. Offer love and light to the world.

- Make a list of what O means to you. Circle the items that bring joy or make a positive difference in your world and thus the world at large. Place them in a jar and select one each day. Tuck it in your pocket or place it somewhere visible.

- If you could make a list of rules to live by, what would it entail? Write it down. Choose your top three. Practice.

PART THREE

Pilgrims, Babes, & Threads

Ireland 2009

"A pilgrimage is, of course, not a vacation, but an immersion in a landscape and a courting of holy disruption along the way."

—Christine Valters Paintner

CHAPTER 14

Irish Whispers

"May the road rise up to meet you, may the wind be ever at your back. May the sun shine warm upon your face and the rain fall softly on your fields. And until we meet again, may God hold you in the hollow of his hand."

—Irish Blessing

March 2009

The morning I knew I was going to Ireland, I was sitting in my home office in Seattle, looking out the window into the misty winter morning. Opening my email inbox, I saw an invitation from Spiritual Directors International to join their upcoming fall pilgrimage to Ireland. The text spoke of "thin places," and as I dreamily gazed out my window, my stomach did a flip and something in me Knew with a capital K that I'd be going.

Shortly after I completed my counseling degree in 2006, a friend of mine suggested I check out the work of a woman named Christine Valters Paintner who specialized in combining spiritual direction and the arts. Christine is someone who I felt an immediate kinship with when I first visited her website. Not long after, I invited her to meet me for tea in Seattle. Our connection was mutual and she soon became a mentor, co-worker, and beloved friend. Over the years we've known each other, I've learned much from her about spirituality, accessing the arts, welcoming our ancestors, and pursuing pilgrimage as a lifestyle.

Christine and I had previously spoken about going to Ireland together, and upon receiving the invitation to the pilgrimage, we immediately began planning our adventure. And then Christine pulled back. She wasn't sure if the timing was right for her. She wondered if perhaps she'd gotten caught up in the thrill of our mutual excitement, so she decided to postpone her decision. I, too, started to question my misty morning excitement and waited to register.

A few weeks later, Christine and I attended the Spiritual Directors International conference where I was assisting her with a booth to sell her small books called "zines" as well as offering my limited edition book *Grace Unbound*. It was a large conference with dozens of vendors and booksellers, but as luck (or fate or magic or God) would have it, we were seated directly next to the Ireland Pilgrimage table and its hosts.

Long story short, serendipity worked her magic. I knew I was going to Ireland with or without Christine. Before the end of the conference, I had paid my deposit and was set for a trip to the Emerald Isle.

October 2009

Twenty months after Tess and I met in Paris, she decided to join Christine and me in Ireland. I flew to Dublin on my own, arriving a day before Christine. On the flight I sat next to a young man from the Colorado School of Mines, a junior on holiday, visiting a friend who was traveling abroad. He seemed blasé about such a grand adventure, the kind of excursion that filled me with a giddiness that I'd been saving up for more than twice his lifetime. Our encounter left me wondering whether to be envious of students who travel at an early age or feel sorry for them because of this presumed tendency to take travel for granted and miss the wonder and delight of it.

Transatlantic travel is grueling at best, but I managed to get a few hours of sleep on the plane. The flight attendants didn't turn the lights off for the longest time, but really, who cared? I was going to Ireland. The landing was spectacular. I listened to U2 while a crimson sash of sunrise etched its way across the pitch-black sky. Sea below and clouds above. The horizon made itself known. Lighter. Lighter. The fog and mist mixed with sea waves and land until finally the patchwork green landscape appeared. Ireland.

From the Emerald City to the Emerald Isle in twelve hours. How magnificent is that?

Tess was there to greet me. We hugged and laughed and talked about how we both love the airport scene in the Christmas classic *Love Actually*. My carry-on bags made customs a breeze. "You can see it all in eleven days," said the cheery agent. I don't think she imagined I was leaving Dublin.

I was quick to notice that Dublin is a mixed bag. Extremely pleasant people in a decisively gray city. Old blended with not-so-old and not-quite-new. Tess did her best to keep me awake for the day in order to conquer jet lag. I'm a firm believer that if I can stay up until night time on the first day in a new country, then my sleep cycles will fall into place.

She and I strolled in the Chester Beatty Library for a bit, perusing the illuminated manuscripts, and then sat in a café and sipped hot tea. Putting one foot in front of the other was almost more than I could handle, so we hopped on the Circle Line Bus tour and sat on the open-air deck. It was Tess's ploy to keep my drooping eyes from closing. We toured around the gray city that had begun to grow on me, and in the late afternoon, we checked into our hotel that Tess called "a bit stodgy."

It was comfy enough, so I settled in for a cat nap before dinner. In the early evening, we headed back out onto the brick-lined streets in search of seafood chowder and my first pint of the black elixir called Guinness. We huddled together over food and drink in a dark wood booth and made loose plans for the next day. Then I crashed back at my room and hoped the street noise drifting up from the pubs wouldn't keep me awake.

Repeating the scene from *Love Actually* one more time, Tess and I greeted Christine at the airport the next day. Our adventure started at the Hertz counter where the salesperson—I think they're technically called "agents," but this guy was clearly out to sell me—convinced us to not only get an automatic transmission (most cars are manual in Ireland), but also to get the Jeep Wrangler because he said we'd feel safer on those tiny roads. Big mistake.

While the automatic car was a good idea, driving the large Wrangler felt like driving a semi-truck down a country lane. Tess and Christine were reasonable in terms of not being backseat drivers, but I definitely felt the weight of having passengers in my care. Tess was used to driving on the left side of the road, so Christine crawled in the back and kept her eyes closed when things got tight. (I wonder if they noticed that I did the same thing?)

We started out on Friday morning from Dublin Airport and wove our way around Kilkenny, Kildare, and a few other Kils. The M6 motorway that now connects Dublin in the east and Galway on the west coast wouldn't open for another few months. The three of us quickly decided that going too far west was an ambitious feat for the brief time we had, so we decided to go where the local winding roads led us.

All went well until Saturday afternoon (our second day together) when tragedy struck. Okay, maybe it wasn't exactly tragedy, but it was definitely a bump in the road—literally. The road rose up to meet us.

We were making our way through small villages and landscapes near Glendalough, south of Dublin, when we came upon one of the bridges for which Ireland is famous. Ancient. Narrow. Sturdy. Being the cautious driver that I am, I respected the instructions at the one-lane bridge and honked my horn as I drove onto the span. So far so good.

We were nearly off the fifty-foot bridge when a much smaller car swung around the corner and onto the bridge, barreling straight toward us. My natural instincts kicked in and I swerved left to avoid being hit head on. We were met by a rousing crash as the oncoming car sped away and my left front fender made direct contact with the two-hundred-year-old stone bridge. At least, I'm pretty sure that's what happened, since my eyes may have been closed in that harrowing moment. Two-hundred-year-old stone bridge versus 2008 Jeep Wrangler. The bridge won, although that was not immediately clear.

We pulled over for a moment, got out, and surveyed the car, which looked unscathed. I practiced a few deep inhales and exhales and cursed the other driver under my breath before we got back in and continued on our merry way. Things went well until I needed to slow down. The car made a horrific scraping noise when I put on the brakes. *Yikes!* We pulled over again into a large open area and I drove around while Tess and Christine stood outside listening and watching to see if they could figure out what was happening. No luck. One prime benefit of being a SoulStroller is that feet are easier to understand than other modes of transportation. They either hurt, have blisters, or feel good enough to move on.

With cars and such, we can tell when something is wrong, but knowing how to fix it is a whole other matter.

The Irish countryside is made up of wide open spaces full of emerald rolling pastures, a few forested areas, lots of cows and sheep, and not so many people. This means that even if you can figure out how to use a cell phone to make an international call, there's probably not any cell service due to all those unpopulated rolling hills. It's a bit panic-inducing when you're in dire need.

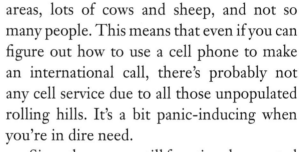

SoulStrollers are comfortable with simple modes of transportation . . . like their feet.

Since the car was still functional, we opted to climb back in and look for civilization. After a dozen or so miles, we coasted into a village where we found a building with a phone marked "Emergency" that appeared to connect to the police department. Once someone answered (after a few tries), I told him about our dilemma.

Is anyone hurt?

No.

Was there another vehicle involved?

Yes, but they sped away.

Is it a rental car?

Yes.

According to the minimally helpful person on the phone who sounded like he needed to get back to relaxing on that Saturday afternoon, our best bet was to call the rental company for help.

Hertz to the rescue? I wish I could say yes, but alas, they weren't our saviors.

By this time in the afternoon, we were tired and hungry. We couldn't use the police phone to call Hertz, so we coasted down the hill to a combo gas station and grocery mart. Once there, we inquired about a pay phone. There wasn't one, so we tried to use our cell phones, again without luck. A young woman straight out of *Brigadoon*, with burnished red hair and a trilling brogue, said we could borrow hers. I made the call.

Hertz's recommendation was to take the car to a mechanic and see what needed to be done. The locals leaned in to hear the conversation as if they were now part of it. I could feel the heat rising in my chest and tears bristling in my eyes as the agent prattled on.

"Sorry, ma'am. There's nothing we can do from here. No, I don't know the area, you'll have to take care of that yourself. I'm sorry, ma'am. No, I can't help you." It felt like the agent was anything but sorry. I took a breath and hung up the phone.

"Would ye be needing a mechanic then?" asked the red-haired woman. She pointed up the road. "You'll be wantin' to go up that way a bit. Top o' the hill, turn right. You'll see the garage behind the house."

My friends and I climbed back into our injured jeep and limped up the road in search of a mechanic. What we found were three men in flannel shirts and dungarees hanging out in their backyard. There was a large double garage and lots of tools so we felt we'd found the right spot. However, it looked like they were kicking back and ready to break open a pint or two to celebrate the weekend.

"Hellooo, fellas," I called from the driver's window with my prettiest smile. "We heard there's a mechanic here."

The three glanced at each other before one stepped forward and nodded his head. "What can we be doin' for ye?"

"Well, we kind of ran into a bridge back down the road and now the car's making a really scrunchy sound." I grimaced.

He looked at me with a question in his eyes, then motioned for me to drive the car around the yard so he could listen for the sound. As things often happen in cases like this, there was no sound. He turned his face into a half frown and hopped into the passenger seat.

"Let's take 'er for a spin," he said.

Not knowing what else to do, I looked at Tess and Christine, shrugged my shoulders, put the car in drive, and left them standing in the yard with the other two blokes. I explained to my new passenger that the sound was louder going downhill while braking, so he showed me which street to take to replicate that action.

Cranky as metal on metal, the crunching sound confirmed our dilemma. I was redeemed and he motioned for me to drive back to the garage.

"It's best if you be gettin' out while we look." He motioned with a gallant wave of his hand.

The three men squatted down, turned their bodies sideways in unison to peer under the front of the car, and shook their heads. One of them rose, got a jack, and placed it under the car to lift it up. The mechanic crawled underneath and poked around for a moment, then came back out. More head shaking.

"Looks like ye've broken the axle."

"That's not good, is it?"

"No ma'am. It's not."

"Can we still drive the car?" I asked with a hint of hope.

"Wouldn't recommend it," he said, pursing his lips and shaking his head.

"Okay." I sighed. "I guess I better call Hertz again."

The spokesman for the rental company told me to leave the car there. When I asked about a replacement, he said they didn't have one and we'd have to make our own way back to Dublin. I pressed the issue and was horrified with the result. "Too bad, so sad" was the implied response.

The band of five had been listening as I spoke, but no one—neither my old friends nor my new ones—could believe the outcome. We were now without a car and still a hundred miles from Dublin.

"Not to worry," announced the mechanic. "We'll call Chester. He'll take care of ye."

Less than an hour later, our knight in shining armor arrived driving a classic black Mercedes. Chester was the revered taxi driver of the village. He and the mechanics transferred our luggage from the jeep into the boot of his car (that's the trunk for you Yanks) and suggested we stay overnight in another town up the road. Christine, Tess, and I nodded in mute agreement and climbed in.

The picturesque village sat near the coast, and the hotel Chester recommended had a room for each of us. We were ready for solitude after a couple of action-packed days.

"Now, what time do ye need to be gettin' to Dublin tomorrow?" Chester asked. We explained that Tess needed to catch the ferry back to England. Christine and I were meeting our pilgrimage group at 1:00 p.m., and I had to stop by Hertz along the way.

"All right then. Shall I be pickin' ye up around 10:00 then?" Chester was going to see this through to the end.

"Yes, please," we replied in unison.

The next morning, Chester picked us up as promised with a gleam in his eye and a smile on his rugged face. At the ferry, we hugged Tess goodbye, then drove to the airport for my showdown with Hertz. Christine and I thought we'd say goodbye to Chester at the rental agency and catch another taxi to our rendezvous, but Chester scowled when we started to say goodbye.

"I'll wait for ye." It wasn't a question. "I imagine you'll be making short order of 'em, won't ye?" he added, eyes twinkling.

The Hertz people were forgettable. Chester was not. He unfolded a newspaper, turned off his meter, and waited.

As he predicted, we weren't long. Hertz was unrelenting. I was kind and cool. Chester never turned the meter back on. He drove us to our rendezvous, we paid our paltry fare (plus a generous tip), and off he went. It was like we'd been held in the palm of God's hand. And that, my friends, was our blessed introduction to Irish hospitality.

CHAPTER 15

The Ancestral Mind

"'Who are you?' said the Caterpillar.
Alice replied rather shyly, 'I—I hardly know, Sir, just at
present—at least I know who I was when I got up this
morning, but I think I must have changed several times
since then.'"

—Lewis Carroll

October 2009

Part of being a SoulStroller is learning to let go of the expected and open up to new ways of being and doing.

After Chester dropped us at the Grand Hotel in Dublin, we continued our journey amid forty other pilgrims, learning about Celtic traditions through ritual, teaching, silence, nature, and attentiveness to dreams and visions. Each day we gathered to greet the day through traditional Celtic prayer and ended our days in Noble Silence, a practice of sharing and deep listening.

> SoulStrollers learn to let go of the expected and open up to new ways of being and doing.

Ireland was changing me. It was a journey into another world or multiple worlds. While Paris was filled with statues, concrete corridors, and a sense of sophistication, Ireland was pastoral and ethereal. It felt earthy and ancient, unlike anywhere I'd been before. It was a thin place, where the distance between heaven and earth collapses. A feather showed its way into my future. Stones landed in my pathway and sung aloud. Dirt sifted through my fingers, each granular piece holding a full story. How could I hold so many worlds in my hands and not come away changed?

We began our pilgrimage with visits to the High Crosses—ninth century sandstone crosses depicting Old and New Testament biblical scenes—at Monasterboice, between Dublin and Glendalough. In Glendalough, also called the Monastic City, we spent several days journeying with the concepts of what we can learn by listening to nature and what the elements of earth, water, wind, and fire can teach us. We learned about the Celtic tradition *anam cara*, or soul friendship, where two hearts connect and seemingly beat as one. My own heart was shifting as I opened myself up to the rhythm of the elements and the wisdom of the ancestral mind. The ancestral mind is intuitive and experiential and lies beneath our consciousness. It operates in feelings and images and offers a source of wisdom and joy that isn't easily definable. To step into the ancestral mind is to shift away from prescribed cultural concepts of how or when things should or should not happen. The ancestral mind operates outside of time as we know it.

April 2015, La Frazione, Italy

> *The future guides us into the present. The past greets us*
> *and the three become the holy now.*
> —My Irish Journal 2009

It's the middle of the night and stories of the past slip into the present. They are from my ancient past, the stories that if I were to question too closely I might consider they never even happened. Are the tales true or are these the musings of an overactive imagination? At 1:00 a.m., they can only be true. At least that's what my inner voice tells me as I flip on the light and reach for my journal.

The small bedside lamp springs to life as I push the button and my tired eyes squint to adjust to the brightness where only moments before it was inky black. The room is cold and I hear my housemate snoring softly in the next room.

Really? You want to write now? my inner voice growls.

Yes. Now, comes my response. *This is a writers' residency after all. What could be more important right now?*

Sleep? whines the petulant voice.

Later, I reply.

It's an unusual story that whispers in my awareness of dancing girls on an Irish mountaintop. Each one takes my hand and we skip down the path together. It's taken me a long time to reach this peak and these Wee Ones have waited patiently to be acknowledged.

They were there with me in Ireland in October 2009. Real. Tangible. Visible as the gray and white sparrow feathers along the path and the variegated stone that rested in my palm. Two small girls clasping my hands with gentle pressure and filling my ears with lilting laughter. They rose through our black-bearded guide's story as forty pilgrims gathered in the fire-lit room. Is this appropriate conversation? Death. Abortion. Abandonment of children. How many people in the dimly lit room had experienced this kind of loss? Certainly not I.

The shift in my awareness began at Monasterboice, the first graveyard we visited on our Irish pilgrimage, when I noticed the gray stone boots filled with flowers—wilted and drying, yet fresh enough to know that the wound they represented was still raw. The girl (or would they call her a lass in Ireland?) was only twelve years old. Four thousand three hundred and eighty days older than the Wee Ones who never took an earthly breath.

How can I say that they never took a breath when they're here with me right now? And where is now? Am I in Seattle curled up under the purple patchwork quilt I made one frigid winter long ago, or am I dancing on the path above Glendalough in Ireland? Or writing in a hamlet in Tuscany? Feathers. Stones. Children. Reality or imagination?

I pour through my leather-bound journal to find them. They aren't there like I think they should be. Why didn't I write their story in clear sentences? Why can't I do it now? The story is neither linear nor clear. There are no concrete facts or proven details. No eyewitnesses except for the ancient stones and singing birds. Flowing water ripples in St. Kevin's well and Celtic music pours through my soul.

A gorilla is sitting on my chest. The fire-lit room has shrunk, or maybe I've grown. Did I swallow a potion like Alice did in Wonderland? Saliva pools in my mouth and bile rises up my throat. Air. I need air. It's dark outside. No ambient light in this darkened hollow. The ancient site of Glendalough lit only by a sliver of the moon. The ancient gate beckons me, the one with the carved cross near its hinges. I place my head on the cool stone. Earth rises up to greet me.

The stones bear witness. This is truth. We want to rely on people, on flesh-and-blood human beings, to confirm our experience with affirming nods and knowing looks, but they are too fragile to hold the weight of deep truth. Blood drains from veins. Bodies die and decay all too soon. Only the earth remains, like the ancient wall beneath my forehead and the wooden pen in my hand. These are my witnesses.

I used to believe that stories needed to start at the beginning. Page one: I was born. But stories are not linear. Only the Universe or God or Whoever, Whatever, Whenever knows. Perhaps when a teenager rolls her eyes and says "Whatever," it's really a plea to a higher power. Hmmm. Whatever.

I try to capture this story of the Wee Ones. I want to bear witness, to prove to you and me and the rest of the world that these things happened. That the Wee Ones existed. But there is no proof—records were destroyed or never existed and memories have been wiped clean. Still, the proof is everywhere. It's in our guide's words inside the Glendalough fireside room as he talks to our group about the unconsecrated children buried outside the official graveyard in a space called the *cillín*. The proof is in the hazel wood wand and feathers that lie atop my altar in Seattle. It's here on these pages and in the leather-bound journal that fails me with its lack of clarity.

The stories of our hearts are bigger than documented proof. The room where I write now is painted a color called French lilac. Like all flowers, lilacs bud, blossom, then fall back to earth. They bear witness to life and the cycle of living. We, humans, bud, some of us blossom, and others fall back into the earth before our time. We turn to compost and feed the ground. We become part of the earth that bears witness to great stories.

October 2009

A modern-day treasure hunter, I stood by the bubbling well in Glendalough, my feet planted in the earthy loam. Rain poured from the sky and I was washed with remembrance. The brook babbled. Memories moved. They appeared to be gone and then they were not. Not all truths are explicable.

Journal entry: October 21, 2009

Rain. Rain. Rain. All the other pilgrims are off to Dublin. A handful of us stay behind in Glendalough. I'm snug and cozy in a room by the stream with a view to the monastic gates. Rain. Spending the day following the whispers of my heart.

Off to the trail. A walk to Laragh. Skipping. Dancing. Singing in the rain. The two hold my hands and we are one. Joy-filled and at peace. I pause at St. Kevin's well. A holy site. I am washed clean.

Further down the trail, I move to the ruined church of St. Saviour. I am mesmerized. Two gates to enter. Stone steps downward. Crossing back and forth between worlds. The rain begins to pour. I am baptized by Mother Earth, sprinkling me with her heavenly water. The trail is narrow and puddle-filled. The rain pours and still I catch a glimpse—a flicker of a baby feather floating in my path. It is my feather. The match for the one gifted to me by our guide Regina. Two feathers for the top of my prayer stick.

I continue down the path. Rain comes and goes. I dry and then I am soaked again. Another pause. This time a rock captures my eye. I almost pass it by, but Mother Earth calls out to me: Stop. *I return to the spot and see the sienna-colored stone with one strong vein. I pick it up and turn it over in my hand. I am greeted by two identical veins on the opposite site. The babes. The girls have greeted me again.*

September 2016

It seemed as though I might have been dreaming on that Glendalough trail with the girls and the sienna-colored stone, but

I was wide awake. More awake perhaps than I'd ever been. I was moving with the magic of that transcendent thin place, crossing between space and time, dancing back and forth through heaven and earth.

Seven years later, their story came flooding back into my mind—the two tiny girls, the Wee Ones, whose destiny was never to be born, only imagined. Imagined yet real as the page you are reading. One was my tiny sister. We would never have had the chance to be sisters if she were born, because my mother would have stopped having children. This sister was the miscarried child who showed up after my brother and before me. Years after our mother passed away, a family friend told my sister, Dianna, that our mother lost this baby while running to catch a bus. Had the child been born as planned, I am certain I would not be here.

The second tiny one was unplanned, scheduled to arrive more than forty years ago. Her birthday in the fall of 1976, but she never took a breath or formed past a tiny embryo. A faceless doctor aborted her from my womb in a cold, sterile clinic in Tulsa, Oklahoma, when I was barely nineteen years old. The boy I married and later divorced sat in the gray waiting room and bought me a cinnamon ice cream cone afterward before we drove the seventy-five miles back to our respective fraternity and sorority houses. This babe was a secret we both kept for too long. Had she been born, I have no certainty about who I would have become or whether any of these stories would be shared.

It is not an easy task to speak of miscarried and aborted children as if they were flesh-and-blood beings. Nevertheless, they prod me to wake up and urge me to bear witness to their story.

Swirling around in this familial stew is the newest child in our family, Jonathon's daughter Violet Grace, who in her brief life has already brought boundless measures of joy to those who know her. I think of the lives she has changed and I journey back to the nineteen-year-old that I was when I made the difficult decision to terminate an unplanned pregnancy. Violet, too, was unplanned. Her parents—young, unmarried, and unsettled with their own lives—had the courage to make a different choice.

I think of the greater Universe that holds all of these stories and the individual choices we each make in our daily lives. To have sex or not? Keep a child or abort? Speak our truth or hide behind secrets and closed doors? Carry our voices into the world or stay silent behind other people's priorities? The child I gave up would have turned forty in October 2016. If she (and I've always believed this child was a she) had lived, then I wouldn't be here writing about choices and voices. I wouldn't have met my husband or mothered the two children who've taught me so much. Violet wouldn't be here either. Lives lost and others gained. Generations and ancestry lines impacted. Making sense of it all is mind-boggling—impossible, really.

I waiver, I wobble, and finally, I return to the simplest (and sometimes hardest) thing I know: gratitude. Gratitude for the sacrifices of the Wee Ones, my unborn sister and daughter. So many seemingly small choices that led to here and now. These days I try to make each choice matter, to make it consciously and deliberately. I write this book for myself and possibly for the children or grandchildren who come after me. I don't know if others will read this account. I can't make the journey or quest for them. I journey between worlds: the here and then and the yet to come. There are tangible ways to record this story that include facts and dates, but the inexplicable cannot be excluded. The intangible is where we come alive and find our strongest voices.

I find mine on the page, especially when I allow myself to wrestle with the possibilities of what if. My family of origin was all about getting from point A to B in the most efficient and expedient manner. If that meant missing the scenery along the way, so be it. This was true in everyday life and on the road of travel. Curiosity was a scarce commodity, and the way of the pilgrim was reserved for grade school pageants and Thanksgiving Day.

I think a lot about choice and destiny and how curiosity differs from overanalyzing. Did I choose to be a pilgrim or was it my destiny? And if it was my destiny, why did I have to wait so long? I was forty-five years old when I got my first passport. I could make myself crazy moving back and forth between all of the what ifs and potential missed opportunities. Life is like a toggle switch. Step one way and this happens. Step another and something totally different occurs. Ireland taught me about getting comfortable with the in-between places and making peace with past choices and decisions. Perhaps it was the destiny of the Wee Ones to pave the way for here and now.

Through travel, I'm learning what is essential to carry with me and what non-essentials I can let go. My toggle switch moves back and forth between the past I cannot change and the future I cannot know. All I have is now. Our journeys move between what is essential to know and what we still dream of and hope for.

I write to discover what I know. It's a tagline I share with Flannery O'Conner and one I've used since my early days in blogging. I write to discover what I know. The same could be said about travel. I travel to discover what I know. Yes, that feels true. I'm not talking about book knowledge, but rather deep, in-the-gut, tear-producing, heart-pounding, wordless knowing. Like now when I felt the nudge to go back to the Ireland journals. It's what I'm here to do. To follow the thread. To live in this thin space between worlds, both liminal and real.

CHAPTER 16

Following Threads

"There's a thread you follow. It goes among
things that change. But it doesn't change [. . .]
Nothing you do can stop time's unfolding.
You don't ever let go of the thread."

—William Stafford

November 2016

Like the thread of which William Stafford writes, his poem has been trailing me for more than a decade. It speaks to the journey I'm on—spiritually, personally, vocationally. I think of the poem I heard about the ancestors, traveling seas, trees keeping track of the crimes against us, the ocean opening to contain it all. And then Rumi pipes up, "Don't go back to sleep. People are going back and forth across the doorsill where the two worlds touch."

Don't go back to sleep, the ancestral mind is speaking.

The ancestral mind is speaking to me from the journals of that first trip to Ireland and the art journal I made several years later. In each journal I created a collage with a woman in a long flowing dress, her body turned toward the open sea. She is gazing across golden fields. The ancestral mind speaks to me through images that show a ship's captain and passengers on an ancient voyage. They are familiar and unknown. I am the woman looking across the fields to the ocean. I am the sea captain navigating the rocky and smooth waters. Their blood runs through my veins. Their threads are entwined in my DNA like the ancient Inuit tale where the fisherman's line caught in the bones of a skeleton woman whose angry father had hurled her, alive, into the swirling sea. The ancestors whisper to me through strains of music playing on my iPhone. *In spirit, she's drifted to the ocean.* How do I unravel all that is here before me? Do I need to? Is that my journey? Is this what being a SoulStroller means to me? I'm holding onto the thread.

I'm blown away by the connections that continue to rise seemingly out of nowhere, the way the thread is woven together when I pay attention. How can it be that before my 2009 trip to Ireland, I created a collage of a woman standing over the ocean in a field of golden grass and then I forgot about her? Seven years later in 2016, I made an almost identical rendering in my visual journal. I had no memory of that first collage, but a gentle tug prompted me to go back to the Ireland journals. I knew I wasn't finished with the story from there, but I went looking for words. Instead I found images and poetry and music and the replica collage. I found music with a refrain: *I'm coming home. And I'm coming home. And I'm coming home.*

Ah, and there it is. I'm coming home. This is the journey. Always the journey toward home. We never let go of the thread. It follows us across centuries, through time and space. When we travel it accompanies us in and out of faraway countries and foreign lands.

I turn to the weathered Ireland journal again.

Journal entry: October 19, 2009

Journeying into other worlds. A feather showing its way into my future. The future already stirring. Past and present. Hawk feather—the gift of sight. The two babes sacrificed for my life. To make sacred. The baby girl before me and after me. Sacrificed to make my life sacred. Without them, I would not be Jonathon's mother. Much sacrifice for him and vice versa? Yes, the swirling story coming at me and before me. Our guide's story, the babies, the cillín. My sister and my daughter. Crazy. Wild. Blessed. What a blessed time. The walk up to the monastic gates. Stumbling back alone in the dark. Walking by the brook. Tears flowing. A child on either side. Worlds opening up. Giftedness. Yes. I know. Amen.

Something deep was happening. The signs of change marked my pathway, hawk feather leading the way. It was like the tethers of my conventional life were bursting their buckles. I felt a touch crazed, euphorically wild like a stallion set free, and blessed by the kiss of Mother Earth I could feel on my forehead. The darkness held me that October night as I stumbled out of the gathering room after my heart shredded when our host described the stories of the lost children, those babes who died before baptism, buried in the *cillín*, the unconsecrated ground. The forgotten children. The silent ones . . . like me.

It was in the desolation in Ireland that I was introduced to an ancient ritual of making a prayer stick to unite the prayers of this world with the spirits of heaven and earth. It was a Native American tradition that, in this case, would unite my past stories of a child growing up in Oklahoma with the current narrative of a woman on a journey to heal her life.

The time came while I was in Glendalough to create my magic wand. I gathered the bare necessities: a stick from the hazel tree in St. Kevin's desert, the feathers tucked inside my journal that had appeared on my holy walks in Ireland, and yarn from my friend

Donna who prays with each knit and purl. Leaving the warmth of the hotel behind, I entered the Monastic City, forgetting that my destination, St. Mary's Church, was down the road and outside the City walls. The mockery of women and children being placed apart from the mainstream is not lost on me. I turned around and touched the engraved stone cross before exiting the gates.

Time shifts.

A break in the rain welcomes me. I move with meditative footsteps, my heart sits in my throat, tears form, and the visceral voice whispers, "The ancestors are waiting."

I climb over the stone and wooden stiles into the field where three sheep stand in a triangle as if arranged for a photoshoot. I sketch an image in my mind. I pass through the field, navigate one more stile, and watch for sheep dung. Placing one hiking boot after the other, I cross over the final stone wall where St. Mary's stands before me. Dating back to the tenth century, this nave and chancel church was likely built as a convent chapel or a gathering church for women in general, but on this day she belongs to me. I hold the hazel wood baton in my hand and feel the feminine spirit that bridges the worlds between heaven and earth, now and then, today and tomorrow.

Through the blackberry brambles I scramble, into the *cillín*, the abandoned graveyard on the northwest corner of the church grounds. It looks like a discarded garden plot. Weeds and grass fill the area and an empty jar sits at the edge. I remember that a jar is a hieroglyph for the heart. How comforting to see a visible reminder in this tiny patch where the children lie forgotten. Today, they are not forgotten. Their cries beckon me to never leave them alone. We join together in the sacred womb of branches, brambles, and unturned soil.

Sitting on a moss-covered stump, I gather my tools of stick, feathers, and string. My ancient instincts kick in and it is like I've done this forever. One hundred times. A thousand. A million.

My vision narrows to what is right before me. I place two small feathers near the top of the stick, position Donna's yarn to anchor the feathers and begin to pray. One wrap around the wand. One prayer. Another revolution, another prayer, and so it goes. I pray for the lost babes. I pray they will no longer be lost.

I don't know how long this lasts. Time stops. My prayers could fill the Universe and so they shall. I wrap and pray until the rain begins, signaling it's time to start the next phase of this ceremony, the one that's been unwritten until now yet has been lingering in the heavens since the beginning of time.

I crawl on hands and knees out of the brambles, kissing the *cillín* with my heart. Prayer stick in hand, I enter the door of St. Mary's, crossing through the doorway made of seven granite stones built like a cyclops, three on each side and one large one at the top center. On the underside of the lintel is a diagonal cross opening into circles in the center with arms extending outward. Its presence highlights the purpose of this place as refuge and sanctuary. My fingers lift to touch the cross as I pass through.

I walk slowly to the altar where the abandoned rock baptistry has filled with fresh rain water. Gently, I dip my fingers into the pool and bathe the feathers. I am struck by the brilliant blue stripe on the larger feather. Blue, the color of the throat chakra, that energetic center that invites us to speak our truths into the world. I notice the remaining small stones from our group ceremony held here only a few days ago—so much has transpired since then. I survey the ground for a place to plant my stick inside the nave and am met by a stubborn pebbled floor. I exit St. Mary's and return to the spot at its side where we dug up soil and held it in the palm of our hands to remember the forgotten children.

Standing in the misty air, I wonder if something or someone is watching me. My attention scans across the outer yard and lands on a tiny cross, the smallest recognizable one in the area. *Here. Here. Lay your prayers here.* The veil between heaven and earth, between reality and mystery is thin. The words spoken are audible and there is no reason to question their source.

Without effort, I plant my prayer stick into the ground near the tiny cross. Hazel wood connects to Mother Earth and feathers reach toward heaven. I pause and ponder what is next in this ceremony that is writing its own script. I notice the plush green grass and reach to touch it with my fingers while an otherworldly voice invites, *Take off your shoes for you are standing on holy ground*. Is this the same voice Moses heard in the wilderness?

It's been my dream to dig my toes into the Irish countryside and so I willingly comply. Prayer stick standing as sentry, I remove my shoes and begin to walk in a counterclockwise circle around St. Mary's, the holy vessel of the Divine Feminine. Rain falls around me. One step leads to another. The Monastic City lies before me. I pause at the northeast corner of the church, next to a tree. The birds are sharing their vocal beauty and the rain begins to fall in earnest. I remove my knitted cap and spread my arms to fly, then lift my face to the heavens. The birds' symphony continues. *Blessed be. Blessed be. Blessed be.* Tears and laughter mingle with rain. I am baptized afresh by my surroundings.

Continuing on my path, I hear the words, *Let go of the stone in your heart.* I reach into my pocket and feel the stone that called my name on the trail while walking with the Wee Ones. It had hopped into my pocket along with the thread and feathers. I resist the invitation to let it go. It's a tangible and visible symbol of what's transpired in the past few days. I haven't yet shown it to anyone else. *Let go of the stone in your heart.* The words come again and I know I'm being asked to leave this rock here.

With light steps, I re-enter the church. My feet are bare and the rocks beneath them are sharp. Slowly, slowly I approach the altar once more. I dip the stone into the baptismal water and wash it clean, then I place it next to the smaller pebbles on the altar after pressing it to my lips to say goodbye. "You'll be safe here, little one," I whisper.

I return to my prayer stick, planted next to the cross. On the way there, two birds fly overhead. *What is God's will for a wing? Every bird knows that.* Teresa of Avila speaks to me.

The Wee Ones fly together in heaven, rising through the mighty oak and gentle hazel. Wands wave over the *cillín*, the children who are lost no more. I am home. We are home. Together.

I bend down and pull on my socks and shoes, thank the elements for holding and carrying my prayers, and gently remove the wand from the ground. I love you, my Wee Ones. Without you, I would not be me.

And so, I continue this act of planting, listening, and remembering. Remembering. Putting pieces together and stringing fragile threads onto a wobbly loom like a novice weaver trying to make sense of shape and form. Weaving words together to be remembered and to remember those who come before and after me—this is my act of SoulStrolling.

To SoulStroll is to remember—to weave together experiences, people, places, and words until we are made whole again.

To be re-membered. To bring the scattered bones back together. To sing the flesh onto our barren skeletons. To build my

stories from the ground up, brick by brick, footstep by footstep, prayer upon prayer.

CHAPTER 17

Darkness of the Night

"Only those willing to walk through the dark night will be able to see the beauty of the moon and the brilliance of the stars."

—Archbishop Socrates Villegas

October 2009

My time in Ireland felt like it passed through my life as dreamily as rain pouring on the autumn leaves in Glendalough. It lingered and washed over me with a richness as golden as those leaves. And then it was time to return to Seattle.

Bill and I had an unspoken agreement that time away was precisely that—time away. He knew how to reach me in case of emergency, and otherwise my phone was turned off and email access limited to allow for a true experience of being out of the flow of everyday life. Bill is an honorable man who respected our agreement nearly to a fault.

My journey home was excruciating. It included an eight-and-a-half-hour flight from Dublin to Chicago O'Hare followed by a seven-hour layover before I could board my final flight to Seattle. By the time I made it through customs at SeaTac, I'd been traveling for more than twenty-four hours. It was past midnight local time and two calendar days after I'd left Ireland. I was exhilarated and exhausted.

"Tell me about your trip," Bill said as he drove north on Route 509 toward our Ballard home.

"Oh man, loaded question," I replied. "It was amazing. Wonderful. Life changing. More than I can answer right now."

"That's good. Really good, honey. I'm glad you had a good trip." It wasn't a rousing response, but we were both tired so I wasn't surprised that our conversation was slow.

After a long pause, Bill took a deep breath and continued. "Honey, I got some bad news this week."

I sucked in my breath. It was dark in the car, and my normal sensibilities that something might be wrong were dulled with jet lag.

"Oh?" was all I could muster. I later learned that he'd prayed for hours that I wouldn't call him from the hotel or one of the airports. He knew this news needed to be relayed in person, and he couldn't lie to me over the phone.

"Mary's been diagnosed with breast cancer."

Mary is a dear family friend and I'm ashamed to say that I breathed a tad more freely when I realized that the bad news wasn't about one of our children. Yes, I was sorry for our friend, terribly sorry, but I was more relieved that my kids were fine.

Bill wasn't through though.

"And Janey . . . well, she's having a hard time at school."

I focused on the car headlights in the road, dim on the dark corridor that lay before us. We were the only car on the highway. Bill was talking, but my ears weren't working. "Some girls . . . drinking . . . football game . . . suspension. She'll be okay . . . I handled it." I nodded and wished that the dark night would swallow me whole, that I could scoop my sweet girl into my arms and fly her back to Ireland with me.

"Mm-hmm. Mm-hmm. Mm-hmm. What?" I tried to listen, but my brain wouldn't engage. And then Bill started to cry. I hadn't heard the bad news yet.

"And our boy . . . well, he's done it this time, honey. It's really bad." Between Bill's sobs and my faulty brain, I caught pieces of the story. Somewhere between finishing rehab more than a year before and taking classes at the community college, he'd started dabbling in drugs again. Now he'd been involved in a drug deal gone bad. He'd been arrested in Tacoma and the outlook wasn't good. He was facing time in prison.

I remembered reason #103 why I'd gone away. Life at home could be excruciatingly hard.

My official pilgrimage ended abruptly on that road home from the airport. Ordinary life began again. I journaled between two worlds and two notebooks. I've never been great at transitions. For example, I have a tendency to hang onto summer until the last ray of warm sunshine is swallowed into winter's chill, and God occasionally has to use a giant 2x4 to capture my attention or knock me out of complacency. My head pounded, literally and metaphorically.

It was hard to leave Ireland—to reconcile the weeks there, to come to grips with life in Seattle, and to witness the pain of my children. Jonathon disintegrating into more alcohol, drugs, and crime. Janey disappearing into teenage sullenness and victimhood of mean girl madness. Bill was hanging on by his own thread, going to work and support meetings. I stood by and wondered if I would be swallowed by their stories. Is that what a good mother does? She stays with her family until she's swallowed alive, piece by piece? Maybe I wasn't brave enough or strong enough to stay. But Paris and Ireland had taught me that I am brave and strong.

I honestly don't know how we didn't all disintegrate during that time. I like to think it's because we were strong. Maybe we were lucky, but luck is a fickle mistress, and I no longer believe in a god with a white beard who lives in the sky and pulls puppet strings while spouting, "You get to be lucky. You don't."

Then and now, I believed in following my instincts, in practicing discernment, and listening to the choices that felt life-giving instead of life-draining. If I let it, the life would have been sucked right out of me like the darkness that swallowed our headlights on the road home from the airport. But I had tasted freedom. I tasted it in the cactus field in Mexico and on the deserted island at Lake Texoma. I'd felt it in the silence of Notre Dame and standing beneath the shadow of the Eiffel Tower. Freedom had spoken to me in the hills of Ireland.

In a favorite fable of mine called *The Knight in Rusty Armor*, a wizard asks the knight in regard to his loved ones, "If you can't take care of yourself, how will you take care of them?" The thought of being responsible for my husband and near-adult children made me feel like I was locked inside my own rusty breastplate. The simplest daily tasks were all I could manage. If I remained inside that armor, how could I ever be present with my family? So, I took my millionth deep breath, pulled on my big girl panties, and made sure everyone else's underwear was clean and folded.

Only three days after arriving home from Ireland, I repacked my bag and prepared to drive to an ancestors retreat near Seattle that I'd signed up for months earlier.

The threads of ancestry beckoned me to come closer. It felt like they were leading me toward the future *and* were already there. My soul teetered between this world and beyond. The veil in Seattle felt as thin as the Irish atmosphere. A sign outside a pub in Dublin that said "Steeven's" floated into my memory. Were they my ancestors? Do my roots link back to that isle of hospitality? My parents always claimed we were from America. Period. No need to look further than that, or so they said.

A cousin I hadn't heard from since I was sixteen years old (Richard, my father's nephew) popped up out of the blue while

I was traveling in Ireland. He sent an email to my siblings and me describing a box of photos and memorabilia that no one knew existed. A woman in San Diego had discovered the box at a pawn shop and traced it back to Richard. Photos and birth records that could easily have been thrown away found their way back to us. My family rarely discussed lineage, but when I read Richard's email, my mind drifted to images of the Oklahoma City graveyard where my father's maternal lineage, the Gilmores, are laid to rest. I wondered about the story of my father's father, John David Stevens, the grandfather we never met or talked about. It was a passing thought that raised more questions with fewer answers.

In the Northern Hemisphere, October 31 marks the Celtic version of New Year's Eve—the beginning of winter, and the time with the thinnest veil between worlds. Whether or not you believe in ghosts or Halloween goblins, or talking stones and whispering winds, it is a potent time of year to explore the legacy passed onto us by our ancestors, and it was swiftly approaching.

Like Carl Jung, I believe that images often speak more clearly to our inner world than words ever can. In that vein, I have a collection of collaged cards that I've made in honor of different seasons and attributes of my life. They allow me to tap into the recesses of my mind in ways not unlike what I'd experienced in Ireland through the stones and brambles, crosses and landscapes.

While pondering my recent pilgrimage, the upcoming retreat, and my decision to leave home again so soon, I selected a card at random and lay it on my home altar. The words began to flow.

Journal entry: October 29, 2009

My ancestors call to me like sand pouring through an hourglass. They whisper and prod and announce their presence through endless means and voices. "Watch, listen, pay attention."

With red poppies in the hands of bright-eyed girls and sultry women, they murmur, "Pay us honor. We are here." They come to me in the pathway of a labyrinth, "This is how you build a house. All is necessary. All."

They dance with me and frighten me and send love bumps and goose bumps up my spine and down my arms. They float in the dust of fall-kissed sunshine and hang heavy in the mist of an October day. "We are here. We are here. We are here."

"Honor. Love. Obey. Listen. Do not be afraid . . ." And still my heart pounds with trepidation for I am stepping into unknown territory, yet known for generations. Held within our bones. Buried in family plots and unmarked graves.

Ancient. Omniscient. Benevolent.

"Call on us and we will come. Bury us and we will plague your dreams and stall your life."

"Come," they say in the song of a wooden flute and the heartbeat of a drum. They twinkle in the eyes of my children and the wrinkles of my soul. Like an eternal flame, they will not be squelched. Like St. Brigid and her Kildare women, I am a tender of the fire. My fire burns bright. It calls to the ancestors just as they call to me.

I do not understand this road nor do I need to. I am drawn. I am comforted. I am safe. I am astounded and enlivened. Enriched and enraged. There is so much I do not understand. I want the answers to be solid like their tombstones. Instead they slip through my fingers like the mist of morning . . .

CHAPTER 18

Dancing with the Ancestors

"If you look deeply into the palm of your hand, you will see your parents and all generations of your ancestors. All of them are alive in this moment. Each is present in your body. You are the continuation of each of these people."

—Thich Nhat Hanh

October 2009

Nestled into the retreat center on Hood Canal with a dozen other women, the ancestors continue to drift in and out of my dreams. Offering gifts. Opening doors. Ethereal and tangibly present. To sleep is to rest in another realm where aunts and uncles, grandparents, and friends from the past morph in and out of consciousness offering their gifts of love, humor, presence, creativity, concern, and sensuality. The list goes on, carrying what I recognize and what I don't.

The ancestors are here. My grandmothers, Anne from my father's side and Myrtice, my mother's. Stern and buxom, they transform into giggling girls as I prepare to enter the labyrinth walk. *Come on. Come on. Come play with us. We'll skip down the path together*, they beckon.

The girls and I are joined by other faces from my life. More stern women of my past. Bright faces of the future. I recall a vision I had once during a meditation: "Grammy, I love you," said a tiny golden-haired girl. The future is present as an unborn Violet Grace flashes before my mind's eye.

Still I am resistant. Resistant to believe. Resistant to let go of the stone on my heart. What will I hold onto if I let it go? I resist because I am one of these women. Stern. Solemn. Scared and scarred. I have learned their attributes well. Our protective shield is formidable. What are we protecting? *Our hearts*, whispers the one I can't quite name.

My lineage includes preachers, farmers, a sign hanger. Hard-working, salt-of-the-earth people. Is that who we are? Who I am? How did my mother's sister, Audra, make it to college? Was she the first and only one? She was the eldest, so it seems odd that no one else in her generation furthered their education. My mother talked of wanting to go to college. She said she would have studied English. Did her missed chance contribute to her sternness? How did it impact her voice, the voice that raised me? The voice that I use to raise my children?

So many questions drift in this fragile air, this time when the veil between heaven and earth is wafer thin. Our retreat leader says the ancestral mind is "charged with looking after our well-being." I tremble at the sentiment on this Hallow's Eve. Still, I choose to open my mind and heart to be greeted by more ghosts of my past and share them with those who come after me.

Will my lineage dissolve into giggling girls as they did in the labyrinth, or will the embittered, sarcastic, hardened ones rise up in their stead? Whoever comes, I know I am a reflection of them. All of them.

I am exhausted, wrung out, saturated. This feels like too-much-of-a-good-thing syndrome, nearing counterproductive results. Always, we are greeted by the question of balance. Will I move forward or is it time to pause and slow down? When will I say enough is enough?

During our morning retreat activities, we were invited to engage in a dance with an ancestor (or ancestors). I began mine as a young girl, standing on my daddy's feet. So sweet and tender, this being transported back in time. Patent leather shoes on top of scuffed work boots. While I can't fully remember, I believe I did that same dance in real life with my father. Maybe I danced that way with my mother, too.

What I do remember about the dance is the feel of solid feet beneath my own, holding the weight of me; then growing older and taller until I could look my partner in the eye. My sister's ex-husband was there. Next came my uncles. Uncle Slats was the tallest. His son Richard (who found the memorabilia box) appeared. Uncle Earl, the Shriner clown. Uncle Marion, a school bus driver. Where was my brother David in this dance? He showed up in my dreams the night before—perhaps that was enough. This first dance with so many of the men from my young life moved me in a tender and tangible way. I felt protected and adored.

For the next dance, we were partnered up and witnessed by an earthly "angel." My dance felt tiny and small under her watchful eye. Once again, I was Daddy's little girl. Small and growing bigger until I was looking into the eyes of my son, Jonathon—my beautiful, smiling boy.

The two—Daddy and Jonathon—morphed back and forth between each other until I could not distinguish between them.

Tears streamed down my face as I wondered whether or not I'd lost them both. My son who had drifted away. Imprisoned. We hadn't spoken or connected for weeks. Still, I carried him in my heart.

I lost my father when I was nineteen. Had I lost my son when he was twenty? *Oh Lord, I want him to be flesh and blood, not a Halloween ghost!* He was dressed up like a tough guy—a criminal—but in my heart he was a young boy, still tender and innocent. I feared for the hardening of his heart. Do each of us carry the weightiness of life in our hearts? Does he carry a piece of my stone in his?

My angel-witness suggested I call on my father to help my son, his namesake, so several hours later while walking in the woods, I asked my father to be with and protect his grandson. He could be with him in ways I could not. He would not judge him. Of all my relatives and ancestors, I did not fear judgment from my father. He might kick my son's butt in love, because they are cut from the same cloth. But he would not judge.

The men faded into the background and I turned toward my sister Dianna, who had physically joined me on the retreat, her presence an amazing gift. She did an exercise I couldn't do where she embodied our mother in the time around our father's death. Dianna learned during this enactment that Mother did the best she could do. She was trying to protect each of us from the grief of our father's death. My family did not do grief. There was no space given, but I was learning (with the help of these ancestors and others) to give space for grieving and exploration. They were lessons I would desperately need.

In December 2009, Jonathon was sentenced to almost five years in prison. He would serve three and a half years. When grief, exhaustion, and the emotional overload of all that had transpired screamed that enough was enough, I listened. Instead of pulling myself up by my bootstraps and pushing through in the tradition of past generations, I heeded my internal voice and agreed that it was okay to crawl into bed, curl into a ball, and pull the covers over my head for as long as I needed. I thanked God for the lessons of self-care and grace that I'd learned through life and travel over the past few years.

Take Your Soul for a Stroll

soUlstroll

Part of being a SoulStroller is learning to let go of the expected and open up to new ways of being and doing. It is through curiosity and travel that I've cracked open my rigid thinking.

U is for uncovering *your* universe. Understanding what makes you tick, so you can better understand and unite with others. Uncover. Understand. Unite.

Following everyone else's rules had kept me locked in my own metaphorical prison. Even as a self-employed therapist and writer, I made rigid rules for myself because I didn't understand there was another way. Going on a pilgrimage to Ireland with forty people taught me that I have my own personal universe to understand, even if there is a group agenda. Had I stuck with the program and gone into Dublin with the other pilgrims instead of listening to the whispers of my heart, I'm not sure I would have met the Wee Ones on the trail above Glendalough. Uncovering my personal universe helped me begin to heal in ways I could never have fathomed, had I fallen in line with what I thought I was supposed to do.

Where might you be following agendas that aren't of your own making? What if you brought in a touch of curiosity and explored a different choice to understand what makes you tick?

Practice SoulStrolling®

- Use the prompt: My universe . . . After a few moments of silence, take pen and paper and write for five minutes without stopping. Be curious. Let your mind flow freely and without restraint. If you get stuck, simply repeat the prompt and keep writing.

- A great tool for developing personal understanding is to become your own non-judgmental witness. Emphasis on non-judgmental! As you go about each day, bring in curiosity. Instead of berating yourself for doing things in a way that you think might be less than perfect or unacceptable to others, observe and invoke the phrase: Isn't that fascinating? Practice kindness toward yourself.

- Pay attention to what signs or patterns repeat themselves in your life. For example, while in Ireland I began to notice feathers and stones. Maybe there's a word or desire that shows up over and over again. Or a person that comes to mind or a longing to sit by the water or walk through the trees. Paying attention to patterns is a great way to explore and understand what lessons may be arising and/or what makes your soul sing.

PART FOUR

Wings, Humps, & Hooves

Egypt 2010

"When we think of those companions who traveled by our side down life's road, let us not say with sadness that they left us behind, but rather say with gentle gratitude that they once were with us."

—Author Unknown

CHAPTER 19

Standing on Holy Ground

"If the journey you have chosen is indeed a pilgrimage, a soulful journey, it will be rigorous. Ancient wisdom suggests if you aren't trembling as you approach the sacred, it isn't the real thing. The sacred, in its various guises as holy ground, art, or knowledge, evokes emotion and commotion."

—Phil Cousineau

September 2010

In sharp contrast to my Paris trip of 2008 when I shared each step of my process with an online blogging community, my trip to the Sinai desert was enveloped in silent revelation. Instead of testing the waters for approval, like I did before going to Paris, my preparations were internal, with fewer words to outwardly convey what was happening.

It's taken me years to find adequate language for this essence of calling that is principally instinctual, but author and comparative mythology professor, Joseph Campbell, comes closest with his description of a shift in our "spiritual center of gravity." Campbell spent a lifetime writing volumes on the topic of the hero's journey and what it means to hear and follow the call. The call comes when we are asked to move into a new realm, like leaving home or traveling to an exotic place like Egypt. Something rises from deep within and answers *yes*.

To SoulStroll is to travel by the heart and listen when destiny calls, even though we don't understand it may be destiny calling. The road less traveled is filled with what I call SoulStrollers and others refer to as pilgrims or intentional travelers. Saying yes to this kind of adventure generates a feeling of lightness and joy; it's not heavy or oppressive. SoulStrollers respond to their personal nudge from within to throw off the bowlines and do something "foolish" (society's word, not mine) like travel to the Sinai or Sahara. They avoid spending their time, money, and effort on endeavors that fill them with heaviness and dread.

To SoulStroll is to listen when destiny calls. Saying yes generates a feeling of lightness and joy. SoulStrollers avoid spending resources on endeavors that feel unnaturally weighty or heavy.

Once I began to bear witness to my patterns and preferences, I noticed there were numerous instances where I'd be humming along doing something naturally, like putting together certain ingredients for a meal or intuitively exploring a lead in psychotherapy, only to discover there was an official name for what I'd been doing without formal instruction. No one taught me how to do what I was intuitively practicing. There wasn't anything formulaic about my approach. The natural way of being came from an instinctual or innate lead. I was listening to my heart, like a pilgrim on an unnamed quest.

I think that's true for most of the natural truths in life. We know the truth or recipe somewhere deep inside us, whether it comes to us through personal experience, our lineage (i.e., ancestry), the collective unconscious, or from an infinite power that operates on a scale greater than we can ever grasp or imagine.

When the invitation to travel to Egypt came, a deep sense of knowing cradled me. It felt light and tasted of freedom. I knew going there was what I was supposed to be doing. Things on the home front had settled down. Bill was enjoying his work, Jonathon was serving his time, and as a senior, Janey was counting the months until she'd be free of high school.

While Paris was a journey of its own kind, Ireland was my first official pilgrimage where the primary purpose was to visit holy sites. It was in Ireland that I knew I'd be going to Egypt, even though I had no idea the timing would come so quickly. One evening in the fireside room in Glendalough, while our guide shared about the similarities between the desert *ammas* and *abbas* of Egypt and the religious mothers and fathers who settled in Ireland to practice Celtic spirituality, I envisioned myself riding a camel. That was it. Me on a camel. In one brief moment, I knew I'd travel to Egypt one day.

Not so many months later, after I'd resigned from my facilitator position at the graduate school and established a private psychotherapy practice, I received a personal invitation from Regina, the same guide who co-led us in Ireland, about her upcoming trip to the Sinai Desert. Even though I knew I'd need to rearrange client schedules and clear the calendar at home, I understood deep inside that saying no was not an option for me.

A second pilgrimage is like experiencing childbirth a second time around. You've been through it once before, so there are expectations that come with anticipation. With the first child or pilgrimage, you don't know what you're in for and ignorance, as they say, is bliss. In both examples, it's possible to get caught up in the excitement of the preparation without a clue of the life-changing impact that awaits. With a first child, there's no memory of prolonged labor or countless, sleep-deprived nights. For me, being pregnant had been exciting. I was one of the lucky women who bypassed severe morning sickness and was told I carried a glow on my face even while my belly expanded. I didn't worry about the delivery because I was in good health and had a great childbirth coach.

Ireland was like my first child. I had prepared for and anticipated it, and I understood it would alter my life. I didn't, however, factor in the discombobulating seasons of ongoing change. Once a person has stepped onto holy ground with both feet, it's hard to go back to an ordinary pathway.

When I was pregnant with our daughter Janey, I remembered the thirty-six hours of labor that came with Jonathon and the fatigue that came after. I also had memories of the incredible joy of bringing new life into our midst and watching that child develop and grow. The motherhood memories left me with a mixture of anticipation alongside occasional perspiration. The same could be said for this second pilgrimage.

Preparing to leave for the Sinai desert was a time filled with trembling and awe. I knew I was approaching more holy ground. While in Ireland, I had removed my shoes and sunk my toes in the damp loam in the graveyard of St. Mary's Church. I walked across sharp rocks in the crumbling chapel and felt the sting of holiness surround me. The contrast of that damp climate and where I was going couldn't have been greater. Arid air. Burning sand. Desolate terrain. I wondered if my feet would beg to curl their toes into the hot desert sand. Would I travel in the pathway of Moses and receive the command to remove my shoes, as he had?

No matter how many times I pack my bags or step into a new experience, I must ask myself how best to prepare. There isn't a prescriptive packing list or formal rules of engagement.

Storyteller and sojourner Phil Cousineau says if the journey is the "real thing" then it will be challenging, with trembling in its wake. In the weeks before my departure date, I wondered over and over if this was real. The pesky naysayers of my mind always had something to share. *Nope. Don't do it. This is crazy.* And then I would read a phrase or hear a gentle guiding voice offer, *Yes, dear one. This is for you*, and I would tremble in awe and joy mixed with terror. I was in the presence of an almighty God who beckoned me to don my desert attire, pare down, and simply come.

SoulStrollers understand there aren't formal rules of engagement when they choose to step into a new experience.

Simplicity became my guide during that season of preparation. My body was strong and lean from tri-weekly hot yoga classes I had been attending with Bill. My most challenging pose was camel, a back-bending, heart-opening pose. There are no coincidences. I knew that Spirit would call on me to lean in and open my heart in the coming days.

My home was tidy and uncluttered from removing items that no longer served me or took up excess space in my life, like ill-fitting clothes and unwanted heirlooms. I was opening up for something. I didn't know what or dare to guess. This journey beckoned me like a deer to water, like a Bedouin to an oasis. Surety left my thinking and entered my depths. I was standing on holy ground even while I trembled in anticipation of what lay before me.

CHAPTER 20

Seriously? Be?

"I had a beehive
here inside my heart.
And the golden bees
were making white combs
and sweet honey
from my old failures."
—Antonio Machado

October 2010

Our small band of pilgrims headed to the Alabaster Mosque in the city of Cairo. Stern, religious voices inside my head chattered about entering such a place. *It's dangerous. Evil. Beware.* The old mixed with new as I trusted our guides and knew they wouldn't take us anywhere unsafe. I felt my horizons expanding and excitement filled me with joy.

The heat was oppressive in Cairo in October, so we wrapped ourselves in red and white scarves to keep the sun from our fair skin. Once we reached the entrance to the ancient mosque, we removed our shoes and stepped into the cool blue interior. Our guide pulled us aside and told us a story that I call "The Hundred Names."

"There are ninety-nine names ascribed to God Allah," explained Regina. "But if you quiet yourself and listen closely, you will hear the hundredth name that is reserved for you." The mystery and truth of her words coursed through me like an electrical current.

At the conclusion of the story, we were given time to explore the mosque on our own. I wandered around, taking note of the various people inside the mosque: families, individuals, and a few Westerners—all shoeless. Were we all nameless? The intricate weave of the carpet caught my attention and I wandered along the pattern until I heard the word *here*. It was an audible whisper from the walls. *Sit here.* Without hesitation, I obediently sat down, crossed my legs, and waited to receive my word.

Nothing. Deafening silence surrounded me.

It felt like time had both stopped *and* was moving too fast. I knew our time at the mosque was limited and I was desperate to hear my word. Grasping, I reached with the tendrils of my mind as if I could pluck the word out of the hallowed air. The only sounds I heard were the faint murmuring of other visitors and the deafening silence that filled my ears. Where was my word? I was ready. Or was I? I was willing, but it wasn't coming.

Then I heard it.

Be.

As soon as I was offered the gift that I desperately wanted to receive, I tossed it away. *What? That can't be right.* That wasn't my word. I was making it up. *Be? Are you kidding me? That can't be right.* And then our guide signaled from across the room. It was time to go.

We filed into our van and everyone began to whisper to each other about their wonderful words. I felt disappointed and had no interest in sharing my contrived word with anyone. My new friend Arleen sat next to me on the bus.

"Did you receive a word?" she asked in a hushed tone.

"Sort of. But I don't think it's the right one." My stubborn roots of perfectionism rose to the surface. I needed to get it right. I wanted something splendid and magnificent, not a simple word like *be*.

My disappointment hung around me like a necklace of sorrow. I had failed to receive the right word. I was a failure at being a pilgrim. I wasn't getting this spirituality thing down like I thought I should. I was certain the other pilgrims could see right through me and that they were laughing at the ridiculous word I'd conjured up in my head.

Ha ha. She thinks be *is a real word.*

I wrestled with my thoughts throughout the rest of the day and night and finally decided to try and let them go. I hadn't received my word in the Alabaster Mosque. So be it.

After a hazy night's sleep, we began the next day at the Pyramids of Giza. The massive structures rose out of the rocky sand, and we could hardly believe we were standing on the ground of the pharaohs. The three large pyramids were flanked by three smaller ones, built for the wives, and three more for the mothers of the pharaohs.

Visiting the pyramids was the most tourist-like thing we would do on that trip, but we couldn't come all the way to Egypt and not see the mighty giants. Tour buses lined up as far as we could see. Hundreds, probably thousands, of people milled about the grounds.

Camels and tourism police surrounded the perimeter of Giza while peddlers hawked their wares for "very good price." Our local guide Hany (pronounced "Honey") warned us to be on guard. That "very good price" could quickly increase, and thievery was not uncommon. As we walked from the bus toward our first destination, an earnest Egyptian handed me a small blue scarab and asked how many children I had. He handed me another for my second child. As I continued to walk, he offered me more gifts for my son and daughter. I graciously thanked him while keeping my stride. Finally, he stopped handing me gifts and the quiet request came. "A small amount of money, please?"

"No, thank you," I replied and handed back the treasures. Our dance of commerce ended and I moved away through the burgeoning crowds.

Hany had explained that if a person was claustrophobic, it wasn't a good idea to go into the inner chamber of a pyramid. The entrance was no more than three-and-a-half feet wide with people coming and going in both directions. There were points along the way where it was necessary to crouch down and waddle like a duck to get through the passageway. Hany said the inner chamber was often quite crowded because there were no regulations about how many people were allowed in at one time.

Nine intrepid travelers from our group entered the opening toward the tomb, knowing it would be a potentially strenuous path. Crouched in a low walk to accommodate the four-foot ceiling, my head bounced off the ancient stone until I found a pleasing rhythm to make my way up the ramp. I kept a rhythmic pace behind my roommate while pausing to touch the solid walls where so many hundreds of thousands had gone before us.

The sacred chamber was barren except for an empty sarcophagus and a few modern lights. It felt like we had entered the center of the earth. A sense of calm overcame me, not the claustrophobic feeling we'd been warned about. The far wall beckoned me to come around and place my handprint in a space where other hands had lain. My other hand mirrored it and I leaned in and touched my forehead to the wall. I was locked in a slow, intimate dance with an ancient mystery. The quiet was infinite and held me like a tender partner for several moments. When I finally opened my eyes to see if everyone else had evaporated, five of my fellow compatriots and I were standing together at the center of the earth. We'd been granted a miracle moment. With thousands of tourists outside, our handful of pilgrims received the gift of silence and profound connection inside the pyramid.

Slowly, I moved around the perimeter. I stopped by the open burial crypt and proceeded clockwise until I stood across from the place of my slow waltz. There, above the invisible impression where my forehead had touched the cool stones, was the word I heard the day before inside the Alabaster Mosque. BE.

There were only a few unremarkable letters inside this sparse space, yet somehow I had chosen to stand below the very letters that had selected me the day before. The word I had rejected. A chuckle escaped my lips and I tapped Arleen on the arm to show her the affirmation. Truth bumps gyrated down both our spines.

Still, I am a stubborn woman. Lessons must be learned over and over again until they finally start to seep into my bones. Even then, I am forgetful and must be taught again. Even with the affirmation I received inside the pyramid, I was disappointed with the simplicity of my word. *Be.* I don't know if it was arrogance or lack of trust that made me question it. Remnants of my traditional upbringing—the stories that shed doubt on the notion that God would speak to a normal person like me—clanked around in my head.

Something was happening. I could feel the truth. I wanted to accept the word as my own, but still I doubted. Such a simple word, laced with profound and deep meaning. I'm not sure what I was looking for, but a two-letter word wasn't the answer.

Our journey deepened as we left Cairo and moved into the silence of the Sinai desert. By day four, we were ready to climb Moses's mountain, the one called Sinai that stands beside St. Catherine's Monastery, the oldest continuous-operating monastery in the world.

Our band of pilgrims met in the darkness of the courtyard at 2:50 a.m. Our pilgrimage host, Dr. Rabia, walked us to the edge of the monastery where our trek guide Hussein took over. Sister Joan, a feisty nun from St. Louis, led the way on her camel like the Queen of Sheba. The rest of us traveled on foot.

With a waning moon, a fraction over half full, our path was lit with no need for flashlights. Our pace was slow, almost to the point of tediousness. One pilgrim reminded us how excitement can get in our way and how going at a steady pace would serve us well. The serpentine line of pilgrims wound its way up and around the rocky paths for what seemed like days. Each stone beneath my foot, a reminder to pay attention. Heel, toe, heel, toe. Maintain balance and focus. Each step, a reminder of those who went before me this day, and those who would follow on the next. Heel, toe, heel, toe. One foot in front of the other.

A group from Greece who made the climb at midnight began to pass us on their way down. Bedouins offered camel rides to the top, and at times I considered taking one to break the monotony of walking on the dusty trail. We passed one snack shack and then another until we finally connected with Sister Joan at Abraham's Tent for coffee, tea, and breakfast. We'd been walking for over two hours.

As we sat on the worn Bedouin blankets, snacking on bread rolls, cheese, honey, apricot jam, and hard-boiled eggs, the sun made its appearance over the horizon. Layers of color tinted the air as dawn turned into day. Tiered outlines of mountain peaks materialized before our eyes. The sounds of local chatter, belching camels, and pilgrims' voices danced in the air, punctuated by the occasional whistle of a bird.

As we made our treks to the WC, we thanked God for strong thigh muscles and mothers who taught us from an early age how to squat over toilet seats (or holes in the ground) and hold our nose at the same time. After our ablutions, we gathered inside the tent for morning liturgy. Holiness presided. As we began to prepare the space, our host Abraham offered us a stunning cloth to spread over our altar. It was a gesture of refined hospitality that we felt deep within our bones.

Candles lit, we inhaled the fire and breathed in its precious gifts. Poetry, scripture, and the lilting voice of Elvira, our resident songstress, filled the air. A simple gathering, reminiscent of Moses's time. Only our Western clothes belied the century. We were united where thousands, perhaps millions, of others had gathered for centuries.

Take off your shoes, for surely this is holy ground.

Time does strange things in this ancient land. A story from days before combines with the clicking of hiking sticks to meld into a knitter's needles, weaving, weaving, weaving. Our pilgrim's steps leave imprints in the sand and merge with the footsteps of Moses and his sister Miriam.

Was my hand touching the palm of an ancient Egyptian or Yahweh herself when I pressed my fingers into the stone inside the pyramid of Giza? Was our host Abraham a resurrection from the Bible? Truth comes in surreal snippets, like the moment I looked into the eyes of the Sinai Christ icon and knew he was beckoning me. Or when my friend Marie-Joseé described the same experience and in the sharing of our stories we *knew* and we were known. Our deepest longings crossed centuries and time. They wove together a tapestry of new and ancient stories.

Leaving St. Catherine's and traveling deeper into the desert, we were greeted by Bedouin children and their elders who offered us sweet tea, hot and strong. Only four enameled cups for the whole group. There was no sense of lack or hesitation. We would participate. It was a ritual. The elders poured. The children served. We sipped and returned our cups. The ritual began again.

A mother wrapped her tiny infant in a sheer scarf and tossed him over her back. We all gasped as his soft head swung dangerously near the stone wall. In the United States, we swaddle our babies in designer wraps and sanitize everything that comes in contact with our children. Our lives become sanitized along the way. There is much to be learned from these noble people.

I was mesmerized by the locks of brown hair that curled around one young girl's face. I saw myself mirrored in her eyes. She'd materialized out of nowhere and was our introduction into how the Bedouins share their treasures, unfurling a scarf at our feet, spread with beaded bracelets and bangles. I wanted to purchase all of her wares. I longed to linger with these curious lasses and gaze into their soulful eyes. I wondered who they would grow up to be. Likely they would become makers of tea, jewelry, and more Bedouin babies. Would they ever encounter a computer or ride in a car? Would they be happy in this simple life or dream of more? Would their mothers silence them with sterile frowns or would their voices rise and fill the skies, like sweet music in the morning dawn?

That night, settled into a campsite of sleeping bags and stars, I was spent. And without an ability to discern why, I felt sad, very sad. Maybe it was simply exhaustion or the fullness of our days. I craved space even though I was surrounded by infinity. *Be still and know that I am God.* I rolled over onto my back and watched the stars. *Be still and know that I am.* I didn't like how I was feeling. *Be still and know.* I didn't understand what was happening. *Be still.* I just wanted to be. *So be.* I just wanted to cry. *So cry.* I just wanted to sleep. *So sleep.* The whispers wafted through the night sky and I listened without question before finally drifting off.

CHAPTER 21

Past Horse, Present Bee

"Some horses will test you, some will teach you, and some will bring out the best in you."

—Author Unknown

October 2010

There is a barrenness in the desert landscape that is in sharp contrast to the life I experience at home in the Pacific Northwest. In Seattle, we are surrounded by buckets of rain and foliage bursting with color. Traveling across continents, I experience the challenge of shifting between internal and external landscapes. Egypt clearly declared, *We're not in the Emerald City anymore.* In that magical land, there were nights where my sleep was interrupted by buzzing mosquitoes and dreams that carried questions like "How do you turn down the moonlight?"

Each day our meals came with the threat of stomach aches or worse. Our guides encouraged us to eat cooked foods prepared in recommended kitchens and avoid fruits or vegetables washed in local water. One of our pilgrims never seemed to make the connection between her love of street food and the bouts of diarrhea and fever-like symptoms that latched on to her after eating them.

She would make her apologies, disappear for a day or two, only to veer back to the first local vendor she could find and repeat the cycle. We also lived with constant warnings about the ferocity of the sun and took necessary precautions to reduce the risk of sunburn and dehydration. I felt fortunate to have the wisdom of the desert fathers and mothers and our local guides to encourage and nurture me. Theirs were journeys that carried the promise of resurrection and blossoming even in the midst of barrenness and desolation.

As we traveled deeper into the core of our pilgrimage, our methods of transportation became more and more simple, from airplane to bus to jeep. The day after our tea ceremony with the Bedouin girls, my perfect traveling companion and wisdom guide showed up in the form of a majestic and sultry camel named Bella. Bella was a desert queen who knew exactly how to find blossoms in the desert. She bloomed by following her own rhythm, and in this we had much in common. Oh, how I loved that camel.

Bella and I began our morning with a Bedouin boy named Mohammed holding the multi-colored ropes that served as Bella's tether. He was the youngest of the guides, no more than ten years old. Dressed in a black tunic and pants with a lavender scarf wrapped around his head, there was a contagious twinkle in his eye. His energy was palpable and I could see he was ready to begin the day's journey. He walked ahead of us, and Bella, in her graciousness, allowed him to lead. Slowly, slowly, she and I built trust until ultimately Mohammed let go and turned the reins over to me. Even though I held the tether in my hands, Bella was in charge. Sitting atop this majestic beast, the rhythmic swaying and rocking lulled me into reverie and carried me back to another time on a different independent beast named Yoyo.

The memories come flooding back. Oklahoma. Summer of 1968. Camp Tecumseh. An empty swimming pool. A five-pound rock. A dare. A rat with a crushed skull. Blood on my conscience. I stare over the edge of the pool and can't believe the rock has fallen from my trembling hands and hit its mark. A creature dead. It's my fault. I don't feel brave.

I'm almost twelve years old with black oval-shaped glasses and crooked bangs that mirror my cutoff jean shorts. I pull the hard-sided Samsonite bag out of the bus storage space, a grimace on my face. The suitcase is almost as big as I am. That's a lot of baggage to tote around. My mother snaps a candid shot.

It's wacky, mismatched clothes day at camp. I don't want to stand out. Is this before or after the rat? Was it even the same trip? I'm not sure it matters. The tan Samsonite bag is filled with clothes that match precisely. The best I can come up with is a hot pink, sleeveless, button-up-the-front top and lime green Bermuda shorts. Not cool in 1968. I look like a neon sign. Someone please give me back my cutoffs.

And then there is Yoyo. Seventeen hands high. Midnight auburn coat. Black mane. Three feet wide hips. Daunting. He's my designated horse for the trail ride. An old guy (likely all of thirty years) boosts me into the saddle.

"Not to worry, little lady, Yoyo knows the way. Hold the reins like so and you'll be fine." There was that word again: fine.

"But, but . . ."

"Just hang on and follow the other horses. Like I said, it'll be fine."

As soon as our group of twelve leaves the stables, Yoyo begins to inch his way past the steed and rider in front of us. He lifts his hooves from a walk to a trot and breakfast jostles inside my stomach. "Slow. Slow." I hear the counselor call out. I tug the reins and squeeze my knees like he showed us. Yoyo picks up the pace. He's having none of this "fine" business. He knows the way, all right.

Soon we are traveling at a canter until he passes the lead horse and breaks into a full gallop. Trees flash by. High grass brushes against my squeezing knees. My knuckles whiten and my mouth forms an O-shape. Nothing comes out. The sound of the wind and a distant voice rushes through my ears. "Stop! Slow down!" Survival instincts kick in and I hang on for dear life. Yoyo doesn't slow. I tighten my hold. He lowers his head and aims for a telephone pole.

"Oh my God, I'm gonna die," I whimper before closing my eyes.

We can't be more than ten feet from the pole. Yoyo veers at the last moment. Wood brushes against denim. His rear end grazes the pole. He slows to a walk. It's over. I'm alive.

"Well done," chirps the counselor coming alongside us. "I guess he's tired of having riders today."

You think so? I bite my tongue. *Are you an idiot? Didn't you see I almost died?*

My whole body trembles with tears too frightened to flow. I stay in my seat and let Yoyo lead the way back to the stables at a pony's pace.

"Wow!"

"That was soooo brave!"

"Cool!"

"Look at you!"

"I would've fallen off!"

"Did you see that?"

The girls' chatter surrounds me. My hands loosen on the reins. I sit taller in my saddle until the counselor reaches out his hand to me. Dismounting onto rubbery legs, my campmates sweep me into a giggling jumble of adolescent limbs.

Maybe I am brave after all.

Bella was a glorious creature. Like Yoyo, she was one of the largest beasts in our herd and had an uncanny way of spotting the smallest patch of green from hundreds of feet away. Although she never broke into a full-out gallop, she would subtly pull away from the crowd, increase her speed with infinitesimal segments, and make her way with precision-like focus to the nourishing Acacia bush. I felt safe atop Bella and her rebellion delighted me. She was breaking the rules of the pack and so was I.

SoulStrollers break the rules of the pack.

No one I knew in my Seattle life had ever sat atop a one-humped camel and crossed the Sinai desert. I felt brave and invincible like I had after my wild romp on Yoyo.

After she'd satisfied her hunger on the local shrubs, Bella and I took our time wandering and pondering through the vast dry land. Miles of reddish sand and layered stone formations spread as far as my eye could see. At times, we moved slowly and walked along the edges of our tribe. Sometimes the pace was brisk and we bumped up alongside other pilgrims.

Each one of us pilgrims was on our own introspective voyage. In quiet moments, we relished the space to explore our personal rhythms and discover what it was like to surrender to the voices of the desert. We embraced these essential times of solitude, but also found community an important part of the journey. It was in community that I was prompted to belly laugh in tones that rang through the canyons. Community offered the forum to share my love of the earth and Great Divine with others. Like the crux of life, no single person has a map or can be certain of what lies ahead. We move through most days one step at a time, but intentional journeys allow us to notice the but/and that transforms us. There is barrenness and desolation along the trail *and* nourishment blossoms in the most unexpected places.

We lumbered along for hours on the mighty desert ships,

rocking, swaying, and dreaming. We paused for lunch near some rock formations that provided shade, where we lingered for a while to stay out of the heat of the day. The camels rested too and when I placed my hand on Bella's neck to pose for a photo, she bared her teeth and hissed at me. Her majesty didn't want her nap disturbed. Bella was teaching me about boundaries, too. My feelings were squashed a bit by her standoffishness, but I shrugged it off and ambled away to sit with Arleen in the shade until it was time to move on. By late afternoon, we reached our destination and began to make camp for the night.

Arleen and I huddled against red sandstone rocks like the red clay cliffs of my childhood and settled into the scant shade. We sat facing an enormous sandstone structure and noticed where nature had carved a heart into its center. We bolstered ourselves with cushions our Bedouin hosts had provided and then pulled out our journals. The silence was ineffable, like we'd been dropped into a vast canyon or onto another planet with no other signs of life. Time melted while we sat on the edge of I-know-not-what.

I picked up my pen and journal and began to write about the previous days: visiting St. Catherine's, the early morning climb to Mt. Sinai, and our camel ride to there and then. I swear we'd stepped into another dimension in time. The silence of the desert reminded me of the profound silence we'd experienced inside the pyramid at Giza. Our hearts beat as one with the earth and our breath linked us with our surroundings as if everything was a single, pulsing organism.

My mind reached for the words to describe this place at the edge of the world. No vegetation. Only rock, sand, and blue sky. The shadow of my hand and pen moved across the page. I could feel Arleen's presence a few feet away. And then I sensed something else. A faint hum. Another shadow crossed the page. A tiny bee was circling my hand.

A bee. No bigger than the fingernail of my index finger. It

danced loop-de-loops across the page, taunting me. *Be. Bee. Be. Bee. Don't you see? Won't you believe?*

My mouth gaped. I turned my head toward Arleen. She was already watching the tiny winged creature. We both shrugged our shoulders, looked heavenward, and burst into laughter. *Yes, I see. Yes, I will believe.* Later I came to learn that bees are longtime symbols for accomplishing the impossible. *Yes, I believe.*

A few days later our pilgrimage took us to the ancient city of Petra in South Jordan. Petra is also called the Rose City due to the color of its stone. It is carved into the hillsides and was introduced to the Western world by a Swiss explorer and has been a UNESCO World Heritage Site since 1985. There is a scene in one of the Indiana Jones movies where Jones, played by Harrison Ford, rides his horse through the winding caves and passageways of this otherworldly city. While we weren't able to ride as freely as Indiana Jones, we were able to ride horses and trot from the parking lot to the entrance of Petra.

It was a hot day in the desert, but the heat was dry and we were prepared with water bottles and layered clothing. Our tiny group was weary from the long bus and ferry rides. It's not easy to get from the Sinai into Jordan. Some pilgrims chose to remain at the hotel near the Red Sea because it would be such a long day. I was buoyed by the promise of adventure and the opportunity to explore a site I might visit only once in a lifetime.

I could feel the grit and determination of this city. It was estimated that hundreds or even thousands of people died while building Petra. There was no safety gear or scaffolding in those days, only indentations in the vertical rock to serve as ladders. The pads of my fingertips ached as I imagined gripping the stone and trying to simultaneously carve a building. Death, life, and resiliency spoke to my soul in this sacred space.

Winding through the singing passageways—called that because of the sound they make when the wind blows through—a song rose in my mind. It was probably something like "Midnight at the Oasis" but I can't quite remember. Nonetheless, I sang to myself as I soaked up the surroundings. Several of my friends walked on the other side of the passageway, maybe six or eight feet away. Out of the corner of my eye, I noticed they were pointing at me. More specifically, they were pointing at the crown of my head. I scrunched my brow in question.

"A bee," one of them shouted. "There's a bee circling your head."

I felt like Jacob waking up from his dream in the book of Genesis when he said, "Surely the Lord is in this place." There was no doubt that the bee and I were indelibly linked and something greater than I was at work.

After I returned home, bee talismans showed up everywhere. Random people I knew sent me excerpts of bee poems without understanding why they felt compelled to do so. A necklace emblazoned with the word *be* and the silver-winged insect practically jumped off a store display and wrapped itself around my neck. A friend sent me a book for no apparent reason titled *BE*.

One day, on a drive across the mountains to eastern Washington, a honey bee landed on my car door handle. Inside the car was a woman I'd offered to transport to a retreat we were both attending. I was emotionally wrestling with her neediness and was near my wits end after she'd required we stop for the third time during the hundred-mile drive. On the door handle in the middle of a Safeway parking lot was my reminder to *be*. Simply be. I chuckled, breathed a sigh of gratitude, and climbed back into the car with a renewed appreciation for pesky passengers. My spiritual world and reality were weaving their way into an extraordinary existence. The wings of bees were lifting me to a higher place.

CHAPTER 22

Egypt Reverberations

"People coming to the desert discover that they are drinking from truth. And people become more at peace with themselves because of this truth, this quiet."
—Ramadan,
a Bedouin from *Walking the Bible*
by Bruce Feiler

October 2010

I have drunk from the truth of the desert and tasted the painted landscape. Communed with the dying Acacia. Crawled inside crumbling rock. Chatted with a shade-seeking lizard, wise camels, and their Bedouin leaders. I have been washed in the silence of the early morning and the brilliance of a billion stars, the grit of sand reaching into every nook and cranny. I have felt the freedom of standing naked in a barren landscape and blending into it until I resembled finely chiseled stone.

The earth pulses in the desert. It speaks of ancient times while holding only now. Surprise has turned to reality. When I returned home, it seemed normal that it was the week celebrating St. Francis when we are called to recognize the strength and beauty of human nature and its mirror in all of creation.

The desert mirrored beauty back to me, even as my skin grew gritty, mosquito bites on my face blossomed into an epic plague, and my hair took on new designs of its own unwashed creation. I was the lizard seeking the cool shade, the camel gently rocking across uneven sand, the mother bird fiercely protecting her nest, and the painted desert floor swirling with patterns few paintbrushes would dare to create.

I am home now. I was home there. I have learned to take home with me like a true pilgrim, one who carries my heart wherever I go. I am home and the Sinai is a part of my soul. It is imprinted on every fiber of my being. I am home.

Re-entry was kind this time around with no catastrophes to report on the home front. While I was busy with clients and reintegrating into our family routine, I reminded myself to take things "slowly, slowly," a practice that had been offered daily by our wonderful guide and friend Rabia. My body started to reset itself, adjusting to the ten-hour time difference, and I enjoyed a diet of leafy greens and granola that I had missed while traveling.

Dreams that began in the desert continued to be vivid and spoke to the depth of the places I'd been. In my sleep, I danced with the moon, rocked on Bella's back, and felt the peace of great silence. I resisted turning to DVDs or Netflix and instead drifted to sleep reading *Walking the Bible* by Bruce Feiler. I had begun the book before leaving for Egypt and picked up where I left off. Stories of Mount Sinai, Father Justin (an American monk residing at St. Catherine's Monastery), ancient burial tombs, and the Bedouin people took on new and more significant meaning. I have walked those places and met these people. They are imprinted in my DNA.

There is a uniquely profound quality about stepping into a landscape where millions of people have gone before you. Centuries-old cathedrals are notorious for this out-of-time experience, but nature is often the greatest mistress of mystery. This profundity reminds me of my time in the Sinai desert where earth and sky replaced mortar and stone. In the desert, I felt like Moses or Rebekah from the Old Testament might walk by at any moment and that would be quite normal. It was yet one more example of this otherworldly sensation that feels timeless and unknown yet simultaneously known and found.

A similar experience occurred in September 2013 while Bill and I were sailing on the open Mediterranean Sea with dear friends. Being on a fifty-foot sailboat in the high rolling waves created an ungrounded feeling and the sense of being internally adrift. On our thirty-six-hour crossing from San Pietro, Italy, to Menorca, Spain, I could have sunk into despair, but the breeze on my face whispered something different. Instead of succumbing to the misery that comes with seasickness, I closed my eyes and asked for a miracle. I asked to be found. I prayed for connection and felt my toes grip the rocking boat. Peace rose like the moon. When I opened my eyes, a single dolphin danced across the bow of our boat. My husband witnessed the miracle alongside me. When I took his hand in mine and told him I'd asked for that dolphin, he smiled knowingly. Together, we had been found.

Once upon a time on a visit to Galway, I encountered a precious woman who somehow had managed to get herself from St. Louis, Missouri to Ireland and still come across as if she were frightened of her own shadow. Over coffee one morning at our bed and breakfast, she clutched her map to her chest and asked if anyone was walking into town.

"I'm afraid I'll get lost," she moaned. "Yesterday was horrible. I walked miles in the wrong direction. Can someone please come with me?"

I watched her from across the table and something stirred inside me. Of course we could walk into town with her, but that would merely delay her fears until another day. This was not a weak woman. She didn't need to be rescued. She was ready to be found, so instead of enabling her fears I looked into her eyes and simply asked, "Have you ever stayed lost?"

Sometimes we must get lost in order to be found.

While in Paris on my own one evening, I had an inexplicable urge to go to the area around Place St. Michel near the Latin Quarter. Once there, I strolled through the lively streets where restaurateurs stood on the sidewalk and beckoned patrons to come inside. Young couples strolled arm-in-arm and laughter poured out of open doorways and balconies. I knew this area well. I'd been there many times during the day. I did not feel lost, but I was slightly unsettled as I wandered without destination.

Notre Dame, came a whisper through the moonlight. *Notre Dame.*

Crossing the Seine at Petit Pont, I made my way across the worn cobblestones and stepped inside Our Lady. A mass was in progress with music resounding in achingly gorgeous strains. I stood like one of the nearby statues, listening with awe. Tears filled my eyes. A lump formed in my throat.

A SoulStroller has perspective and grace as she allows herself to get lost in order to be found.

Words my mind could not translate melted into my soul. Time shifted and the sensation of being unsettled dissipated. I had been found, even when I didn't know I was lost.

This is the SoulStroller's path—opening up to the way of curiosity with willingness, desire, and delight. It's about perspective and a touch of grace. Allowing ourselves to get lost in order to be found.

When we start to move on the outside, things naturally shift on the inside and vice versa. Perhaps the travel comes first. We acquire a passport and imagine what it would be like to cross borders into foreign lands and then begin to notice our worldview or personal beliefs begin to shift. On the other hand, we may start to shift internally and discover we've longed for travel and seek new ways of being in the larger world. The two ways of being are integrally intertwined.

Take Your Soul for a Stroll

SOU**L**STROLL

This is the SoulStroller's path—opening up to the way of curiosity with willingness, desire, and delight. It's about perspective and a touch of grace. Allowing ourselves to get lost in order to be found. When we start to move on the outside, things naturally shift on the inside and vice versa.

L is for lessons, lingering, getting lost and being found. Lessons that come from unusual teachers like bees and camels. I can't tell you how many times over the years that a bee has shown up at the precise moment I was about to drop into panic or overload mode. A fleeting moment and barely audible buzz immediately remind me to simply be. I am eternally grateful for that winged creature.

I also can't pass up the opportunity to again emphasize the benefits of getting lost. If the notion of getting lost raises a touch of trepidation in your belly or throat, ask yourself this simple question: *Have you ever stayed lost?* My hunch is that you're not reading this book in the midst of a treacherous jungle with no compass or guide, so I think you have your answer.

Practice SoulStrolling®

- Allow yourself to linger while you practice silence, sip a cup of tea, look out your window, stroll down the street, or explore destinations that call to your heart. Linger. Look. Listen.

- One of my favorite tips to getting lost in my own neighborhood is to take a source of music (iPhone, etc.) with me on a walk or run. I walk one direction for the length of a song, then turn a different direction when the music switches, and so on. This allows me to see different streets and get off my beaten path. You can also do it by randomly counting blocks or switching directions every five minutes or so.

- When traveling in other cities, practice getting off the main boulevards. Be safe, of course. This practice is a lesson in listening to your instincts. If you don't have a camel to ride or a Bedouin to lead you, rely on a map only when absolutely necessary. Astronomers and navigators still use the stars!

- Get lost. Be found.

PART FIVE

Le Cadeau de Paris
(The Gift of Paris)

Paris 2013

"You can't escape the past in Paris, and yet what's so wonderful about it is that the past and present intermingle so intangibly that it doesn't seem to burden."

—Allen Ginsberg

CHAPTER 23

Seasons & Calling

Journal entry: November 2, 2013

We are on a journey. We are travelers in this life whether or not we ever choose to pack a suitcase or carry a duffle bag.

There is something about the season of autumn that speaks of change, and for me, ultimately of travel. Perhaps it's the shifting seasons and the way the brilliance of summer begins to change into fall colors, bursting and boring. Change is visible as leaves fall to the ground and trees expose their bare branches. In Seattle where I live, clothing choices transition from light cotton to sturdier fabrics and bare arms disappear beneath multiple layers. It's fascinating how deciduous trees drop their coats and human beings pile them on. I wish I were a tree.

I've always been a warm weather girl at my core even though my current home boasts moderate temperatures throughout the year. Still, the dying leaves and fading flowers signal change. Fall is integral in our earthly cycle with its hints of grown-up wisdom dancing beside carefree childhood rhythms. It promises to bring order and ritual back into the days after the leisurely chaos of summertime. I don't really know whether it is order or ritual that I seek, nor does it matter. What I understand as I write these pages is that once again I'm called to travel in this time between summer's heat and winter's ice. It is a time in between.

A time in between. Yes, that feels true. It is the liminal space of which the mystics speak. The place between here and there, then and now, the already passed and the yet to come. It is a gracious place that greets me as nothing else can. The day-to-day pressures of the world peel away like waves rolling off the shore, and there is an instant of infinite possibility where anything could happen before reality rolls back in. It is like the moment before dawn when you know the sun will rise, but you can't yet see it. It is a space of absolute knowing with a hint of what-if. Like a bag filled with treasure, it is weighty and wonderful.

As I write, twinkling lights grace the edges of my ceiling and drape around the window in front of me. Bill joined me at yoga this morning, then left for the office. I hear Janey stirring in the kitchen, getting ready for her shift at the frozen yogurt shop. Jonathon, who was released from prison in January, is asleep on the futon in our basement. I think he still has a job at the neighborhood cafe. They're both adults now, but my mother's heart knows them primarily as my children. The children who daily teach me the process of moving close and letting go. I twirl my hands together as if I can see their futures inside my palms like a crystal ball. I pray they will learn to trust their loving instincts. I pray for sobriety and dignity and all good things. I whisper to the Universe to keep us all safe and that each person in my family will find our best pathway.

The fan from my space heater begins to purr, signaling that the room temperature has dropped below my tolerable working level of 68°F. My body is limber and warm from an hour of hot yoga, and steaming coffee fills the cup that says "follow your heart."

Yes. Follow your heart, dear one.

This time my heart leads to Paris. Again.

In the fall of 2011, I shared my love of the city with Bill, my sister, and her husband on a brief trip. Then in March 2013, I took my daughter Janey and we spent a glorious week wandering the streets together. My love affair with the city continued to grow and as they say, absence makes the heart grow fonder. It was time for another solo adventure.

"What's in Paris?" my yoga instructor had asked earlier in the day. What's in Paris? I know and yet I don't. What I know for certain is that I've been called there again like a heroine to an epic journey. Will it be epic? That I don't know either, but what I do know is that I must go.

When asked how I decide when or where I will go next, the easiest thing to say is that I just know. This is an unsatisfactory answer for many people, unless like Joseph Campbell suggests, they have also encountered a personal shift in gravity. If you've ever seen a dog perk up his ears because he's heard something that only he seems able to hear, it's like that. When you hear it, you know that *it* is asking for your attention. Individuals who've had this experience nod with approval and send me off on my adventures with words like "Bon voyage" and "Have a fabulous time!" Others look at me with question marks etched on their faces when they hear that I don't seek out these excursions. It's nearly impossible to explain that the adventures seem to seek me.

It's analogous to the line from the classic hymn, Amazing Grace where the lyrics speak of being lost then found and sight being restored to blind eyes. Each journey or adventure seems to find me. My role is to listen and respond to the call. To open my heart and see.

Once the idea is planted, there is plenty of planning involved, but the type of journey I'm describing has a sense of effortlessness that comes alongside. Airfares drop or frequent flyer seats open up. The perfect studio apartment is available for my time frame. A previous commitment is cancelled or simply falls off the calendar. There's money in my bank account and a travel map with my name on it. A sense of magic envelops the experience and I am invited to take the lead.

This doesn't mean there isn't a sense of trepidation or hint of fear. As pilgrimage guide Phil Cousineau says, "Never doubt for a moment that there will be darkness and disappointment on your travels. If we truly want to know the secret of soulful travel, we need to believe that there is something sacred waiting to be discovered in virtually every journey."

It is my calling to listen, watch for, and trust the sacred.

These trips, adventures, pilgrimages, or SoulStrolls all have a quality of being timeless, like I've been there before *and* that I'm seeing the places for the first time. I rarely, if ever, call them vacations, because SoulStrolling is about fully inhabiting life, not vacating it.

Embarking on these journeys feels like the seeds of motion were set into place long before destinations like Dublin, Vienna, or Cairo entered my geography.

As a kid, I thought Austria and Australia were the same place, just spelled differently. I wasn't a geography buff and wasn't one to keep a bucket list for places to go or things to see. My world was small. My experience with travel began in the 1950s when my parents doled out Dramamine before my truck-driving dad loaded us into the sensible sedan and hauled the family across Route 66 from Oklahoma City to San Diego like time-sensitive cargo.

SoulStrolling is about fully inhabiting life, not vacating it.

Ever since an unfortunate incident as a toddler, when I filled my aunt's lap with vomit, I'd been drugged with anti-nausea meds and forced to sleep my way across the lower western states more times than I could count. A SoulStroller enters the world with open eyes—a far cry from what I had on those road trips that were a blur of scenery from behind heavy eyelids.

Even without Dramamine, other constructs of my childhood created blinders on what I saw. I lived my first thirty years within a 150-mile radius of Oklahoma City. My community was a homogenous environment where opinions lived inside a narrow script. Everyone I knew was Protestant Christian, conservative, and white middle-class. I had one friend who seemed rich because she owned the whole collection of Nancy Drew mysteries and had a swimming pool in her house. Her father was in politics and real estate; my dad drove a semi-truck and my mother sold Avon for twenty years.

Growing up in the mid-twentieth century right off of Route 66 in the land of General Motors with a church on every corner, there wasn't a lot of room for broadening horizons or crossing borders. History and geography classes at my high school were taught by football coaches instead of historians or geography scholars. Text books were dry and learning was rote. We believed we had everything we needed right there in the insulated center of the United States. I'm grateful for those foundational decades, but it wasn't until I left Oklahoma and moved to Seattle that I began to comprehend the vastness of the world. My blinders finally began to come off.

CHAPTER 24

Three Aunties & A Rooftop Dancer

nefelibata: (n.) one who lives in the clouds of their own imagination or dreams and does not abide by the conventions of society, literature, or art.

November 2013

There is a sense of giddiness that bubbles up inside me as I prepare to go on any adventure. Excitement, delight, curiosity, and a reasonable dose of fear keep me fueled as I pack and gather everything I may need for the journey. There's a gentle push and pull of what I think I should take and what can stay behind. Packing, in its own way, highlights the metaphor of everything we carry and are invited to let go of, throughout our days.

During the preparations for my fourth trip to Paris, the intrigue of my ancestors that I tasted in Ireland resurrected itself. I pondered the family stories that said we didn't know where anyone was from. My family tree has gaps and holes, but as I studied the intricacies of what it means to be rooted in family, I began to learn and experience that our lineage doesn't automatically die when people leave this earth.

At a conference in southern Washington, I had the privilege of meeting poet Judith Prest. She and I shared an afternoon lingering in the sun while anticipating the gray winter days to come. At the end of the conference, we traded books. Even though I'd never read anything of hers before our exchange, I simply knew I would enjoy her work. I literally laughed out loud when I ran across her whole chapter titled "Ancestors." Her poem, "You are Here" has become one of my favorites, especially when I'm packing to go overseas.

"You Are Here" by Judith Prest

Wherever ever I go
I bring a crowd along:
old lovers, dead parents and pets,
my first grade teacher with her
long red fingernails
and harsh judgment;
all the girls and women I have
ever been . . .

It can be exhausting
this travel
with an entourage stretching
back nearly six decades, and
let's not even mention
the dead ancestors
whose grave magnetism
aligns the particles
of my dreams and desires:
Great Aunt Carrie, bipolar vaudeville star,
Dad's Uncle Theo, sea captain,
lead miners from Yorkshire,
French Huguenots,

Great Grandpa Theodore
drinking up his pay
from the clay mines before
Saint Ellen my great grandma
can use it for food

Perhaps this explains
my difficulty preparing for travel:
my baggage is full
before I pack the first
pair of socks.

My baggage is full before I pack the first pair of socks. We carry so much baggage with us in and out of our days. Traveling gives us the time and opportunity to decide what is essential. The early pilgrims didn't have valets or taxi cabs or elevators to help them transport their belongings. In the true spirit of simplicity, they carried little with them.

In this modern world, individuals (including myself) have a tendency to fill our lives with an overabundance of stuff, but I like to travel light. For several years I've made it a practice to only pack what I can physically carry onto an airplane. When I travel by car, it's a different story. I can load my little VW bug to the brim and then roll down the ragtop if I need more room.

I began to zero in on this practice of simplicity when I started to travel solo, which coincided with noticing the SoulStrolling way. The first time I went to Paris, I traveled by myself on a slim budget. I'd prefer to spend my euros on a nice glass of wine or second espresso than pay for a cab or town car. Please don't get me wrong, I do adore being treated with luxury, but if I have to make a choice, I'll pack light and put on my walking shoes.

When one travels independently and stays in apartments instead of hotels, there are no bellmen to lug your bags. Bottom line, you're on your own to get yourself and all your belongings from point A to point B. The other benefit of having carry-on baggage is that you don't have to worry about lost luggage on arrival.

I find something quite satisfying about being my own valet. It's a great reminder to stay in shape as best I can and only pack what I can carry.

Packed and ready to go, leaving home went without a hitch. Bill was up and ready to drive me to the airport, and Aslan, our cat, waited by the door to say goodbye. Okay, maybe he was waiting by his cat dish that happens to be by the back door. Cats can be that way. Still, he's my furry muse and has been known to time travel and show up at my destination to say hello when I'm away from home. Once, he met me on a road outside Taos, New Mexico. In the light of the moon, I could have sworn it was Aslan. I'm still not sure it wasn't.

The ancestors felt weighty in my packed bags, so I decided to leave some books at home. My SoulStrolling® pal Sharon had loaned me three or four creative books with French phrases and descriptions of Parisian markets. I decided to take Great Aunt Trudy instead. She promised to leave her coveralls at home and be the glam girl from her classic '20s-style portrait. Trocadero Plaza was calling our names and I imagined the two of us dancing on that rooftop.

Olive Gertrude (who I call Trudy) was the younger sister of my father's mother, Anne Gilmore. We had our very own set of Gilmore girls. Six of them—Anne, Mazie, Ruth, Edith, Gertrude, and Dorothy—plus Great Uncle Harold, who was born between Edith and Gertrude. I didn't know Trudy existed until around 2010 when my sister Dianna and I discovered a picture of her standing next to a house she built in the Mojave Desert. In my mind's eye, I see Trudy standing on the roof instead of the ground next to concrete blocks. She reaches out her slender hand and invites me to dance through the stars with her, circling chimneys and church steeples like a scene out of *Mary Poppins*. Her vibrant spirit touches the rebel inside me that says: *Follow* your *path. Dance to the rhythm of* your *soul.* I consider my nieces and nephews, great nieces and great nephews, Jonathon and Janey, Violet Grace, and even the grandchildren who have yet to be conceived. What legacy will I leave for them? I chuckle and imagine them saying, "Do you remember our crazy Aunt Kayce? Did you know she went to Paris alone and called herself a SoulStroller?" Perhaps they will value my stories like I cherish Trudy's memory. Every generation needs a rooftop dancer.

Since no one in our family ever talked about lineage or family lines, the pieces of the puzzle have been hard to assemble. It was only a few years ago that Dianna and I discovered we had so many great aunts on the Gilmore side of the family. Our three "kissing" aunts—Grace, Arcylla and Sallye—were from the Stevens' line. We called them the kissing aunts because they always greeted us lips first. And not just any lips, but brilliant red-painted lips on smiling, age-crinkled mouths.

As children, we had no idea that these were amazing women who outlived who knows how many husbands and traveled like sprites throughout Europe well into their eighties. Great Aunt Grace was a painter who moved boldly past the traditional stereotypes of her time. I have vague memories of being inside her cottage in Oklahoma City in the early 1960s and marveling at the bold fabrics, paintings, and glass treasures in her home that were so different from the Naugahyde and paneled wood surfaces in my parents' house.

I wish I knew more about Great Aunt Grace. I wonder if she had lovers outside her marriage or if she painted in the nude. My imagination runs wild as I peer into the distant reflection of her cat-eye glasses, and I'm grateful that her blood courses through my veins. In our brief encounters, Great Aunt Grace planted small seeds of bold living inside my virgin soul. I think of her each time I color my own lips with Mac's *Brave Red*. Today I leave my own crimson imprints on loved ones, including granddaughter Violet Grace, who is working her sparkling brand of healing on those who adore her.

What a robust legacy these great aunts left me, a legacy I didn't understand until I began writing and giving voice to them. It was when I traveled and wrote that these ancestors spoke up in my consciousness. They were adventurers and artists. Sassy ladies, too. Methinks perhaps they wanted to join me in Paris. No wonder my luggage gets heavy. Even spritely ladies carry heft.

Come along, girls. I've got the Brave Red lipstick tucked inside my bag.

Clothing is something I admire although I'm not a designer label kind of girl. I like to be comfortable but not sloppy, and with airport security as it is these days, it pays to be mindful of several things. How easy are my shoes to get off and on? Is it worth wearing a belt? Will my jewelry set off the metal detector? How can I be comfy for fourteen hours and not look like a rumpled mess when I arrive?

Traveling in colder weather can be trickier, because of layers and such. I knew that my coat would need to be worn and packed shoes kept to a minimum. I really do think about these things because it makes for more pleasurable travels when I have what I need. It's a bit like "Goldilocks syndrome," the search for something just right.

My just right for this trip included a purple wrap tee, matchstick jeans, black tie-up flats, a scarf that doubled as a blanket, and a black tweed walking coat. My gray knit poncho tucked nicely into the second item the airline allowed and served to cushion my books, iPad, and sundry assorted items that didn't fit into the rollaway bag.

I wore a belt with my jeans and my good watch and a silver bracelet, knowing I'd likely have to take all of them off to make it through security. Little did I know it was my lucky day.

We arrived at the airport at 6:00 a.m. on the dot—the requisite two hours before departure. Bill dropped me at the curb and I headed inside to begin my adventure. A friend of mine named Ali once told me her favorite feeling in the world comes when she's driving to the airport. I think mine comes once I've confirmed that my flight is on time and I've made my way through the loops and potential frustrations of the security check.

Once inside the airport, there were no lines at the United counter and the agent pointed me toward an empty kiosk where I could check myself in. Another humorous agent who called everything a "thingy" (the machine, my passport, etc.) helped me get my tickets.

"Take your thingy like this," he said, scanning my passport, "and put it in the thingy right here."

I teased him about the thingy thing and he retorted that he hated me anyway because I was going to Paris and if I wasn't nice he wouldn't help me anymore. Do you know how rare it is to meet cheerful workers at the airport, especially at six o'clock in the morning? *Zip zap zing.* My boarding passes printed without a hitch.

The next bonus came when I got to the security checkpoint and noticed a special stamp on my ticket. I'd been preselected for a new program where I didn't have to stand in line forever and didn't have to remove my shoes, belt, liquids, or laptop. Score! I was ticketed, scanned, and through security in under ten minutes, a SeaTac record for me.

When I texted Bill to let him know, he asked how I did that. Based on the time it took him to reply, my hunch is he was barely out of the airport drive before I was inside the terminal and approaching my gate. "Magic" was my reply. My sojourn was off to a promising start.

Traveling is a crazy series of highs and lows and lots of in-betweens. At the gate, we queued up like cattle heading to the slaughter house. I know it's not an uplifting analogy and I didn't really feel that way except the queues were designed in structured lines to keep us from straying. Lining up to board is the moment where I either start to panic and give in to the warnings that I should check my bag because this is a "relatively full flight and there will be little luggage space available," or I practice what I teach and take a few deep breaths to remain calm.

I chose something in between and sidled over to wait in my queue thirty minutes before boarding time, becoming third in that line. While standing there, I vacillated between checking my bag at the gate and imagining abundant overhead space on the plane. My internal naysayer tried to convince me that even though my bag had fit into the overhead bin a hundred times before, it would be too large on this day. With a deep breath, I envisioned a wealth of space and everyone except me checking their bags.

It ended up neither packed nor spacious. The bins were full at row 36 (my designated seat), but there was plenty of room two rows up for my rollaway and coat. Once in the aisle seat at 36K, I crammed my smaller bag in the tiny space under my feet and resigned myself to sitting with my knees tucked to my chest for four and a half hours. The middle seat was open and a pleasant woman sat at the window. Across the aisle, two men had the same configuration.

As the rows around us filled up and the passenger line trickled down to nothing, we each looked at the other and wondered if we dared fasten our seat belts. Would the middle seat remain unoccupied? It's a traveler's dream come true—more elbow room and an empty seat to drop your extra books or iPad.

Superstitious me opted to keep my belt unlatched and the bag stored at my feet. I didn't want to jinx anything. Again, I started to imagine spaciousness and my deep calm was rewarded. "The cabin doors are closed." You could see the mental fist pumps and beaming smiles on our entire row. I quickly moved my bag into the middle space (leaving room for my seat mate who declined the luxury) and buckled up. The magic continued.

Punctual departure. Stored luggage. Extra leg and elbowroom. Simple pleasures. *Merci beaucoup et bon voyage!*

CHAPTER 25

No Proof Required

"Without leaps of imagination, or dreaming, we lose the excitement of possibilities."

—Gloria Steinem

November 2013

Je suis arrivée.

The flight from Dulles to Charles de Gaulle went without a hitch and we landed a few minutes before 7:00 a.m. It took me two hours post-landing to arrive at my apartment without rushing. Since part of this trip was about stretching myself (like SoulStrollers tend to do), I chose to take the train into the city—a first for me. I was also staying in an unfamiliar neighborhood.

I'd been warned that the green ticket machines at the airport could be persnickety, and this day was no exception. I tried two separate machines before I got one to accept my credit card. The same thing happened at the cash machine. There's something slightly different about the card readers between Europe and the US, so I always hold my breath until the transaction is successfully completed.

At Charles de Gaulle Airport, the trains to Paris are clearly marked until you get down to the actual train tracks. Even though the signs say "All Trains to Paris," it looks like the coaches are heading in two different directions. Since I've climbed on more than one train going the wrong way, I opted to slow down, get my bearings, and ask for help.

The ride into the city was a visual mixture of French countryside, urban graffiti, working class villages, and commercial skylines. I caught a glimpse of Sacre Coeur and the Eiffel Tower before we dove into a tunnel and I transferred from the RER B to Châtelet-les-Halles to Metro #1 for Bastille.

My cozy walkup described as "under the rooftops" was *trés mignon*. I ascended four flights of narrow stairs to reach an apartment that no doubt belonged to a domestic servant at one time. My host, Romain, announced that I'd arrived with perfect timing. It was 10:00 a.m. in Paris and the middle of the night back home in Seattle. I was grateful when he carried my bags up the final harrowing steps because I was exhausted from lack of sleep and lugging two bags up and down the metro stairs.

Though I'd learned that jet lag can be successfully allayed by staying up the whole first day of arrival and collapsing that night, on this trip I went against my own advice. I took a nap while it was still morning and set my alarm for noon. I was worn out from finishing a writing project and arranging schedules at work and home so I could leave without worry. I knew a catnap would be perfect. Unfortunately, I didn't have my fuzzy cat with me.

I don't know why or how, but every time I travel I seem to forget the brain fog that envelops me after a transatlantic flight. Without the sun to brighten things up, I was hazier than normal this time and was surprised by the discombobulating effects of stepping into a foreign country, even though I'd done it before.

I had quite the conversation with my overactive brain that kept telling me I should be out walking and not wasting my time inside journaling and sleeping. I reminded myself that taking care of my needs was not a waste of time.

It felt essential that I gather my bearings and settle in before the week kicked into gear. Serendipity from my own book, *As I Lay Pondering*, worked on my behalf. The day's entry was about being our own providers of permission. In that moment, I gave myself permission to follow my desire and move toward peace. Hunger nudged me out of the apartment in the early afternoon and my dim senses worked on overdrive to stay aware of my surroundings. Searching for peace was proving to be a challenge. On my first stroll in the Bastille neighborhood, I managed to wander into a park I probably shouldn't have. Note to self: *when your spine tingles, it's time to go a different direction.* I did.

My discombobulation heightened when, much to my chagrin, I yelled at a blind man. An innocent blind man. He yelled back. I had stopped to read a sign at another park on a not-so-busy street when he rammed into my back and caught me off guard. While I've never had an experience with a pickpocket, I thought for a split-second that this must be what it was like.

I whirled around like a Karate kid, tossed my arms in the air, and yelled, "Hey!"

He bellowed the same back at me. It was then I realized he was walking with a cane and wore dark glasses.

"Oh, *je suis désolée*. Sorry. Sorry," I mumbled profusely.

"*Merde*," he swore under his breath before ambling off.

While I felt badly to have yelled at the man, I also felt very French. I'd experienced my first argument à la française.

For me, the first meal in Paris is always the hardest, especially in an unfamiliar neighborhood. By mid-afternoon in the Bastille, I was questioning my judgment to stay in a new arrondissement.

Everything looked odd and strange. Then I chuckled as I remembered that's what it means to be a traveler—to be a strange
person in a strange land. I wondered if the Bastille would grow on
me or if I was destined to compare it forever to my beloved Rue
Cler where I'd stayed on all my previous visits to Paris.

While I was strolling, I kept my eyes peeled for a boulangerie
or a patisserie to pick up a tasty treat. I wasn't yet prepared to sit
down and dine by myself. I found a place that looked promising
but saw they were closed on Wednesday and Thursday, which were
my first two days in the neighborhood. The French have their own
distinct way of boundary-setting and leave-taking. It's not unusual
to see a scribbled note on a shop door that says the equivalent of
"back in a minute" or "on vacation until further notice." It can
be unsettling to find such announcements, especially for North
American city dwellers who are used to twenty-four-hour access to
everything. *And* it's something I adore about this culture, because
it invites me to slow down and be grateful for what I'm offered in
each moment.

However, hunger, jet lag, and basic disorientation were pushing
my limits. I forged onward, noticing how everything seemed gray
and kind of dirty, not the glistening city of my memory. I wondered
if people could tell by looking at me that I was more or less lost and
didn't speak the language. A hangover of old insecurities. *Are they
watching? Do I look foolish? Does anybody care?*

Finally, I noticed a storefront situated diagonally from where
I stood, and could tell it was an organic health food store. Score!
I crossed the street, entered, wandered around, and surveyed the
assortment of fruits, vegetables, and delectable treats, ultimately
choosing a ripe pear and a bag of organic almonds. The shop
keeper was charming and we chatted *en franglais*. I left the store
buoyed by my first purchase from a human being and the promise
of a sweet, juicy *poire*.

Food, winding streets, and a good stroll reminded me of my

trip in March with Janey. During that time, she and I visited le Marché Beauvau-Saint-Antoine, a treasured nearby market where she bought a silver ring. The vendors were *trés français* and my hunch was that unlike Rue Cler, they didn't see many tourists at their stalls. After we had perused the circular market, we were famished and hungry for an omelet and café crème. I noticed a young man with a kind face and asked, *"Parlez-vous anglais?"*

"Non." He shook his head. *"Parlez-vous français?"*

"Oui, un petit peu." Between sign language and smiles, I conveyed our hunger and he pointed in the direction of a local café.

"Merci beaucoup. Au revoir."

"Au revoir, Mesdames." He waved after us.

At that time of year, chocolate shop windows were filled with Easter bunnies and decorated eggs. It was gorgeous and decadent like a scene out of *Chocolat*, but what I remember most about that time was how after *le petit dejeuner*, Janey tucked her arm inside mine and we strolled down Boulevard Richard-Lenoir like *les flâneurs* of old Paris. *Les flâneurs* were the original SoulStrollers who gained notice in the nineteenth century as literary types and urban explorers who made their promenades without regard to specific destination. Boulevard Richard-Lenoir has a wide parklike promenade in the center of the bustling street, and even though we were walking away from the metro station that led us home, I never considered it to be the wrong direction. The fond memories of strolling arm in arm with my nineteen-year-old daughter, who had seemed distant from me for so long, were worth every footstep we took together.

Parisian streets have a way of crisscrossing and turning like no other place I've visited. Boulevard Richard-Lenoir and the Bastille market were very close to my apartment on Passage du Chantier. A half dozen streets fan out from the center isle of the Bastille metro area, which Rick Steves calls "Paris's most famous non-sight." Tourists are said to emerge from the metro hub only to stand there, trying to find the fortress of Revolutionary War and *Les Miserables* fame. Alas, there is no fortress to be found. Only the square remains where the legendary prison once stood, punctuated by the *Colonne de Juillet* that commemorates the July Revolution of 1830.

Those spoke-like streets have carried me off in haphazard directions to places unknown more times than I can count. However, I wasn't in a mood for exploring at that moment. A fresh pear, almonds, and my cozy walkup beckoned to me, so it was a wonderful surprise when I managed to wind my way back to the apartment without significant detour.

Poet William Stafford once wrote, "'You don't have to prove anything,' my mother said. 'Just be ready for what God sends.'" It's like he penned those words for me and that trip to Paris. No need to prove anything. No necessity for fancy discoveries or wordy explanations. Just the pure simplicity of being in a city I love and the ecstatic wonder and joy of travel. And, yes, the readiness for what God sends. Because, ready or not, it comes.

Whenever I say Paris, I can see by the look in people's eyes that they either understand its magic or they don't. Most often people imagine the romance and lyricism of the city. Their minds drift to the Eiffel Tower and images of lovers strolling hand in hand down the Seine. All true. All Paris.

What they often don't imagine are the winding passageways littered with a stray whiskey bottle or two and the remnants of a dumpster-dive meal. They can't fathom passing a homeless mother and four children huddled on the sidewalks beneath ragged blankets and not quite enough plastic tarp to keep them dry in the winter rain. The City of Light has a dark corner or two.

In my wanderlust, I see God everywhere in this city. In the bustling subways filled with smells a far cry from any church's sweet incense, and the cozy cafés that tempt my taste buds with a beckoning call from each pastry case. Atop Montmartre where Sacre Coeur glistens like a mountain of snow against cornflower blue skies. Inside the catacombs where human bones lay stacked like cords of wood chopped for a long, cold winter.

I hear God's whispers in the cobblestones and church bells, through the language I almost understand and the lilting notes from the flutes and fiddles of street performers who play at every turn.

In my Paris, you don't have to prove anything. Just come as you are. Walk. Listen. Pray. Weep. Dance. Eat. Laugh. Love. And be prepared for what God sends.

SoulStrollers see before them what isn't readily obvious to others.

"You don't have to prove anything."

I wish my own mother had said the words

Stafford's mother offered to him. I wish she, too, could have heard the whispers and smelled the scents and cherished the sights of this city. I wish she had been one of the ones who *knows* and had taken my young hand to stroll along the Seine. Together we could have seen the sights and believed you don't have to prove anything.

Not so. My mother was a formidable woman, striking, beautiful even, with classic features like a Hepburn girl combo of Audrey and Katherine. Her hair was teased high atop her head from the mid-1960s until her death from Alzheimer's in May 2004. She wore classic outfits in beige and coral to go with her fair skin tone, and she special ordered Ferragamo shoes for her size 9 1/2 AAAA feet. A strong advocate of sunscreen, her skin belied her age, but her demeanor spoke of a woman serious about proving the correctness of life. I can't imagine her ever conversing with gargoyles or tossing a coin into a street performer's cup. I can, however, envision her walking by herself along the Seine and wondering where life went.

At a class reunion a few years ago, my close-knit group of girlfriends (the ones I snuck out with at night to smoke Swisher Sweets and drink beer) confessed that they always thought my mother was a bit scary.

"Scary?" I asked. "What do you mean?" I posed the question even though I thought I understood.

"Well, there was something kinda spooky about the way she'd suddenly appear in a room all stealth-like. I always wondered what she'd caught us saying or doing." Heads nodded around the room.

"Yeah, me too," I mused. My mother, so regal and mysterious, was like a cat burglar showing up with cookies and iced tea. I used to think she was old and annoying, but now I think perhaps she was discontent and lonely. Perhaps she was silent and stealthy because she wanted to be around our girlish energy or to hear us singing love songs along with our Beach Boys and Beatles records.

I wonder what songs she sang when no one was listening?

The only album I remember in our house was Rodgers and Hammerstein's *The Sound of Music*, but I could never imagine my mother flinging her arms wide and singing like young Maria on that mountaintop. Did she ever believe that the hills were alive or that God whispered through the cobblestones?

It's hard to think about her without pondering the impact she had on my life. If she'd sung lullabies to me or boogied alongside with the Beach Boys, would I feel more confident in my own voice?

Apparently I come from a long line of non-singers. I've always wanted to carry a tune or hold a perfect note, but somehow that gene is missing. My dad didn't sing either, but he loved listening to truck driving songs and crooners like Roger Miller. My favorite song in the fourth grade was "You Can't Roller Skate in a Buffalo Herd." I remember playing it over and over again at Sherry Dutton's ninth birthday party while singing off-key at the top of our lungs. There's certainly no way to be stealthy or austere while singing that song.

On my own in Paris that day, I pondered life and voice and how things might have been different had my mother sung to me or taken my hand and offered curiosity rather than rigidness. I can only imagine. There is no real need to prove anything, especially when I remember that in my Paris—in our lives—we simply get to be who we are and God will send the rest.

CHAPTER 26

Oh My God!

". . . an American writer who had come to visit France . . . asked quite naturally what it was that had kept me there so long . . . it was useless to answer him in words. I suggested instead that we take a stroll through the streets."

—Henry Miller

November 2013

Never underestimate the power of a petite nap, a perfect pear, and a soulful stroll. *Oh my God!* My love for the city was rekindled in short order. On the flight earlier that day, I listened to a Tedx Talk by photographer Louie Schwarzberg who suggests that "Oh" means something has caught our attention, "my" means it's connected with us personally, and "God" resonates with the universal bigness or otherness. *C'est fantastique!* That's what my Paris does for me. She gets my attention and connects me to the larger world in a big way!

Part of my excitement about being back in Paris was because my friend and mentor Christine Valters Paintner was flying over to meet me for a few days. In the summer of the previous year, she and her husband had moved to Galway, Ireland, and I missed her exquisite company.

Christine arrived late in the afternoon on my first day in Paris. Being the adventuresome woman she is, she booked her brief stay on a private boat in the Bassin de l'Arsenal, a few blocks from my studio. As early evening approached, I left home to meet her at the boat with trusty directions in hand. Even though she was only meters away, I became hopelessly disoriented and it took me longer to get there than planned. She teased that she was about to call upon *les agents de police* when I finally stumbled upon her dock.

We were both weary from our travels but excited to be in Paris together. We decided to dine within walking distance of Place de la Bastille (our center point of reference) and relied on my five-year-old guidebook for references. The first restaurant we approached was out of business, so I pulled out my Paris City Guide app and we tried again.

Winding our way toward Place des Vosges where Victor Hugo lived while writing *The Hunchback of Notre Dame*, we stumbled upon the Provençal bistro, Chez Janou. With no reservations, the maître d' turned up his nose in an almost imperceptible tilt and seated us at a tiny table near the overstimulated heater. He looked like a caricature of a snooty French waiter, but as soon as he realized we both spoke a modicum of the language, he softened and we settled in for a charming evening.

All around us, lively conversation flowed alongside wine and the *pastis* (an anise-flavored liqueur) the establishment is known for. My steak and Christine's duck were acceptable, but the potato gratin and roasted potatoes were scrumptious. *Un pichet de vin rouge* warmed our insides and the buttery peach *tartine* we shared for dessert was melt-in-your-mouth delicious.

We knew we had redeemed ourselves with the waiter as not any old tourists because after our meal, he showed up at our table with a complimentary serving of melon liqueur, a cousin to *pastis*. Christine and I thought we'd died and gone to heaven when the liqueur passed our lips. It was chilled goodness and rich flavor in a slender shot glass.

There's a perpetuated rumor in the United States about how uppity and rude the French are. What I have found, however, is the opposite. I think we find what we're looking for. I'm enchanted by most things French and, therefore—more often than not—my enchantment is rewarded with surprise gifts, like *pastis* on the house and strangers going out of their way to help. A smile and *un petit peu français* go a long way in creating relationships and building bridges across misunderstanding.

I slept like the dead that first night in Paris. Fourteen hours of travel, getting lost, yelling at a blind man, and sipping shots of *pastis* are apparently good for my sleep cycle. Since Christine was already on European time, she offered to bring croissants to my studio the next morning, where we met at a civilized 10:00 a.m. We sipped our coffee and savored buttery pastries while looking at the Paris rooftops from the slanted windows of my studio. *Oh my God.*

The weather was overcast but not raining, and we simply wanted to wander together and notice where the streets might lead us. That is SoulStrolling.

We headed back through Place des Vosges, the oldest square in Paris, which was a new find for me. Place des Vosges is filled with art galleries, two large fountains, wide open lawns, and precisely sculpted trees.

SoulStrolling is wandering and trusting wherever the streets lead.

One of the things that enchants me most about Paris is that there are gardens and squares and parks and sculptures everywhere. The city is filled with a multitude of beauty

waiting at every turn. The changing of seasons and light and moods makes everything new and fresh upon each visit.

Through these intentional journeys, I've learned that this sense of beauty is available anywhere, whether at home or away. A SoulStroller seeks meaning in the quotidian. She brings herself fully into the presence of her surroundings and opens up her life to be moved and impacted by that time and place. Like a pilgrim, he or she is fluid, not rigid. A SoulStroller seeks the light yet knows that darkness is a necessary part of the journey.

A SoulStroller seeks meaning in the quotidian, assumes flexibility over rigidity, and appreciates light alongside darkness.

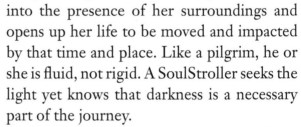

For example, I never get tired of walking around Green Lake, one of the most visited parks in the United States. It's less than two miles from my home, and I can't begin to count the number of times I've circled its three-mile circumference. Each time I walk, I see something new or different. I've come to trust that my personal favorites, the gray heron and majestic eagle, are usually watching from a hidden perch and I only have to open my eyes to see. No matter where we are, there is the possibility of a gift awaiting us.

After leaving Place des Vosges, Christine and I strolled toward Île Saint-Louis and Notre Dame—two of my favorite spots in the city. We stood in the plaza of the grand church, listening to the bells ring, and watching the clouds drift by, revealing blue skies after the gray morning. Instead of entering the crowded tourist site at midday, we chose to visit Saint-Séverin in the midst of the Latin Quarter, a charming, out-of-the-way, uncrowded church. On display was an amazing mural of the Apocalypse by artist Claude Manesse, a twenty-first century painter. It was exquisite to see the modern mural in an ancient setting and the old story created by a new painter. Yet one more treat we found by letting our hearts and feet lead.

Christine and I strolled and talked and laughed and ate until our weekend came to a swift end, as memorable meetings tend to do. We said *au revoir* near L'Opéra Bastille with breakfast, hugs, and *bisous*.

When I began to believe my sense of direction was becoming more dependable and that I had all the gadgets and maps I needed to keep me on a charted pathway, I decided to test that theory. The first time I came to Paris, a friend recommended a small box of maps. Fifty adventures, each on a card with directions. I vaguely remember using it one time before the box got tucked away with my other out-of-date guidebooks.

Before I left for this trip, my SoulStrolling pal Sharon (who's spent hundreds of hours wandering the streets of Paris) left me a care package with metro tickets and a stack of miniature books including a replica of the fifty adventures on foot.

It was a rainy day and Christine had left earlier that morning. After our goodbye breakfast, I had returned home and snuggled back under my covers where I snoozed and dreamed and planned my next adventure. Since I trusted Sharon implicitly, I decided to pull out a map for inspiration.

Père Lachaise Cemetery was calling me, so I selected the card for that walking tour. I'd been there on my first trip to Paris and loved strolling through the aged headstones, listening to crows cawing and the *clip-clop* of footsteps on the cobbled pathways. It felt like a perfect way to spend an overcast day.

With card in hand and a few steps on my way, I remembered why I quit using those maps. They didn't have sufficient instructions for a direction-impaired person such as I. They began with commands like "Walk down Rue des . . ." but didn't include the direction (north, south, left, right), and as I've learned, "down" is often a matter of interpretation. The cards included no practical distances, like "three blocks" or "two miles." It was just "go this way" and "turn right at the stairs." *I need more!*

Needless to say, my intuitive sense of "down" was out of kilter and I walked a mile or two before coming to Parc des Buttes Chaumont, which was at least a half mile north of Père Lachaise's neighbor, Parc de Belleville.

It started to rain in earnest even though the forecast said the day would clear. As I became more and more discombobulated, the rain poured harder and harder until I desperately needed to pee. *Quelle horreur!* I tried to console myself by thinking about how serene the park looked (and it did) and convincing myself that I was on an adventure (*mais oui*). At some point, I panicked and remembered I had all my worldly resources in my bag (except my passport). If anyone decided to grab my purse, I'd be without cash, credit cards, cell phone, or apartment keys. None of this chatter helped to ease my nagging bladder.

Let me clarify that I do believe in miracles *and* I've been known to step behind a well-placed bush if need be. This time a miracle was on tap. I exited the park and quickly found a public *toilette*, but that wasn't the biggest marvel. The astounding thing was that it was in working order *and* there was no charge. Indeed, a functioning *toilette* is a miracle in Paris where you can walk blocks and blocks only to find the public-designated bathroom is out of order or you do not have the correct change to enter. *Merci beaucoup* for traveling mercies for this middle-aged woman.

Once my brain and bladder were clear (and yes, this clarity can directly correspond), I tucked into a phone booth à la Clark Kent-style and checked my map to verify I was going in the *wrong* direction. I had gone "up" instead of "down" Rue des Pyrénées, so I turned around, determined not to be thwarted from my destination. Back on the correct path, I scanned the window displays in this working-class neighborhood. None of the stores called my name, and I was on a mission to find the "right turn" that my map suggested.

At some point, my stomach started to growl and I realized it was three o'clock in the afternoon and I hadn't eaten since breakfast. A corner boulangerie beckoned my attention and I popped in for *un palmier, s'il vous plaît*. With nourishment in hand, I continued my mission, watching like a hawk at each right turn for "the" staircase. *Impossible! Merde!* I cursed to myself and simply stopped walking. *I give up! This is* not *SoulStrolling!* That's when the second miracle occurred.

A young woman rushed up to me, frantically speaking in French. I knew enough to understand she was asking for directions. I tried to dissuade her from relying on me. I was not the person to ask. She insisted on my help and shoved her iPhone into my face with the address she was trying to find. We were on the correct street, that much I knew. When I looked at the number, I chuckled because finding visible street numbers can be a real challenge when you need them. Nonetheless, I decided to give it a try for this stranger in distress.

I looked across the street and *voilà*, there was a number, then *voilà*, a second number next to it. I knew better than to use words like "up" or "down." Instead, I pointed her in the right direction and off the now happy traveler went. I turned back to my position on the corner, discouraged that I could help someone else but was hopelessly lost myself. One final time I turned in a circle like a worn-out pup chasing its tail. *Et voilà!* There was the staircase I'd been seeking.

This encounter reminded me of a story I heard from poet and storyteller Deena Metzger. Deena talked about what I call "entertaining angels unaware." Across cultures, we see the story of helping a beggar and later learning it was Christ or Buddha or an angel in disguise. I don't know if the young woman I met was any of those things, but I do know that when I stopped worrying about my own predicament and allowed myself to tend to someone else, my situation became better. "Do not forget to show hospitality to strangers, for by so doing some people have shown hospitality to angels without knowing it" (Hebrews 13:2).

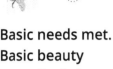

Basic needs met. Basic beauty seen. Basic love received. It is the SoulStroller's way.

The situation became better, but the map was still bogus. Thank goodness I had other forms of survival and strong walking legs. I finally managed to wind myself back to Père Lachaise, having missed the promised panoramic view of the city and casual wine bar for the weary traveler that the map promised. Sometimes a pastry, a potty, and an encounter with an angel is enough to make a day a success. Basic needs met. Basic beauty seen. Basic love received. It is the SoulStroller's way.

Tell me, please, what woman hasn't dreamed of being wooed by a handsome man with a French accent? Is it just me? Maybe your ideal is British or Spanish, or perhaps there's something seductively attractive about a drawling Southern accent. My man was on Pinterest the first time I noticed him. There was something in his stoic look that intrigued me and captured my attention. I knew one day we'd have to meet. I pulled out my favorite map of Paris and circled his address in ink. We had a date.

The curious thing is that the first time I was in town after we'd locked eyes, I didn't make the effort to see him. While I knew our meeting was inevitable, my trip to Paris with Janey in the spring of 2013 didn't seem to be the appropriate time.

It wasn't until the final day of my trip in November that I used one of my last metro tickets and rode to Lamarck-Caulaincourt, the northernmost point on my map. I was in search of Le Passe-Muraille, which according to my translation dictionary means "the password wall." I was looking for my soon-to-be friend, the man who passes through walls.

My journey consisted of deep listening and much map consulting. While I wasn't in a hurry or on a crucial mission, I didn't have time to waste going miles in the wrong direction. A few twists and turns were welcome, but hauling off on chaotic trails and becoming lost and frustrated like I'd done earlier in the trip near Père Lachaise was not appealing.

Wandering through the streets of Montmartre near Sacre Coeur, I knew I was in the vicinity of Le Passe-Muraille, but he wasn't showing his face. After a few unsuccessful back and forths along what I thought was the correct street, I popped into a small gallery to ask for directions. A man and woman sat huddled in conversation around a petite table for two. When I said *"Pardon"* in my halting French, the gracious proprietress asked if I spoke *anglais*, then proceeded to give me excellent directions in flawless English.

My man resided down the street, but I had missed him from the angle of my approach. His domain is at the bottom of a steep incline and backs up to a pocket-sized park. He is fantastic. It's like his body, face, and extended hand are made from the roots of the park and they've all turned to bronze as he passed through the stone wall.

A young couple sat on a bench not far from him, seemingly unaware of his power and presence. I wanted to be alone with him, to have an intimate chat and ask him how it felt to be frozen in this wall, bursting through yet never fully emerging. Oh, what would it mean to never fully emerge into the world? To be only half seen? A fraction visible? How many people spend their lives unwitnessed? The questions touched a place inside my soul and for a moment, I was saddened for us all.

I took him by the hand and whispered, "Everything will be okay. I see you. I, too, want to be seen. I don't want to be frozen in a half-life."

The couple moved on, so I took a seat on the low windowsill in the shadow of his wall and began to ponder the stories and questions that I'm able to hear more clearly when I slow down. *What does it mean to be a citizen of this world? Of my own world?*

Paris, with her golden statues, precious parks, and endless window displays, invites me to step out from behind my own walls. She encourages me to burst into Technicolor, into a full life where I can boldly say I'm a writer and take risks every day to discover something new when all else seems foreign. In Paris it's okay to sit or write alone in a café and sip a glass of champagne at noon. To wrap a turquoise scarf around my neck and dangle my feet over the Seine, to savor an *aubergine et fromage* sandwich while watching light glisten on the water. To blend in or stand out. Paris teaches me that everything is my choice.

At home, it's easy to get lost in familiarity. To be okay with only having one hand in the world. To freeze our growth at a certain point. It took me most of a lifetime and much of the world to learn what I know about love and fear, compassion and gratitude, the profundity of choices we make and stories we believe in, and the difference between living a half-life and a full one.

When I was five, anything seemed possible. At Mrs. Peck's whimsical kindergarten inside her oversized gingerbread house, I wielded the power to wake sleeping children at the end of naptime, using a magic wand made from ribbons and stars. I shared ice cream cones and conversations with puppies and flew down a pint-sized roller coaster, my long curls blowing in the wind. Somewhere between the time I skipped around the block, scuffing my patent leather shoes and the time my sister got married and I was abandoned without a comforting word, the girl who danced with arms wide open began blending into the background.

I wonder how my life might have been different had I chosen to keep skipping to the music of my own making instead of kowtowing to the conventions of society or taking the limiting words of others as truth. If I'd demanded to be heard above the voices that said good girls don't question authority. What if I'd shouted from a young age that "the time is now" and demanded a full life from the very beginning? Sitting with Le Passe-Muraille, he whispered: *Anything is possible, my dear. Anything.*

CHAPTER 27

Jetlag Gyrations

"Our most important beginnings take place in the darkness outside our awareness. It is, after all, the ending that makes the beginning possible."

—William Bridges

November 2013

Home again. I couldn't settle down. Or is it in? Which way do we settle? Down in the ground? Into the earth? Or through the love of the Universe? Our beloved? Our loved ones? Ourselves?

I curled up with Aslan, my golden-furred feline. He couldn't get close enough to me, and I think he would have crawled inside my skin if he could. His nose lay tucked under my left arm and he breathed with deep, resonating purrs. Was he relaxed or worried that I might leave again? Janey said he was annoying while I was gone. He wanted attention, love, and connection. *Don't we all?*

Breathing with intention, I felt connection to the world around me. Istanbul, where Bill was traveling on a photo tour. Paris, where I'd just returned from. Vancouver, where I spent a few jet-lagged hours munching on french fries and drinking warm beer.

Human beings want to connect, to settle in, to know that we are loved.

A phrase rolled through my mind: *Love thyself and the rest will follow.* I pondered what it meant to love every part of myself, including the weak and scared parts, the ones afraid to ask directions or speak in another language or eat alone. The parts that are brave and glorious and sensual; the ones that like to flirt even though I'm happily married; the sassy one in red boots and crimson lipstick; the woman who boldly rides a bicycle through the streets of Paris with hair blowing in the breeze and gurgling laughter.

The nasty parts that judge others and get frustrated and grumble or shout or curse. The tender parts that weep for a tiny mouse scurrying through the subway and cry at the sound of guitar music floating upward into the night sky.

The cold parts that, with eyes averted, walk by the homeless mother and her children covered in ragged blankets and plastic tarps on the street corner. The brash parts that laugh aloud at bawdy jokes and wish they were seventeen again, if only for a moment.

The kind parts who smile at strangers and give their last coins to someone in need. The funny parts who make silly faces and help a restless child laugh on the subway. The curious parts who take us on wild adventures, down streets and narrow alleyways and into churches and undiscovered markets.

The spiritual one who weeps at Joan of Arc and carries a Latin mass inside her. The statue lover who touches her fingertips to hands of bronze and feels the strength waft through her. The romantic who longs to be kissed on the Seine and toss the key to her lover's heart into the flowing current. The beautiful. The ugly. The wretched and mild. Strong. Courageous. Weak and worrisome.

What would it mean to say *yes* to loving every last wicked, wonderful part of ourselves? Saying yes in this way is a doorway to loving the greater world. My way. Your way. All ways. Always.

I slept nearly eighteen hours straight the first day and night home, an hour for every one spent in the air and on the road. At some point during the trip, I had envisioned slipping into a warm bubble bath and having a delicious meal before curling up with a book in my own cozy bed. Instead, I slunk out of the taxi, let myself into a human-empty house, trudged up the stairs, peeled off my travel-worn clothes, and heaved myself under the covers. No bath. No food. No book. No fanfare. To return home to no fanfare was a welcome treat.

After three days, I entered into the awake-at-4:00-a.m. routine. Ah, sweet jet lag. It always seems to happen. I get home, crash for the first two or three nights, think I'm going to skip jet lag, and then *boom*. I'm wide awake at the oddest hours. Brain buzzing. Stomach grumbling. Nothing to eat in the house, because the refrigerator looked full until I dug in and cleaned out the leftovers from before the time I left. Ugh. Nothing to eat. Nowhere to go. It sounded like a first day in Paris, only this time I was in Seattle.

I wonder if first meals are a part of every transition. First meals. Last suppers. Breaking bread. Whoever thinks that food doesn't have a place in ritual, metaphor, and traveling is shopping at the wrong market. Oh, I crack myself up. Blame it on the jet lag.

Tossing and turning in the middle of the night is never any fun. Luckily, that's one of the benefits of traveling as a party of one or having a private room. There's no one to disturb. With Bill still in Istanbul on a photographic SoulStroll of his own, turning on the light wasn't a problem. Even though he always tells me it's not a big deal, I still feel guilty when I flip on a light while someone else is sleeping. The other thing is that when I awaken early with buzzy brain, it usually means that my mind is wrestling with something and the round is best served in a private arena.

I reached over to the spot that I instinctually know holds the light cord, gently pulled the chain, and tried to make as little noise as possible. The cat came running up the stairs like the switch I pulled was connected to his tail. He, too, seemed restless and unsettled. For him, the click of the light is synonymous with either breakfast or cuddles—both, if he's lucky.

I hate this part of returning home. The wonky, in-between space where I'm not there anymore and haven't fully arrived here.

Life is rarely linear or clear even though we try to make it so. The same is true of my story. Some days are exciting and others dull. It is one traveler's labyrinth, folding across itself, seeing where questions and answers appear to intersect, then moving far away and back into the unknown. The storytelling task is to share the unexpected *and* sink into the mundane and familiar. Like a lingering SoulStroll, the invitation is to walk the path without expectations and allow each word to wash over us like waves kissing the beach, picking up treasures and detritus with each turn.

A SoulStroller begins with an invitation to follow a path . . . without expectations.

A small image on the corner of my journal catches my eye. Patches of blue with a head in the clouds, in another world. Feet planted on the ground. I hear the whisper, "Weight and wings. Stay grounded and be open." I see more blue, the color of voice. Triangles. Three sides. Three siblings. Three aunts. Maiden, Mother, Crone. The images blur and meld together like an alchemical potion. I stir the pot. I add the necessary ingredients—a butterfly wing, sting of bee, two cinnamon sticks, ginger, turmeric, more healing balms. A horse's hoof, a femur bone to stir. Sprinkle with laughter, moisten with tears. Stir. Red dirt, white sand, broken teeth, and hairspray to set. No molding or cooking required. Chill if you like or serve at room temperature. I prefer a balmy 80°F myself.

I once spent a week at a retreat with a transgender woman who taught me that *trans* means to cross over, go across, move beyond. Is that what I do in these liminal hours of the night? Do I trans? Cross over? Move across the bridges in my dreams and waking hours? My eyes blur. I wonder again about my dreams, the ancestors, Great Aunt Trudy building a home brick by brick. The three kissing aunts. What are they telling me?

I stand on a bridge in a dream and a trio of women wave and beckon me from the other side. They speak. *You will fall, but you will not die. Instead, you will fly like Pegasus and rise like the phoenix in the flames. Your voice will be heard, not through sound, but through words and image and metaphor.*

Once more I turn the page of my journal and a quote by Tama Kieves slams into me like a gale force wind. I can't make this stuff up. "Transformation of any kind always exacts a holy tussle. The newborn butterfly struggles to open its wings so it can conjure up the strength to fly. So, too, with artists, inventors, mystics, and entrepreneurs."

Holy shit! The words spill out of my mouth and onto the page. "Go back to sleep, Kayce." I hear the same words Liz Gilbert heard in *Eat, Pray, Love*. "Go back to sleep. We've got this. You've done your part. We'll stir it around a bit now. Go back to sleep, lovely one. Rest your wings. Sweet dreams."

Take Your Soul for a Stroll

SOUL**S**TROLL

A SoulStroller seeks meaning in the quotidian. She brings herself fully into the presence of her surroundings and opens up her life to be moved and impacted by that time and place. Like a pilgrim, he or she is fluid, not rigid. A SoulStroller seeks the light yet knows that darkness is a necessary part of the journey.

S is for stretching, strolling, surveying our surroundings, and sharing with others. *Le Cadeau de Paris* was a time of stretching when I decided to stay in a new neighborhood. I could have stayed in my familiar surroundings near Rue Cler, but chose instead to explore the Bastille neighborhood. I witnessed a different side of the city there—slightly less pristine parks, more people sleeping on the streets, unfamiliar storefronts and cafés. This broadening invited me to encounter darkness that at times stretched my views of the City of Light. I also stayed in one of my favorite studios and witnessed the vibrant side of a fresh community. Now it's a neighborhood I love sharing with others.

Practice SoulStrolling®

- Ground yourself in whatever practice suits you, then pick up pen and paper and explore this prompt as if it were a winding street with no particular destination. *To stretch myself would mean that I . . .*

- While SoulStrolling® can seem like a solitary act, it actually prepares us to engage more fully with the world. So, practice something new. Find a trusted friend and share your written musings or one of your lists with them. Stretch your voice and allow them to be your witness. No feedback required, unless feedback is what you'd like.

- For some of us, gratitude can be a stretch especially when things feel dark or beyond our control. Say yes to gratitude and make a list of five items each day for the next five days. You might consider creating a gratitude journal to continue this practice. Stretch yourself!

PART SIX

Lucid Meets Liminal

Italy 2015

"I am reminded that as a human being living on this earth I am part of the pattern of day and night, darkness and light, the waxing and waning of the moon, the rising and setting of the sun. The whole of my self is inserted into the rhythm of the elements and I can here learn something, if I am prepared to, of the ebb and flow of time and of life itself."

—Esther de Waal

CHAPTER 28

This Story Is Not Linear

"The future enters us, in order to transform itself in us, long before it happens."

—Rainer Maria Rilke

April 2015

Memory is fluid. No two people will remember an event or conversation in exactly the same way. I keep imagining that it's crucial for me to find the precise formula for this story, that somehow this journey is linear. But it isn't.

This part of my tale begins at a tiny desk in Italy, atop a hill in the center of Tuscany, where I've arrived for a two-week-long writers' residency. The painted brown window across from me is half open. A medieval church tower peeks from behind a giant evergreen tree and birdsong fills the crisp country air. To counterbalance the cool temperature, I've poured a cup of steaming green tea and wrapped myself in a blue paisley shawl from Siena. A wave of gratitude grabs my chest and I can hardly breathe. Is this really my life? How did I get here? When did it all begin? The storylines march through my brain like endless red ants from my Oklahoma childhood.

My tendency is to rush forward, to answer all my own questions in one fantastical swoop. But that is impossible. I wrestle with the questions like a bear cub who's trying to decide if she's fierce or playful, grown or young. Which stories are important? Whose shall I include? My family? The ancestors? Jonathon's daughter Violet Grace who was born six months ago? Inner journey or outer? Which is more important? Will you love me if you know the truth about my story or might you think I'm a raving lunatic? On and on march the message-toting ants.

A new sound breaks past my mind chatter and joins the whispering breeze. *Bzzzzzzz.* My old friend bee has entered the room and is bouncing against the glass panes. His efforts are futile. *Bang. Bang. Bang.* He throws himself into the glass over and over. Does he realize he is here on my behalf?

Through his buzzing and banging, I hear the message. *Be. Simply be. Write. Simply write.* I chuckle at my winged friend who is no stranger to me and turn back to the pile of notes and journals that surround me. Sound softens. The buzzing disappears. The bee is free and so am I.

Before the bee joined me, another scene was on my mind. I am standing at the edge of a narrow bridge. Water rushes below me and jagged rocks emerge in the Oklahoma red-clay river. When I look more closely, I see there are more rocks than water. It is arid and dry. On the other side of the bridge, there are lush evergreen trees and a verdant pasture filled with poppies and wildflowers.

A recurring dream from my childhood steps into this liminal space. I've followed my father up a winding path to an oddly familiar place. The trail upward is narrow and steep. There are no handrails and the uneven steps are hewn out of the same red stone—carved like the scaffolding in the ancient city of Petra. I am three or four years old. Dark curls fall down my back and my pudgy legs stretch with each deliberate step. My father and I have climbed this peak together, me trailing behind him. Did he take my hand? I can't seem to remember, but I think not. It's like he knows

I'm there, but more as an afterthought or surprise or nuisance. I know a Jungian analyst would have a field day with this.

At the top of the trail is a tavern. My father reads the "No Minors" sign next to the door and furrows his brow. "Wait here." He pats my head and turns away. He opens the door. Laughter and the smell of smoke and stale beer drift out. My father disappears inside and I am alone. *Always alone.* The canyons echo around me.

I hear other people approaching from below. I'm frightened and look for a place to hide. There is a small aluminum trashcan beside the door. It's low enough for me to step inside. I curl into a ball and hold my breath. The moment I start to feel safe, as if I'm wrapped in an invisibility cloak, the can tips over and begins to roll down the side of the cliff. I wake up.

Past, present, and future merge. Burnt orange rock. Steep incline. Pounding heart. I stay in this dream-like state and continue to observe what unfolds.

At the bridge again, I look back over my shoulder and see my father. Or is it my son? They look so much alike, tall and lean. He's standing outside the tavern from the dream. I know he sees me. He winks and offers a slight bow. *Go on.* I feel my chest loosen and understand I must cross this bridge alone.

The terrain looks like it could split me open with one misstep, but I know it's the path I must take. I'm not a child anymore. I look back again and see the man kick the aluminum trashcan over the side. It ricochets off the canyon, bounces over a sharp precipice and falls. The sharp noise echoes through the air. *No need to hide. Nowhere to hide. It's time to walk on your own.*

Across the bridge in the lush green meadow, a young girl beckons to me with outstretched arms. She is dancing and twirling. Sunlight sparkles off her shimmering garments. Her eyes gleam and repeat their invitation. *Come. Come join us.* I look more closely and see she is not the only one there. An older woman with steel gray hair and sky blue eyes sits beside her in the meadow, stringing daisy crowns with her weathered hands. I look into her eyes and even though they are a long distance away, I read them clearly. The message is the same. *Come. Come join us.*

Is this a trick? Surely if I step onto this bridge I will tumble to my death. "Yes," the old woman responds. "There will be death, but we will not let you fall." I look across the divide again and see the meadow is now filled with my female ancestors—the Wee Ones, Great Aunt Trudy, my mother, and more. "It's time," they say. "Your journey has begun."

A SoulStroller is someone who dreams while awake and captures infinitesimal moments of time.

The same is true of a writer. Both have the ability to dig deep and look inward and at the larger world in more expansive ways. Big world. Big dreams. Occasionally, big obstacles. It's a writer's curse and blessing to be able to dig into his or her own psyche and connect, then transfer it into poetry or prose, so that others might connect too. We need to know our own stories, to understand our blind spots, to be aware of where we get caught up in shoulds or musts. We also need to know when to let them go. *Laisse aller.* To release and detach.

A SoulStroller dreams while awake and captures infinitesimal moments of time.

Being away from home is the perfect time for such exploration. By going outward and beyond, we step away from ordinary circumstances and create time to simply be. We encounter new experiences and bump up against old stories. We find fresh modes of being with ourselves and wrestle with static problems in potentially different ways. My old stories of loneliness and being voiceless have been tested every

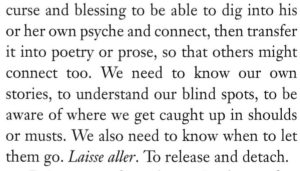

time I have traveled alone and have had to speak up for myself when intimidating situations presented themselves.

Little did I know in the spring of 2015, when I embarked on the longest trip (to date) of my life, that an unusual story would arise to test me in curious and deep ways. I would be away from Seattle for six weeks: the first two in Tuscany, Italy, for a writers' residency program; then a week driving north to Cinque Terre with my husband, Bill; and finally three weeks in Paris. Two of the Paris weeks were dedicated to leading SoulStrolling groups with my business partner and soul friend, Sharon Richards. I'd transitioned out of working in an official capacity as a psychotherapist and was focusing more time on travel, writing, and SoulStrolling—a trinity that made my heart soar.

Travel invites us to dance upon the edges of discovery and seek balance in our days. A tourist vacates his or her life, thus the word "vacation." A pilgrim or SoulStroller inhabits it more fully. It was no wonder I bristled when a young family member commented on how lucky I was to be going "on vacation" for six weeks. While I do feel extremely fortunate to be able to travel so much (*I mean, seriously, would someone please pinch me?*), he missed the depth of what I was doing and didn't seem to understand that I wasn't vacating life even though I was leaving home base. I was stepping with my entire being into writing, pleasure, and my work in the world. I would inhabit it all.

This six-week trip would become my own hero's journey, complete with mentors, tests, trials, and threshold crossings, including the recurring childhood dream that kept surfacing. The work inhabited my days as well as my dream life. Worlds colliding. Waking in wonder and walking with weirdness. Dragons and demons, inside and out, reared their not-so-pretty heads.

The trip's territory was rife with highs and lows. Even the call to attend the writers' residency began with my own initial refusal. *How could I possibly go to Italy and write? With* real *writers?* Once

I'd set my intention on it and applied, the program coordinator sent an unexpected denial of my application which turned out to be a clerical mistake. Up and down I went. No one ever said the SoulStroller's way is easy.

CHAPTER 29

Buongiorno

"All journeys have secret destinations of which the traveler is unaware."

—Martin Buber

April 2015

After my first night's sleep in Rome, the thoughts that entered my mind upon awaking were:

- You only have one opportunity to see something (or meet someone) for the first time.
- Remember the strangeness of being the stranger.
- WTF am I doing?
- The adventure has begun. I am here now.

After I walked past the Trevi Fountain and then backtracked to discover it devoid of water and covered in scaffolding, the "one opportunity" thought pushed its way through disappointment to the top of the list. *Quelle horreur!* It was the one thing in Rome I cared about seeing and I'd booked my hotel and arranged my short agenda around experiencing the Trevi Fountain. Alas, I had to remember that even national treasures need tender loving care and stories of transformation always incur obstacles.

It was also clear that I need more than a single day to fall in love with any city. The first day anywhere, everything resonates as odd and out of place from the jet lag. Getting lost does not feel like being found. It takes all of my residual energy to remember to stop, pause, and gather my bearings.

So, I stood in a park in the center of Rome and remembered what was important: the breeze through the trees, the sound of a foreign bird bringing music to my ears, Jack Russell pups scurrying past my legs without a care in the world, warm sun on my skin, an adventure beginning. *I am here now.* The park was an oasis in the midst of the Roman hustle and bustle. Yes, the Trevi Fountain was scaffolded, but I would survive.

I found myself comparing Rome to Paris. How could I not? There aren't as many benches in Rome. The streets are more confusing. The traffic is louder. It was all noise in my mind.

I paused again, took another deep breath, and tried to give Rome a second chance. After all, I'd been lost for hours in Paris. Not the lingering, lovely kind of lost, but the exhausting, my-feet-hurt, I-have-to-pee kind of lost. Often on the first day of travel, I've pondered through my jet-lagged discombobulation, *Why am I here? What have I done?*

Each day, wherever we are, we have a thousand chances to re-write our story into a manageable (even pleasurable) adventure or spin a thought into madness and anxiety. What if there's no driver to meet me? What if my luggage gets lost? What if my passport is stolen? What if I get food poisoning or hit by a bus or lost forever? What if? Yes, my mind sometimes plays these games on me. But being a SoulStroller has taught me that while I've taken many ill-chosen turns and headed the wrong way more than a few times, I have never stayed lost forever.

One of my favorite spiritual muses is John O'Donohue, who said, "When you travel, you find yourself alone in a different way, more attentive now to the self you bring along." The self I bring along with me on these journeys is complex yet simple. She's been with me forever yet chooses to take on different personas along the way. My shy girl showed up on the cab ride from Leonardo di Vinci Airport, but she wasn't frightened. Something had shifted since those early

SoulStrollers may take ill-chosen turns but they don't stay lost forever.

days of travel. This woman was brave, content, observant. More attentive. I witnessed myself being quiet and found this manner fascinating to observe in lieu of a mind-spinning tale of *OMG, I should say something. I'm such a fool. Blah. Blah. Blah.* I didn't beat myself up. I knew I could try to speak to the Italian driver if I needed to, but instead I curled into the back of the taxi and watched Rome come into view.

My time there was short, a smidgeon over twenty-four hours, long enough to have dinner with an old friend, drive by the Colosseum and the Vatican, eat pasta and multiple scoops of gelato, drink wine, and realize that I indeed needed more than one full day to fall in love with a city.

And then it was time to catch the train to Chiusi and begin my Tuscan writing adventure.

My journey and arrival at the writers' residency in Tuscany was filled with magical moments and delightful synchronicities, such as being assigned a seat across from a fellow writing mate on an almost-empty train and then being tucked into a small private room when I had paid for a double. Even though I could almost touch the opposite walls when I stretched my arms out wide, I was thrilled to have a spot to call my own.

The location of our residency, La Frazione, was a scenic hillside estate nestled into thick woods between Siena, Florence, and Montepulciano. The picturesque compound included several farmstead villas, a tower, village church, and courthouse, all dating back to the medieval age. The family had owned the picturesque hamlet since the end of the seventeenth century and graciously opened it up for retreats such as ours.

The first full day of the residency included a brief orientation and a leisurely afternoon at the local hot springs. In the evening, I chatted with other participants over cocktails and snacks and was particularly drawn to a young woman from Prague named Dusana. Her translated name means "soul" or "spirit." She and I huddled together as if we'd known each other forever and talked in quiet whispers about the power of metaphor and how paying attention to symbols can be potent for our writing and personal lives. Later, the group sipped delicious wine from the local vineyard and gathered around the ten-square-foot table for a meal prepared by loving hands and served in a room called the Dungeon. It was like stepping into a time capsule, greeting old friends that I'd newly met, and nestling into a familiar landscape where I'd recently arrived. My bones proclaimed that this was a journey of the most extraordinary kind.

I don't know if it was the amazing Italian wine, the evening conversation that soared around dreams and metaphor, personal jet lag, or something greater that awakened me that first night. What I did know was that a portal was opening. An eagle entered my waking dreams. She held a light bulb in her talons and shouted, "Wake up! Wake up, my wild one. You are here to write these stories. You are here to tell the world of stepping through portals and crossing thresholds to another space and time. You are here to speak of dancing with Wee Ones on the trails of Glendalough and hearing the heart of the earth beat in ancient Egypt."

During our evening orientation, our hostess, Victoria, shared stories about the history of the land on which we would reside for the next two weeks. She spoke of vineyards and ancient villages, of a chapel reclaimed and restored, and she told us of the shadow side of her heritage that included a space on the property where her intolerant ancestors persecuted and burned women believed to be witches. When I heard her speak those words, I nearly gasped and wondered if anyone could see through me. Did they know I was a seer, a woman connected to a power even I didn't understand and rarely discussed? Perhaps if I'd been born in another age, they would have burned me at the stake too.

Friends, clients, and even my own sister have called me a modern-day witch. They say it in jest and with a touch of curiosity, but I often sense a hint of underlying fear about how I know what I know and see what I see. What would they make of this eagle who came to me in the night as vivid as if she were alive and sitting on my bedside table? I shuddered as I thought about the answer to that question and remembered the hill behind where I resided, that place where witches were burned. I tucked the bed clothes tighter around my legs and wondered if the persecuted women were so different to myself. The voice of the eagle gave me no time to linger on these thoughts before she continued her speech.

"You are here to testify about the magnificence of mystery. To declare you are a witch and seer of the most daring and wondrous kind. The messenger has arrived and her name is Grace."

Was it destiny, irony, or merely my imagination that equated the eagle with my own ancestors both before and after me who held the name Grace? I thought of my Great Aunt Grace from my father's line, one of the three kissing aunts, and, of course, our sweet granddaughter Violet Grace. I remembered the first booklet that Bill and I created together called *Grace Unbound*, and the U2 song about grace making beauty out of ugly things.

Eagles are mighty spirit animals that represent power and freedom. Their ability to stage a comeback after being declared an endangered species has been remarkable. Living in the Pacific Northwest, we are fortunate to have regular sightings of this majestic bird, and I occasionally see them fly over our house.

Have you ever witnessed an eagle being attacked by crows? Walking around Green Lake one December day, my friend Sharon and I spied an eagle, high on her perch—watching and observing. She had no apparent worries as she sat upright, taking in her surroundings. For her, there were no errands to run, tasks to complete, or judgment from others to consider. Her only goal in that moment was to soak up the brilliant blue sky. She mesmerized us, and we stopped in our midday busyness to stare.

After a few quiet moments, the scene changed when out of nowhere, half a dozen crows began to dive bomb the eagle—squawking, pestering, and pecking. Still the eagle exuded calmness and serenity, unlike me who only moments before had become annoyed by grumbling store clerks and erratic drivers.

The eagle didn't snap or respond with spite. She held her head high and continued to survey the world around her. *I am the Eagle.* Sharon and I heard her speak with an uplift of her beak. Soon the crows drifted away like scattered clouds or errant thoughts and my own state of mind began to shift.

So what if a driver cut me off on the road or I have to wait on the phone for an hour listening to elevator music? Big deal if no one appreciates the work I do.

I can be the eagle. I can yield to beauty. I can hold my head high in the midst. Sharon and I continued our walk, but now we shared a new mantra: *Be the Eagle.*

In Italy, it is this proud image of the eagle that made her way into my late night musings. I call them musings, because I couldn't quite discern if I was awake or dreaming. It felt like both.

Sit tall, my beauty and hold your head high even when the crows attack like nasty thoughts that shout "Beware. None of this magic is true. And even if it is, no one will listen or believe." Turn away from those thoughts, my dear, because Grace is here.

I paused, focused on my breath, and waited. *I am here now.* Like the eagle, I could rise above it all. It was time to soar and tell my stories. I offered and received permission to do it my way, because I was not alone. I set aside my journal and opened my iPad to search for an old Bible verse that came to my mind. I found it in Isaiah. "But those who wait on the Lord shall renew their strength; they shall mount up with wings like eagles, they shall run and not be weary, they shall walk and not faint" (Isaiah 40:31). It had been a long time since I turned to the Bible. Yes, something was shifting.

I felt renewed. I was tired but not weary. My eyes filled with tears and truth whispered in my consciousness. The eagle soared above it all. She was not the forgotten ones who twirled in my dreams, or the constant chatter that played in my head. Nor was she the god of my ancestors. The eagle represented something greater—a soaring magnificence that rises above everything and offers grace. She is the one who takes us under her wings and whispers, "All shall be well." This was the voice that spoke to me in the dead of night and said, "Wake up. You are not dreaming. This is real and true. I am here now. Look up and soar."

The presence I felt had no need for name or face. *I am here*, like the bee flitting through the desert and the dancing Wee Ones in Ireland and the eagle perched by my bedside. *We are here now.* One with the Universe. No separation. No definition. Pure is-ness. I am the one sitting under the Tuscan sun with cheese and bread and tea, blending into the spring hillside. I am the pounding waterfall, infinite in wisdom. No beginning and no end. I am the one who slips into dreams and connects past, present, and future.

SoulStrolling is about presence. Am I here or am I there? Can both be true? Will I bear witness and help give voice to the stories that cry to be heard? Or will I choose to plug my ears and pretend I do not hear? If the story is one we are meant to witness, it will continue to show up until we're ready to listen.

SoulStrolling is about presence.

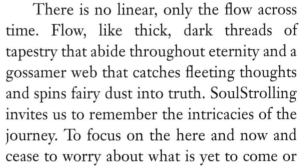

There is no linear, only the flow across time. Flow, like thick, dark threads of tapestry that abide throughout eternity and a gossamer web that catches fleeting thoughts and spins fairy dust into truth. SoulStrolling invites us to remember the intricacies of the journey. To focus on the here and now and cease to worry about what is yet to come or what has been. It invites me to act as if each encounter or upset is a lesson on my behalf, even the ones that can be hard to accept. Perhaps especially those.

Every hero's journey requires a nemesis and mine showed up at the writers' residency in the form of a housemate. Tall, slender, and physically striking, I could imagine her peering into a gilded mirror and asking, "Who's the fairest of them all?"

Her name was Thana and she came from Greece. Like a dark goddess from Mount Olympus, her presence spoke muted strains of death to me. Her words dripped like a poisonous potion that, once ingested, could tear me apart from the inside out. Like most true life nemeses, she showed up without warning, offering a pseudo-smile and a grumble about no hot water. Somewhere in mid-life I remembered to beware of anyone who begins a relationship with grumbling. I was raised by someone who carried an arranged smile on the outside with a word of derision tucked beneath. Yes, Thana reminded me of my own mother, although it took a few hundred hours of introspection for me to come to that awareness. Unlike a mortician who drains the corpse of blood, the nemeses in my life often wield two faces that carve away the pieces of my living voice and character, bit by bit.

I wish it weren't so, but duplicity nearly killed me as a child and still wreaks havoc in my life if I'm not taking good care of myself. Hearing my mother tell me how pretty I looked seconds before reaching her hand up to adjust my hair or straighten my skirt and ask, "Are you sure you want to go out like that?" left me reeling. It was like standing in front of a funhouse mirror wondering if the distortion was true or not. Then there were the times I watched my mother greet a friend in public with smiles and "so good to see you" before turning away to criticize the woman's lack of lipstick or the extra pounds she carried. I learned to question every compliment, and trust became an elusive sparrow that skittered away at the slightest movement—nothing like the solid eagle.

When I was around Thana, my gut turned sour and I felt like I needed to tiptoe away at top speed and navigate eggshells while doing so. She complained about our lack of communication, then chastised me for knocking on her door to ask if she was okay. She said she wanted all of us housemates to spend a quiet evening together then invited the entire community to our cottage for a party without informing us. She gushed about how amazing another woman and I were as housemates then told the others she lived in the "loser house." She grimaced if there was any hint of excrement in the toilet. I felt like I was back in first grade asking permission to relieve myself. She stayed up late into the night stirring the wood in the fireplace that adjoined the wall to my bedroom and looked at me with blank eyes when I asked if she could keep it down so I could sleep. She stopped stirring, but began moving furniture between two and three in the morning, claiming she was doing it on our behalf. In short, her actions made me feel crazed and childish.

I tried to be kind, but she was two-faced and catty and brought the worst out in me. It was like being back in middle school. The therapist in me wanted to diagnose her as deeply wounded. How could she not be? Not that I wanted her to be wounded, but that at least gave a reason for her insecurity and cruelty. I wondered if she would be smug, compassionate, or embarrassed to know that I resorted to using a chamber pot in my room at night because I was afraid to knock on the bathroom door when she was inside (which was often for hours).

I don't think the woman ever slept. She had to be either exhausted or tireless. If she was deeply scarred, at least it might make more sense and offer a reason for the crazy-making.

But her behavior made me wonder about my own inner turmoil and the ways I'd been cruel to myself and others. I felt insecure during those weeks in Tuscany. Thana was stirring the pot, taking me back to my childhood, the place where one thing was said to my face and another told to others.

Duplicity was smeared over her face like cheap lipstick. Her energy was toxic for me, because I can't tolerate duplicity and I don't want to be a toxin. *Tell me you love me or tell me you hate me, but please don't lie to me or be indifferent. Don't speak in abstracts. Don't act like we are besties then name call behind my back.* The exhaustion of dealing with Thana plus interrupted sleep made me weary down to the bones.

The motley group of writers stumbled and awakened, moving through yoga poses, wrestling with stiff bodies, opening to the morning. We struggled with a silent breakfast and then we sunk into it. We waited. We moved. We selected our chairs for the day. We raised our pens. We flew.

A bird. A nod. A tear. Truth bumps spread across my soul. The eagle had arrived and her name was Grace.

Clarity rose through repeated words of conversation that permeated like meditation, connecting threads and opening portals. *I am here now. I am.* It was as simple as that. My only task was to arise and be, to acknowledge the annoying voice of Thana and let it go. To offer kindness and compassion, to receive whatever came, graciously and without judgment. Let it go. Let it transform. Let it flow down the hillside like fresh spring rain.

Shuffle, shuffle. Sniff, sniff. Footsteps. Breath. *We are here now.* A growing, moving organism. Alive. Fresh. Here.

I lay face down on the front lawn of La Frazione and observed the tiny plot of land before me with all my senses. The sharp edges of the world drifted away. In a blossom waiting to bloom, green turned to white to magenta. It was as if I could see it growing, emerging in that moment. Tiny critters, no bigger than a baby's thumbnail, crawled out from beneath soft blades of grass. Each blade held new life, and the cloudless Tuscan sky shared her bountiful message that we are infinite beings. Sunshine blended with my golden straw hat. A torn fingernail and age-spotted hand (was it mine?) shared the green space beside me. Bird song ricocheted from tree to hill to house. And in that wild, wonderful moment of reverie, I heard the words: *This space in time is Tuscany. Only now. Only this.*

Our days passed and a gentle rhythm developed. Yoga. Silent breakfast. Writing group. Simple lunch overlooking the hills. More writing. Nap. Yoga nidra. Cocktails. Dinner. Sleep. It was my rhythm and not necessarily one shared by all. Some mornings I wrestled with my voice while in group. I pondered the format for this book. I wrote in third person to avoid digging deep. I experienced the splendor of Tuscany.

And then one morning, after the loveliest day in Florence, I woke up feeling like I'd been hit by an eighteen-wheeler. Gray outside, I longed to stay in bed. I pondered my choices, knew I could stay in if I chose. I wondered if the day would hold magic or muck. I crossed my fingers for magic even though heaviness clung to me like tendrils beneath lotus blossom petals. A bus ride into the countryside and a stable full of horses awaited. Surely magic would win.

CHAPTER 30

Old Paint

"Let my journey into what lies beneath the surface be rewarding. Help me to appreciate the weight of my wild and enduring spirit, my traumas, my vulnerabilities."

—Pixie Lighthorse

April 2015

Old Paint. Old woman.

We circled the paddock on our plodding horses like children, tethered in our seats. Slow motion on the outside. Racing stories on the inside.

Get me off this horse. Fuck, fuck, fuck. I hate this!

I was plodding along like a worn-out nag. I was made to fly through the Tuscan countryside, not plod along like a horse ready for the glue factory. I was a harlequin heroine, but wait . . . that status had been given to the young beauties. *I am the old gray mare.* The fucking horse put out to pasture under the Tuscan sun.

Irrelevant. Invisible. Old. Unseen. Why were my emotions rising like a spiking fever? Why now? While the feelings weren't exactly new, I didn't remember them ever being so intense when I was traveling.

Typically, when I travel, I feel vibrant and free. Paris, Ireland, Egypt, and the Mediterranean Sea bubble up in my consciousness with their stories of freedom and beauty. At the writers' residency in Italy, I was surrounded by writers young enough to be my children. I bumped up against stories of aging. The gray mornings didn't help. In Tuscany, I turned a corner and *poof!* I became an old gray mare, put out to pasture. I was the Crone. No longer the Maiden or even the Mother of archetypal legend. I was crossing the bridge into elderhood, and unlike some of my peers who cross that threshold with ceremony and *joie de vivre*, I was not happy about it.

Something in my story shifted when Old Paint came galloping into my life. Actually, Old Paint did not come in at a gallop. Rather, she ambled into the shadows in the form of an aged gray mare staring at me from a shabby stable in Tuscany. With her dappled nose and freckled muzzle, she beckoned me to reach out my hand and touch her. Little did I know this gesture was like rubbing a genie's enchanted lamp and I would need to be mindful of how I spent my wishes.

My first wish came half an hour later when I ground my teeth and growled to get off that damned horse and out of the paddock where eight other horses trod in circles like worn out ponies at a toddler's birthday party. I was frustrated and mad to be walking in circles.

I wanted to be on the chestnut stallion with my hair blowing in the wind. Heck. I didn't want to be *on* the stallion, I wanted to *be* the stallion, mane flying free and hoofbeats strong. I yearned for vibrancy and zest. I wanted my magic! But this mare wasn't doling out wishes when I rubbed her muzzle, she was conjuring up lessons, and this one was hard to swallow. I wasn't thirty-five anymore, or even forty-five. *I am the fucking gray mare.*

I was in Tuscany, for God's sake. Where men were supposed

to revere women of all ages and worship them, curves, wrinkles, and all. I thought there were no language barriers in the land of *amore*, but I was not feeling the love—only the ache in my left arm from a yoga pose gone bad and the added weight around my belly from too much wine and pasta. Ugh. Lack of sleep clawed at my serenity and my stylish yoga pants felt snug. My yellow-brimmed hat that had looked so charming at home only highlighted the need to protect my skin from more age spots. If I quit going to the hairdresser anytime soon, I'd become a two-legged version of Old Paint.

No matter how hard I tried to shake the story that I'd been deemed too old for the chestnut stallion and put out to pasture, I couldn't do it. I tried to smile at the paddock proprietor, but all I wanted to do was glare and scream. *I'm not old. I can ride a goddamned horse. I'm from Oklahoma where the real cowboys ride, for God's sake!*

Dusana looked across the table where our hosts had set up an outdoor feast and narrowed her eyes in question. I knew it was a story of my own creation, but nothing would budge the nagging message. It didn't help that a significant portion of our writing community was twenty or more years younger than I and liked to stay up until the wee hours drinking wine coolers and stiff cocktails. The demons were coming out of the woodwork to taunt me. Old paint. Old woman. Nerd. The incessant name-calling felt like I was thirteen years old.

"How was your ride?" Dusana asked in her Eastern European accent. Ever since she and I had connected on our first evening at La Frazione, we'd carried on conversations in shorthand where few words were needed.

"He put me on an old gray horse." I could only call her Old Paint.

"What?" Her auburn eyebrows furrowed.

"Didn't you see? I walked up to the chestnut stallion, and the guy who doesn't speak English looked at me, then took me over to the old gray horse that could barely walk. It was awful."

Dusana took one step back and leveled her ebony gaze at me. "No. Seriously? You're not going there, are you?" I could tell she had crawled inside my mind. "What are you making that mean?"

I shrugged. Wasn't it obvious?

"You have to stop," she continued. "You have no idea why he did that. Maybe it's his most beloved horse and he knew that you'd take the best care of her." Dusana was earnest. I wanted to believe her, but my resolve was steadfast.

On and on I wrestled with the story. I second-guessed myself about everything and offered myself pep talks to wash away the gray. It worked well as a cheap advertisement, but not so much in real life. I convinced myself I was too old to write anything fresh, much less ride the chestnut stallion. Raw and pissed off, I wondered why I was crying because they put me on an old horse. The young mums and the not-yets of the group stirred up my old friend F.I.N.E. I felt as though I was disappearing. I felt patronized and lonely. I wanted to curl up in my pajamas, take a nap, and cry.

I didn't belong there and I did. I was sick of the both/and. Awake at 3:00 a.m., stirred to life by Thana poking that goddamned fire on the other side of my bedroom wall. I needed time on my own. I was wrestling with my mortality. The old gray mare. Loser. I was feeling bereft when somewhere in the recesses of my mind, a quote from Kurt Vonnegut arose. "Peculiar travel suggestions are dancing lessons from God." I was wrapped in a strange dance with God right then. I knew beyond reason that I was supposed to be there. But the challenges—oh my, the challenges.

Why did I need a neurotic housemate?

Be grateful for what you have.

Why does my head have to pound on Sunday morning in Tuscany?

Be grateful for what you have.

Why do I crave sleep when I feel like I should be writing?

Be grateful for what you have.

Grass blew outside my window. Birds sang. The shadow of my hand moved across the page. Our refrigerator door squeaked. Light reflected off the windowpane. I felt nauseated. There was a brown smudge on the wall. The only sound I heard was my pen moving across paper.

On and on I danced with God until I finally fell into a deep sleep and journeyed to my recurring childhood dream about following my father up the craggy hillside and awakening in an open meadow where a wise woman with gray hair sat stringing daisy crowns with her weathered hands.

I wonder about the symbols from my lucid dreams. Father and son. The spirits of the women who beckon me. Maiden and Crone. I wrestle with the places where I need to walk alone and my own unexplored beliefs about living and aging, about Maiden, Mother, and Crone. I cling to the Maiden and what I lost as well as what I gained during the hard years of mothering. I'm not yet ready to cross over and become the Crone. I know I will have to make peace with her. I understand the wise Crone is part of me and has been from the beginning. I have ignored her until now.

Each day at La Frazione, our facilitator Susan asked us to write down ten things we noticed. A theme, that would become recurring, showed up the day in the horse paddock when I rode in circles on the gray mare I named Old Paint. The message persisted throughout my extended time in Italy with Bill and on to Paris: peeling paint. Peeling. Old. Toxic. There was no denying it, the theme of peeling paint was gnawing away at me. The more I scraped at it, the more it confused me.

I saw peeling paint everywhere—on the well-tended buildings of La Frazione, in the piazzas of Florence and Siena, inside the apartment Bill and I shared in Manarola, at La Spezia train station, in the bathroom at Genoa airport, on the Paris metro, and the ceiling of the Parisian flat where I would live for three weeks while co-leading two SoulStrolling adventures. Peeling paint was everywhere, a message inside the chips that wasn't yet clear.

The end of our retreat arrived with the swiftness that said, "Wait, we just got here," and a lingering sense that we'd been together forever. Eighteen writers sat perched on the balcony, enveloped in layers of white, blue, pink, gray, white, green earth and sky. Cold stone pressed against my hand and belly. Full heart. Warm coffee. Someone sniffled, wiped away a tear. Birdsong symphony. Red tile rooftops, dotted with moss. Reverence and awe. Susan's voice offered her last instructions. It was time to say *arrivederci*.

Thana was leaving on the first shuttle. We had come to an unspoken truce a few days before the retreat ended. Still, I was glad to see her go. While every journey needs a nemesis, our story read that it was time to part ways. May her darkness drift away and may we both ultimately be blessed by our time together.

Traveling introduces us to situations and takes us to new places that we can't predict. It's like stepping into the walled city of Siena or winding through the streets of Florence—going in circles and getting lost, feeling gloomy or disappointed until suddenly and without expectation, you step into a brilliant square where music drifts upward and carries you skyward toward the rising sun. On the balcony, my spirits rose as I prepared for the next adventure.

Bill had arrived at La Frazione the night before our group goodbyes. He and I puttered around La Frazione until after noon, the last of the participants to leave. My heart ached from saying goodbye and I wondered where this next step would lead. After a day of travel together, he and I sat happily ensconced at Villa la Palagina, a few miles outside of Florence. Evening drifted across the Tuscan sky like the coffee stains on the edge of my journal. An olive grove climbed the hillside in orderly rows of sage green fluff. A fountain danced nearby with its single plume of water and raspberry-colored geraniums clustered around the pond in terracotta pots. The clouds were divided between springtime pink and storm-cloud gray. Two small birds made of strung-together triangles fluttered by and drew my eye to the moon that I hadn't seen in nearly two weeks.

Buonasera. I nodded to a passing man whose gray hair matched the gravel that crunched beneath his feet. There was a chill in the air that reminded me of the fickleness of springtime. I was content. Nowhere else to be.

We'd drifted through the day like the clouds in the evening sky.

Bill aimed his camera toward the olive grove and I shivered as the breeze picked up. It was only 8:00 p.m., but it had been a long day since awaking to watch the sun rise. I wondered what would come next. The sky shifted again and the next leg of the adventure had commenced. To my right, the clouds turned pink. They spoke of hope. In my mind, I saw Susan's smile and heard her encouraging words.

"Jump in. No need for transition or mediation. No need to always try so hard to make our words transition well or mean something."

We infuse our words with magic, so we do our lives.

CHAPTER 31

Permission & Promise

"Those who don't believe in magic will never find it."
—Roald Dahl

May 2015

The magic of Paris was doing its thing. The longer I was there, the more confident and me-like I began to feel. I left behind the heaviness I'd felt in the paddock in Tuscany. The layers peeled away. I stepped out of my own way and let the city embrace me. Comparison, failure, and success took on new meanings. I gave myself permission to fail. I relinquished control that I could make or break success with the two SoulStrolling groups Sharon and I led. I let go of attachments to age as a number. I chased pigeons and hopped onto fantastic carousels. I chose my perfect ride—a high-seated ostrich with brilliant colors and its head upright. I drank rosé and ate strawberry tarts while my feet dangled over the Seine. I danced in the metro and opened my arms wide atop the Eiffel Tower. I rewrote the story of old, peeling paint and let it go for a while.

One of my favorite poets, Rumi, says, "There are hundreds of ways to kneel and kiss the ground." On our last full day in Paris, Sharon and I kissed the ground over and over and over again and Paris kissed us right back, full mouthed, open hearted, seductive, awesome. My six-week adventure was coming to an end.

We spent our last Sunday morning on Rue Mouffetard, one of the oldest streets in Paris. A sidewalk café. Scrambled eggs, bacon, fries, salad, croissant, orange juice, *pain au chocolat*, Nutella, jam, *café crème*. How many ways is that to share a kiss? People and pigeon watching in the plaza of Saint-Médard. Stunning. Strolling. Shopping. Gifting. Laughing. Blue skies. Puppy kisses. Gelato. Sunday, sunny Paris. *C'est parfait!*

We took the Metro to Pont Neuf where we tried to have wine in Place Dauphine, but the waitress was rude. No food. No seats. No worries. We strolled through the crowded pathways to Rue de Buci and found a scrumptious bottle of rosé at Nicholas. The shopkeeper opened it for us and we bought six plastic wine glasses, plenty to share. Mozzarella and tomato sandwiches from Paul and a strawberry tart completed the picnic.

We hung our feet over the wall to the Seine and watched a boat named *Destiny* float by. Destiny moves slowly. We doubled over in laughter at our own hilarity, or perhaps it was the wine called "Moments." All is precious.

To finish, we strolled through our home base in the 7th arrondissement to say *au revoir* to our local friends, then up to Trocadero Plaza to witness the Eiffel Tower's twinkling lights. One more carousel ride. An evening snack of *croque monsieur* and *un plat du fromage*. *Le pièce de résistance* of the glorious day was sighting a tiny mouse (*une souris*) inside a classic restaurant. We giggled at the hilarity of Monsieur Ratatouille dining inside while we were outside beneath the stars.

I don't care for the term "back to the real world," but Seattle and home were beckoning. Wherever I am, it is my intention to inhabit my life, not vacate it. SoulStrolling and being a pilgrim is about stepping fully into each day with body, mind, and spirit—growing and learning.

We can't step into life for anyone else. I've learned this lesson time and again while leading groups and raising children. No matter how much I can see something of benefit for another person, they must see it for themselves. I can only step into my life and respond to the whispers of wisdom that call to me.

SoulStrollers inhabit their lives through body, mind, and spirit instead of vacating them with absence.

Horse wisdom and magic followed me from Italy to France and home to Seattle. Six weeks after Italy and my self-flagellating horseback ride in Tuscany, I opened Susan's online photo journal from the writers' residency and gazed at an image on the screen. Old Paint stared back at me and invited me to journey even deeper with her. My chest tightened. The photo was of me from behind— undeniable with my leeward bend, black yoga pants, and the golden hat I wore on that horseback ride.

In the image, my right hand caresses a white-spotted mare. I could feel the touch of her silken snout as I sat on my deck in Seattle. How could I have forgotten this moment? In the photo, the mare is locked inside the stables. They've put her in a small space instead of letting her out to roam in the pasture. *I'm so sorry.*

Carl Jung whispers from the grave, "Everything that irritates us about others can lead us to an understanding of ourselves." Methinks this is true of horses, too. The mare stands inside a replica of my own hard-sided box, the one I've lived inside for so long. An etched plate is nailed to her stall. Furia. Fury. She has a name and it is Furia, not Old Paint. That day in Tuscany, I turned the pain of being forgotten and voiceless against myself and then I turned it against her.

How quickly I'd forgotten our sweet connection. In the stable, the mare was wise and compelling, but outside in the sunshine next to the handsome stallions, she was dull as a burned-out scullery maid. As soon as she plodded into the paddock, I began to compare her to the taller, shinier horses and me to the thirty-something fillies I was writing with. Riding or writing? Did it really matter at this point? Jeez. I wanted to crawl under my desk for being so shallow, but it seemed that vulnerability was the only way through to the other side.

When the stable's patriarch chose her for me, I turned the judgments that had been used against me onto myself and her, too. It wasn't the man judging me. It was me judging me. Damn. My old stories were coming back to challenge me.

Inside the stable with her, nose-to-nose, I had seen her beauty and worth. I had offered her compassion and gentle care. I had noticed her. She had been more enchanting than all the prancing stallions. She was a mare who had done her time and lived a full life. She deserved to be revered. How did I so quickly forget my own worth and hers?

Taking in the photo, our story changed. It became about love, not criticism. I never would have judged her if the man had not paired her with me. Dusana had been right. I didn't have a clue why he invited me to ride her. He wasn't judging me. I was. I became the old gray mare by my choice and no one else's. Now I see that he tenderly put her in my care, and I had failed. My hunch is that he witnessed me connecting with her inside the barn and wanted us both to be happy. He saw a good match. I could criticize myself for this failure, but I would rather offer this apology:

I'm sorry for not appreciating your worth and I am grateful for you, lovely beast, who taught me to see the promise of grace in aging. From here on out, I shall release you from the moniker Old Paint and address you by your given name, Furia.

CHAPTER 32

Mirror of the Soul

"The horse is a mirror to your soul. Sometimes you might not like what you see. Sometimes you will."

—Buck Brannaman

October 2015

I close my eyes and open my heart. Moist air softens my skin and mud splatters up my backside. My pallor turns gray like the Tuscan mare, and seconds later I'm transported on a Pegasus-like stallion across the wild marsh of the Camargue in the south of France. Golden-flecked, we fly through the heavens where time holds no sway. My skin melts. I am Icarus who's soared too close to the sun.

Even though I'd made peace with Furia (aka Old Paint), the lessons of horse weren't through with me. Six months after I rode the Tuscan mare and a few weeks after her photo showed up in my inbox, I returned to France for another SoulStrolling adventure with Sharon and an extended visit to Uzés, a small town situated to the west of Avignon and north of Nîmes in the Gard department of Languedoc-Roussillon.

After our group left Paris where we'd danced through the streets and been swept away by the whimsy of Marc Chagall's paintings of blue brides and fiddle-playing goats, Sharon and I took the train to Avignon where we rented a car to continue our adventure into the French countryside. Approaching Uzés near sunset, we were greeted by a platoon of hot air balloons that guided our way toward the village center. Climbing the stairs into the studio apartment we had rented for the week, we felt as though we'd entered an ancient world with an arcaded central square and buildings that resembled castles.

Before we left Avignon in our sporty red Fiat, the agent suggested that if we were interested in seeing the Mediterranean, we should consider visiting the town Saintes-Maries-de-la-Mer. Three days into our trip, we took her advice.

Blue skies and wind. It was late October and warm enough to wear light jackets and sweaters. We reached Saintes-Maries-de-la-Mer via swamplands lined with pampas grass, the bright white tendrils waving in the wind. We passed through St. Giles along the way—a dark narrow town with little charm, high walls, and close, utilitarian streets. Nîmes and her series of roundabouts and enormous warehouse stores on the periphery. *Où est Saintes-Maries-de-la-Mer?* Where was our destination? We circled the roundabouts, sometimes more than once, looking for our signs.

Isn't that what we do in life? Circle our roundabouts, wandering and searching for the next stop or right direction?

And then we were crossing between worlds. Sliding through ancient doors. Slipping down rabbit holes and skipping across thresholds. It was as if the wardrobe in our Uzès walk-up had transported us to another dimension like Peter, Susan, Edmund, and Lucy in the Narnia books of C.S. Lewis. Two pair of red tennis shoes stepped through the portal, wondering where the heck we were. How did we land here? When would we leave? How soon could we return to this odd place where we felt right at home?

We had slipped through time and come out in a world where

the lion was not king, but rather a bull held court in the center square and white horses ran freely across the open marsh. Where pups with ears shaped like bunny rabbits lounged underneath café tables and gypsy women wound through the streets reaching for our palms with their dark, grizzled hands.

The magical city of Saintes-Maries-de-la-Mer is literally named after three saints—Mary Magdalene, Mary Salome, and Mary of Clopas—who are believed to be the women who were the first witnesses to the empty tomb after the resurrection of Jesus Christ. According to French legend, the three women set sail from Egypt after the crucifixion and were cast adrift off the coast of what is now France. They landed in what would ultimately become the city bearing their names. Yearly pilgrimages are made to the city by Roma, dark-skinned gypsies who are believed to be descendants of St. Sarah, rumored to be an Egyptian slave who arrived with the Marys. The name "gypsies" evolved from the word Egypt. The city is rife with legend and folklore. I can't help but wonder if these three Marys were some of the original SoulStrollers.

Feathered grass blew alongside the road and palm trees bent toward the sea. Sharon and I braced ourselves against the elements. We found an empty car park with a dwarf-sized entrance, perfect for our rented Fiat. We inhaled the bracing sea air before searching for a restroom after our winding drive from Uzès. Inside the facilities, we found no trace of toilet paper, only a collection of cigarette butts curled into the corner.

The Mediterranean Sea and a vast sandy beach lay spread before us. Old men rode by on rusting bicycles. A striking woman passed by wearing four-inch heels and shiny red lipstick. From where had she come? Where was she going? It was lunchtime and we were hungry. The wind was calmer inside the town and we wandered into a charming café where we sipped rosé and munched on *poisson de la mer* with *pommes frites*, crisp and curled like golden coins. For dessert, I savored a *flottante* as light as the blowing clouds, laced with caramel and a perfect *crème* like the one our friend Liz, a French chef, had prepared for us in Paris.

After a lingering lunch, we walked along the harbor lined with sun-dappled sailboats, masts clanking in the wind. Hawkers shared invitations to embark on one-hour cruises and strains of the theme from *Gilligan's Island* filled our senses right as the Skipper's boat came into sight, a perfect replica from the '60s television show, only slightly worse for wear. The boardwalk was lined with ornate lampposts, simultaneously giving off the impression of both Paris and London. Again, it had the feel of a Narnia fairytale.

Children frolicked in pairs, running ahead of their parents and grandmamas. Girls in pink jackets and black tops decorated with cat faces leaped across *gigantesques* rocks toward the sea. Speckled pups—black and white, tan and black—nipped at their heels and tried to herd their charges along the sea wall. Nature-painted stones swirled beneath our feet like a magnificent encaustic painting—yellows, blues, sandstone, and gray. There were enormous rocks like those at New Grange in Ireland, seemingly dropped into place by aliens from a future land.

Maisons turned into *casas*; *plats* became *tapas*. Tiled domes. Adobe cottages. Thatched roofs, too. A carousel spun beside the boardwalk and language swirled around us in everything except *anglais*. Still, we seemed to understand.

Saintes-Maries-de-la-Mer is an odd mixture of Mediterranean and French. Sharon and I felt like we were on the boardwalk at Coney Island (even though neither of us had been there) or maybe the Seaside Beach back in the Pacific Northwest. We also had the odd feeling that we could be in Mexico. Or was it Spain? Where did France go?

The morning after our visit, I paused in my writing and looked over at the wardrobe in the loft where we slept. Next to it, a small square window looked over the tiled rooftops of Uzès. A satellite dish was tucked *à gauche* (to the left). The stairwell outside smelled like an old castle. How did I even know that? Stone walls, thick as old growth evergreen trees, surrounded us. Dust-laden beams tickled my nose and caused me to sneeze. What century was this? Again, I sunk into a space that is timeless.

My reverie shifted as cars whirred by outside and I heard the sounds of rain swooshing across the pavement. The weather had changed, and with it, my world.

Two days after our first visit to Saintes-Maries-de-la-Mer, I woke up with one thought in my mind: *I have to go back*. When Sharon got up a while later, she said she'd been thinking the exact same thing. A few minutes later, Bill texted me an article on the top ten things to do in France. Riding the white horses of the Camargue was near the top of the list. Before this trip, I'd never heard of those wild horses or the Camargue and now they were beckoning me from every angle. What else were we to do but hop into our red chariot and head south?

There is a quote by an unknown author who says, "To ride a horse is to ride the sky." After visiting the ornithological park where hundreds of flamingos chanted the refrain *ça va! ça va!*, Sharon and I found ourselves atop two white stallions riding behind a striking French cowgirl no older than my daughter Janey.

No iPhone. No camera. No paper or pen. Only my mind's eye on the Camargue, that magical place nestled between the Mediterranean Sea and the arms of the Rhône River delta. I could see the moment coming toward me like the poem Liz Gilbert talks about in "Big Magic" and her TED talk. The memory rushed at me in slow motion, enveloping me, galloping like the white steed I was riding. *I am here now. This.* Yes, this was worthy of memory and all I had was my fifty-nine-year-old mind. I couldn't afford to be the old gray mare. This moment was too important. Too phenomenal. Too epic. Yes, it was epic—a word I shy away from as too big. But this. This moment on the Camargue was epic.

It's like the memory was speaking directly to me. When I could finally write about it, my journaling came out in second person. I'd been rushing toward this sensation, in slow motion, for a lifetime. Epic. I am the white steed, the swaying pampas grass, the stinging melody of monster-sized mosquitoes. Ageless, timeless, formless, yet there was so much form I could almost taste it. The raspberry cream of the skyline mixed with blue Bullet popsicles on a hot summer day, Oklahoma-style. Creamy yellow like my bathroom walls, pumped up on steroids to taste like the small square banana candies from my childhood. Another flash—a banana seat bicycle, a squirming neighbor with her arms wrapped around my waist, the whir of a motorbike on the chase, a parked car. Skin hitting pavement. Blood. Chips of tooth. Silent screams.

Brakes. Put them on too fast and you'll crash on your face. Reins. Hold them too high and you'll come out of your saddle. From old gray mare to galloping filly and back again. Weightless. Winged. Wise. Still, I haven't described that epic moment . . . or have I?

Little horned bulls, black like night, raced into the rushing stream beside us. Rushing like life gone too fast; like my children anxious to grow up and my beloved unable to slow down. Epic. The moment. The memories. The ancestors. Were they all there on the Camargue? The great aunties in their red lipstick and Trudy dancing on her rooftop? I could hear my mother calling, "Don't be foolish. This isn't worth broken bones." Her voice reminded me that I'm no longer nine. Each choice I make is mine. Daddy is there too, the open road spread before us. I wonder if he ever got lost. "Baby, I lived my life lost," I heard him whisper. Me, too, Daddy. Me, too.

But there on the Camargue, everything was magic. I once was lost, but now I'm found. Amazing grace. Permission, too.

Permission to gallop and freedom to slow down. It would not serve me well to be thrown into a ditch in France or Spain or Narnia. Where were we anyway? That land where flamingoes danced to rhythms of ça va and night owls gazed at us with golden eyes reflecting in the sun. Where an old gypsy woman held my hand and pressed a blue stone into my palm and for a moment I seized her magic with my own.

My magic. Big magic. Wild mystery.

Gray, white, chestnut, and golden, the horses whinny at me, speaking of peeling paint and faded beauty, of fairy tales and melting light, of ancient wisdom circling around and through me. They beg me to speak and they whisper that I can simply listen.

In my dreams, Furia paws off my loose skin, licks my toes and fingers with her coarse tongue. Hooves kick at my heart center, pawing and digging to get it out. To release whatever I'm holding back. My tongue is dismembered. I choke and gasp. My eyes begin to dissolve and Furia laps them up with her sandpaper tongue until I am only bones. A skeleton. Furia lays her head in my stripped pelvic bowl. Together, we rest.

The stories, my stories, drape themselves around my shoulders like scarves from the Sinai desert. *I am the pain of the world, wrapped in blue scarves and white.* Bella the camel leads the way looking for goodness in an oft barren land. *I am the fire of the world, burning with desire and hope.* Eagle holds her head high. *I am the beauty of the world, bare-shouldered with upswept hair.* Bee buzzes past, and horse takes the lead. *I am the joy of the world, reaching toward the heavens.* I am riding the sky.

This is how I was born to write and share my voice. To live. To be. To capture poems by the tail as they threaten to rush by. To ride a horse like the French cowgirl I am. To make space for myself with five minutes or ten or a hundred. To meditate and stretch my body and clear my mind. To leave room for magic and mystery. To follow my story, because it knows the way.

Take Your Soul for a Stroll

SOULS**T**ROLL

SoulStrolling is about presence. Am I here or am I there? Can both be true? Will I bear witness and help give voice to the stories that cry to be heard? There is no linear, only the flow across time.

T is for trusting and trying new experiences. It's about time and the ethereal quality that time takes on when we travel. T is for exploring truth and the ways that truth can show up—horses, bees, ancestors, time travel. When we SoulStroll we inhabit our lives more fully. Vacating is not an option. We try new experiences and trust that the Universe is acting on our behalf.

For me, T is also for Tuscany where I traveled between dreams of my past that pointed toward lessons in the future. Trust and transparency became crucial for me to stay with the otherworldly, and at times excruciating, experiences that came my way—lucid dreaming of Maiden, Mother, and Crone that danced alongside visions of aging and Old Paint. T is for tenacity. To stay the course and trust like the hotel owner in *The Best Exotic Marigold Hotel*, who said, "Everything will be all right in the end. If it's not all right, it is not the end."

Practice SoulStrolling®

- Try something different. Images, art, and photographs are an amazing way to step into a dreamlike state. Open a magazine or go online to Pinterest or Instagram and flip through the images until one says, Pick me! (Trust me, it happens). Either with pen and paper or speaking into a recording device, allow the image to speak through your words. Begin with the prompt: *I am* . . . Repeat until the conversation feels complete. When you are finished, either read aloud or listen to what came up.

- Pick a day or part of one where you have no commitments. (You should be good at this by now if you've been practicing the other steps.) Turn off all electronic devices and take off your watch if you wear one. Allow yourself to trust your intuition and inner longings. Trust that whatever you do will be perfect! Set an alarm if there's something you absolutely need to do, but avoid checking the time. Notice how this feels.

PART SEVEN

Signs & Souls

Bali 2016

"Inspire me to quench my thirst for knowledge and answers. Expose me to the teachers who can engage my mind and explain to me how it's done, how it works, how it's made, how it's all connected. Sign me up for the course of life with the sole purpose of marveling at the wonders of the world."

—Pixie Lighthorse

CHAPTER 33

Why Bali?

"Bali is one of my favorite places in the world. In one of my past lives, I believe I was living on the island of Bali."

—Chip Conley

September 2016

Bali. A single word without context, written in my journal on December 31, 2015. Perhaps it was part of a goal setting exercise for the coming year or a subliminal message that slipped through the veil. Maybe it was both.

Without any official form of acknowledgement, Bali had beckoned me through the decades. Like the song "Bali Ha'i" in the movie *South Pacific*, she whispered on the wind, "Come to me. Come to me." It seems as if the call to go was woven into my DNA before time; a recessive gene, easily overlooked beneath a microscope until one day something shifted in my genetic makeup and the image became brilliant, visible, and oh-so-alive.

Looking back on how and when the Bali conversation began, one stark memory rises to the surface. It comes from the '90s when Bill and I were heavily involved in an ultra-conservative church. A fellow parishioner mentioned that one of the missionaries was going to Bali. For a moment my early marriage fear that my husband would return to his missionary roots faded and a tiny flame warmed my insides.

"Bali?" I gushed. "I've always wanted to go to Bali." *Really? Was that true?* A question mark formed on the woman's face. "Hmmm," she responded. "I've never known anyone who responded to Mali quite like that. It's such a harsh and poor environment."

Oops. I'd misheard on some level, but the recessive gene had made itself known.

Like scores of women who read *Eat, Pray, Love*, I was certain that Elizabeth Gilbert was living *my* life as she rode her bicycle through the Balinese rice paddies and sat on the porch with medicine man Ketut Liyer. I could feel myself meditating in the tropical air even though I'd never explored meditation or Eastern culture. I didn't obsess about being Elizabeth or feel like I needed to re-trace her footsteps. I simply luxuriated in the experience like one does when reading a yummy book, until those thoughts drifted away like wispy clouds on a summer's day.

I fell in love with Paris and Ireland instead of India and Indonesia. I went on pilgrimage to Egypt and sailed across the Mediterranean Sea with friends and ate tapas in Barcelona. I drank smooth rum in Cuba and danced with the local Santeria in a rain storm, climbed Big Mama in Namibia and listened to open air opera in Vienna. I packed and unpacked my bags, accumulated airline miles, wrote a couple of my own books, slogged my way through shiploads of personal angst, and lived my everyday life in Seattle until one day, my friend Sharon asked, "Where do you want to spend your big birthday next year?" Without hesitation, one word gushed out of my mouth after decades in hiding—Bali.

Gratitude is a powerful salve for healing wounds and softening rocky starts.

Sometimes life requires that we navigate mucky pathways in order to arrive at spectacular destinations. I'm not sure where I'd be physically, philosophically, or spiritually without the muck of the early 2000s. The Twin Towers bombing in 2001 on my

SoulStrollers live gratitude-filled lives.

forty-fifth birthday. Sending my thirteen-year-old son to his first boarding school in 2002 and therapeutic treatment in 2003. These events were precursors to harder and ultimately more generative times.

The highway to Ubud was a rough start, too. Arriving in Denpasar after nearly twenty-four hours of travel, we entered the crowded customs hall filled with hundreds of tourists hell-bent on having an epic tropical vacation. A familiar twinge of humidity brushed my brow before we even stepped outside. The baggage carousel went round and round while the ATM spat out 1,000,000 rupiah that equaled about US$75. A sea of signs and cries of "Transport! Transport!" swayed before us until we found the one that welcomed us to Bali. "Sharon Richards & Friends."

Wayan, our driver, asked us to wait with our baggage while he went to get the car. Exhaust fumes blended with jet lag and I wished I'd snagged one of the Hello Kitty! barf bags from the airplane. I crawled into the back seat of the car and nestled between Bill and Sharon. Dave settled his 6'4" frame into the passenger seat beside Wayan. A line of cars snaked out of the airport boulevard on the left side of the road. Scooters loaded with families of four without helmets buzzed by and navigated the subtle pandemonium of tour buses headed for Kutuh Beach and Toyota taxis headed for who knows where.

Large roundabouts displayed gigantic sculptures of charging horses and wild-eyed dragons. To the east, boats rested on the sea floor, low tide causing the makeshift harbor to mimic a boatyard boneyard. We stopped at a toll booth, Wayan paid the fare in rupiah, and I thought in another mile or two we would see Bali— the real Bali. I was wrong.

We drove for nearly two hours past building, shack, and temple, building, shack, and temple until I was convinced that all of the tropical greenery and rice fields of the travel brochures had been sucked up by this crowded version of ramshackle progress. My spirits sank and I tried to figure out what I would say to my family and friends, the band of brave sojourners, who had joined me halfway around the world to celebrate my birthday and follow my call to a mythical Bali Ha'i.

It's all a mistake. I'm so sorry I brought you here. The words formed in my mouth. I practiced them inside my head. Wayan said we were getting close. We rolled past a grocery store and a row of tidy-looking shops, and then we turned off the commercial drive. The road narrowed and I felt my breath begin to expand. We drove a few more meters, the sun glittering through a silhouetted palm tree before Wayan turned into a small paved driveway, and paradise waved hello.

I'd learned to be grateful for the tough starts and still I forgot. "Always we begin again," St. Benedict whispers to me. We come through the hard times like the lotus blossom emerging from the sludge or a butterfly breaking free of its cocoon. One moment we're in the muck and the next we are experiencing beauty.

Later, curled up on the chaise lounge outside our bedroom, I heard a sound to my right. *Splash!* Waves rippled outward from the center of a human cannonball in the swimming pool. I giggled with joy and the wonder of it all. Dave's head burst through the surface and his robust laughter filled the air. The cicadas echoed in symphony, a natural crescendo of *Yes! Yes! Yes! Joy is in this world.* They performed as if a conductor waved her baton, a supreme maestro leading them through a gentle beginning up to another crescendo until *voilà*! They finished in superlative harmony. *We are here now.*

I sit on the patio of our Ubud home and begin to welcome myself into this new land. I awoke with an aching body and tender soul. What do I long for as I step into this journey celebrating my sixtieth circle around the sun? It is this moment I have longed for—to sit outside in my pajamas in the morning light, a jungle of palm and banana trees before me, the sound of water from the river and pool trickling through the air. All of the elements are here. Fiery sun. Luscious earth. Aqua water. Fresh mountain air.

A rooster crows in the distance. His proud sound carries me back to Cuba and Molokai, other far away and strange places. I remember what it is like to lie on the concrete driveway in Molokai with another friend named Sharon and my young children, the stars and frogs too numerous to count. And then I hear the roosters in Trinidad, Cuba, their voices competing with the fading sound of drums from the local discotheques, the noises mingling together in the sleepy moments before dawn. Night surrenders to day before day turns back to night.

It's nearly 7:00 a.m. here and 4:00 p.m. yesterday at home in Seattle. *Welcome the stranger*, hums the voice in my mind. *You're stepping into a new land. You've stepped through a new portal.*

A black ant the size of a thick nickel wanders across my iPhone and the red cap of my Lamy fountain pen that lie beside me on the low table. The ant looks as if she might open her mouth and speak to me like Jiminy Cricket from *Pinocchio*. Somehow I don't think I'd be surprised. She is exploring the strangeness too. Ms. Ant walks back onto the familiar tabletop, over to the rounded edge of my phone and scurries away before returning. Again and again, she repeats this ritual. Again and again, I leave home and return. Following the seasons and the rhythms of my soul. The act of return and recede. It is ancient and new.

I've been here before—not in this exact spot, not yet at least—but in the action of enter and recede. Like the ant who climbs to the peak of my fountain pen before exploring the underbelly of the table.

I wonder what the underbelly of this trip is?

It was a long road, but I am here now in our space called Villa Kolibri Saudara, which loosely translates to "Hummingbird Sister." The hummingbird is my personal companion associated with the third eye chakra, which represents intuition. Hummingbirds, unlike any other bird, have the ability to move their wings in a figure-eight pattern. The figure eight is a symbol for infinity and links the past and future. Hummingbirds remind us to experience the joy and magic of living. Sitting on the patio in Ubud on our first morning, I serendipitously read a chapter about the third eye in Doreen Virtue's book, *The Lightworker's Way*. Virtue writes, "Lightworkers are those who volunteered, before birth, to help the planet and its population heal from the effects of fear. Each lightworker is here for a sacred purpose."

Am I a lightworker, a seer? *Wait!* What was the twinge I felt just now while writing? What was that? Oh, it is the underbelly showing itself. The fear that rises inside me when I admit out loud what I've known since I was a little girl in Mrs. Peck's kindergarten class. I am a lightworker, here to see and heal. The fear this time is that a "real" seer (known as *balians* in Bali) will not see me as that. I will be exposed as a fraud. *No. Wait!* It is the fear that I will be found and affirmed. *Oh my.* The underbelly is a tricky little bastard. Not unlike our tokay gecko, who we've named Clarence, that pokes his head from behind the kitchen cabinets before stalking the residence throughout the night. He tempts us with a quick peek and then dives back into the shadows before we can fully see him.

We know he's there, even when we can't get a full visual. He, too, is afraid he will be found.

What if I am found out as a seer? What if my voice is loud and strong and clear? What then? There's no turning back. Like the black ant with antennae stretched outward, I have my own perfect sight and vision. How many pages has it taken for me to admit this? I know what the mystics have claimed all along—there is a heart of something greater that beats within and alongside me.

And just like that, the ancestors have arrived. That's how intuition works. There is no logical path; there is a quick leap. When I capture it on paper, there is a faint trail. However, my mind and pen can be moving along in one direction when—*wham!*—a new notion pops in. This time it's Auntie, my father's older sister, who shows up in my thoughts to wiggle her front dentures at me. Me, sitting here with my own missing front teeth waiting to be replaced with implants in the coming year. Is that the sign of a seer? Someone who's unafraid to show their whole self, missing parts and all? One who has no front teeth? One who's lost the ability to chomp down hard? I don't want to bump against the hardness anymore. I want to soften, to sink into the underbelly, to pull off my clothes and roll into the pool next to me, to be okay with all of me.

Ah, but there is the fear again. The fear of being exposed. What kind of lightworker am I if I sense fear so readily? I am the kind who sees it and names it. The one who understands that to name fear is to begin the healing process. Still the fear of being exposed rises. Who might see me? How will they respond? If I were alone in this moment, I would slink out of my boxer shorts and t-shirt and slide into the water like a mermaid. Naked and whole.

With this wide-open vision, my desires rise. I long to dance naked in the rain, to feel the sun on my bare skin, to allow my body that is 60 percent liquid to become one with water. I see myself doing the backstroke across the pool's expanse. Naked. Naked. The last time I swam naked was with my girlfriends in Seattle, hours before I came home to an ugly family dispute, one that threatened to erase the watery glow of that summer night.

In a flash my flow stops—today and that night—like crashing my head into the end of the swimming pool. But this space, here and now, is about softness and removing hardness—not with angry fists or words of blame, but with tenderness and letting go. I know that I need to be in Bali right now.

CHAPTER 34

The Signs Are Everywhere

"Faith sees the invisible, believes the incredible, and receives the impossible."

—Unknown

September 2016

Ubud is a thin place, a spiritual vortex where anything can happen, where signs are as prodigious as the tiny squares of banana leaf offerings that one steps over everywhere in Bali. A flutter of wings captures my attention. I pause my journaling to witness a black butterfly unlike any I've ever seen, floating around the garden pool. *It's a person.* I hear the voice inside that I've come to trust and welcome. An image of my father floats through my mind. My nonthinking mind says *Yes.* I choose to trust the ethereal. It's time to learn from the signs.

Sunrises are fresh starts and speak to me of resurrection. To witness the sun coming over the horizon is to see the palette of a new day forming. Sunrise is the time of day when I want to wax poetic, but there are not adequate words to describe the moment our small group stands in a rice field north of Ubud waiting for the sun to illuminate Mt. Agung. I almost passed on the 4:30 a.m. invitation from my husband. We're on a day-long photo journey. It's not even 6:00 a.m. and we've already made two new friends from Australia and driven several kilometers out of town.

Camera at the ready, I fill my lungs with mountain air and watch the peak come into silhouette. Pink and golden light draw childlike beams across the brightening blue sky. A rooster crows. A cicada answers. In the distance, a scooter revs its engine. Wispy clouds mirror the changing colors and the watery rice paddies turn into pink rows of light. Palm trees stand like sentries in the field and wave their spiky wings with a passing breeze. As if on cue, the whole world bursts into reflection.

Reflection is my word for the year 2016. How will I reflect these experiences back to the world? How will I reflect this day back to myself? It feels as if I'm being stripped bare inside a mirror. This year of turning sixty has been a year of getting comfortable with being naked and asking for what I want. Even as we follow the tradition of covering our shoulders and legs to enter a temple, Bali seems to invite the sensuality of bare skin. Massages in open air. Bathing in a roadside stream. Shirtless old men and sarong-wrapped ladies. Bali invites me to leave behind a shame-based culture and be reborn like this new day. With the light on the mountain, my spirit opens and affirms that I am one with the light, here to heal the world in my own small and large ways. It's only taken me six decades to acknowledge.

Our party of eight early risers climb back into the van and we head to a sacred site where two rivers meet. I wish I were better with logistic details, but my intuitive senses take over and I am temporarily lost. Truth be told, this is how I prefer it. What I do know is that this is a holy place where pregnant women come in their sixth month to participate in a water ritual and offer their babies a home in the physical world. Even before I step down to the intersection of the rivers, I am drawn to the ancient outdoor temple of crumbling stones. White and yellow umbrellas frame an altar littered with stale offerings and incense. We have stepped onto holy ground. A circle of light pours through the trees and casts a spotlight in the water. Holy. Holy. Holy.

My pulse slows and I kneel to run my fingers through the water and to ask our guide, Nyoman, more about the sacredness of this place. He is delighted by my questions. He's used to working with tourists and photographers who are only interested in capturing the best shot and not fully understanding the scene they are framing. It reminds me of the indigenous tribes who believe that taking a photo of the face captures a piece of the soul. It feels the same is true when we do not show reverence when the holy is offered to us.

A soundtrack plays in my mind as we climb the hundred stairs to the van and our next destination. *I went down to the river to pray* . . . Thank you, holy rivers, for sharing your spirit with us. *O friends, let's go down, let's go down to the river to pray.*

The Balinese people are exotic and gracious with heartwarming smiles and kind dispositions. The colors of the country are alive and pulsating. I see these things mirrored in my own eyes. Where we see fear, fear is returned. Where we spread love, love blooms and grows.

Our little party weaves its way through the local market near Tampaksiring. We are the only tourists, and I'm grateful for Nyoman who stays nearby and helps us navigate our way through live ducks and chickens in crates, skinned meat, and pig heads. We pass toothless old women with broad smiles, and clean schoolgirls in plaid skirts and crisp blouses, long braids trailing down their backs. Babies sleep on fathers' backs. Toddlers steer worn scooters through stalls filled with plastic toys and fruit I cannot name. Teens are like teens everywhere in the world, aloof and cool.

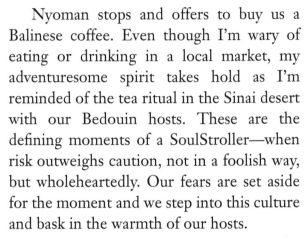

SoulStrolling involves moments when risk outweighs caution, when fears are set aside to allow full immersion in a different culture.

Nyoman stops and offers to buy us a Balinese coffee. Even though I'm wary of eating or drinking in a local market, my adventuresome spirit takes hold as I'm reminded of the tea ritual in the Sinai desert with our Bedouin hosts. These are the defining moments of a SoulStroller—when risk outweighs caution, not in a foolish way, but wholeheartedly. Our fears are set aside for the moment and we step into this culture and bask in the warmth of our hosts.

Sharon and I nod yes to Nyoman and I send a silent prayer to the gods for protection from Bali belly, the local slang term for upset stomachs and more. We make ourselves comfortable on the wooden bench and munch on a local version of peanut brittle. The coffee is hot, gritty, earthy, and delicious.

"Open the door and see what magic arrives," I laugh while Sharon and I wait for the house staff to arrive and make breakfast. I remember that our house manager, Made, said we need to open the door to let the girls know we are awake and ready. "You have to physically open the door." Like with the spirits of our ancestors and the abundant life that lives inside each one of us, we need to offer a welcoming presence. An open door. An open heart. An open mind.

My mind was closed for so many years. My mind and my throat. I could feel the yearnings and knowings. They were whispers inside my being that begged for me to open the door, like the images in my dreams—hiking the cliffs with my father, witnessing the dancing ancestors in an open field, the fingers of God rising in a Saguaro cactus field. The signs were all there.

I marvel at the intricacies of all that we do not know or understand about life's journey. Curled on my cushions in our Balinese rental, I read from a book handed to me by a friend before I left the States. The section is about intuitive therapist Doreen Virtue, and her experience with patients who seemingly had depressed spirits hanging around them. These spirits impacted the mood and growth of the people they surrounded. She calls them "earthbound" spirits and describes how they often hang around the earthly realm because they are remorseful for past behaviors and want to make amends of sorts.

When my son was a young child, he talked about seeing and feeling "other people" next to him. My husband and I were so steeped in fear-based Christianity at the time that we were anxious for Jonathon's welfare, as parents are prone to be. We didn't know what to make of it and instead of being curious and kind, we resolved to get rid of the problem. We cleared his room of any physical objects (like Pokémon cards and children's ghost stories) that might have caused his "irrational" experience. Looking back, I believe we dismissed his young experience of something that might have been very real. Could there have been ancestors from our family line trying to communicate or heal through our son?

Doreen Virtue describes that in her "spirit-releasement therapy," she notices that upon healing or being released, most of the spirits she encounters depart the physical realm and move toward yellow-like colors. Yellow is representative of the solar plexus chakra associated with earthly desires such as sex, alcohol, and drugs. It is also the power center of the body. My son's story has been littered with devastation by "earthly desires" and struggles with power. I wonder if we'd understood more about the spirit world when he was young, perhaps his path might have been different. I ponder the impact of acceptance and curiosity versus expectations and rigid reasoning. I wonder so much as a mother and seeker. Perhaps I'm reaching for answers that will never be found. Perhaps I'm onto something. Perhaps I'll carry this thought as lightly as the winged butterfly who has again fluttered past.

CHAPTER 35

Healing, Balinese-Style

"Like the bee, gathering honey from different flowers, the wise man accepts the essence of different scriptures and sees only the good in all religions."

—Srimad Bhagavatum

September 2016

I knew I desired to see a traditional Balinese healer on my birthday trip to Bali. The why wasn't something I could describe, but in my quest for healing and wholeness—a quest that had turned into one about authentic voice—I knew that not all true things can be quantified or verified. As a psychotherapist and spiritual director, I, too, could be called a spiritual healer, so when the notion of a meeting in Bali popped into my mind, my heart answered without hesitation, *Yes. Mais oui. But of course!*

Leading up to the trip, our Airbnb hostess recommended a healer named Desak and a week after we arrived in Ubud, Bill and I visited her. As we sat on the porch in her family compound, serenaded by cooing doves while two puppies wrestled beside us, I knew that she was not my healer. She was in her late thirties, possibly forty, with Bali brown hair and chocolate-colored eyes.

Her presence was grounded and I liked her very much. Her focus was on energy healing in the body.

"Some people feel an electrical current moving through their body when I perform my treatment," she said. In a Reiki-like tradition, she and her partner/husband perform a massage-type treatment that energetically works to clear pain blockages in the body.

She's not for you. She's for Bill, I heard the doves coo. *She's not for you. Not for you.* I turned to Bill and said, "This is your session, not mine." The healer nodded.

"Are you sure?" He furrowed his brow.

"Yes," I replied. "I'm sure."

A gentle peace settled over me as he rose and went inside with Desak and her husband for the session. I sat on the porch, played with the puppies, and knew my time would come. A while later, Bill came outside with a post-massage radiance on his face.

"Wow," he said. "I actually looked around to see if she had me hooked up to a battery charger." He was glowing and pain-free. The healer recommended at least three treatments for the complete healing of his knee malady that had plagued him for years. Unfortunately, that was something he wouldn't be able to do because we lived so far away. Still, it would be several months before the nagging pain returned to his knee.

Journal entry: September 10, 2016

I wanted to have a healer experience yesterday but/and it ended up being Bill's experience and I'm okay with that . . . Today I ask the angels to bring a healer into my life for me. I want something magical, something I can't quite name. I want it to be named for me.

That last line is so fascinating to me. *I want it to be named for me.* After years of working on clarifying my own voice, I wanted to let go of control. One of the messages I learned as a child, especially in regard to religious things, was to not worry my pretty little head about the details because someone older, wiser, and probably male had already figured out the answers for me. This felt different— strong, solid, and mysterious. I was putting my trust in a power greater than I and relinquishing my need to make things happen. It felt honest and true and good.

Later that same day, I received an email from a friend who had shared a few recommendations for restaurants and places to visit in Ubud. "I forgot to mention my favorite healer," she wrote. "In case you're interested in that kind of thing." *Yes!* I chuckled as I read her words. Yes, please. My request had been answered. His name was Cokorda Rai.

My intuition was operating on a high frequency in Bali, and I trusted those vibrations. While I was journaling, another dragonfly landed on my pages. Throughout our stay in Bali, Dragonfly had become a frequent visitor along with Black Butterfly. Iridescent wings danced around the cozy corner where I wrote in the mornings. Dragonflies and butterflies splayed themselves along the paths near the rice terraces, showing up at opportune moments like a well-placed exclamation point.

The dragonfly is a symbol for breaking illusions that prevent growth and maturity. It is considered the bringer of visions of power. I was no stranger to Dragonfly. She had trailed me for years through the wasteland of west Texas and the high desert near Taos, New Mexico. Her fairy-like wings lifted me higher in Bali as I listened to my own heart's *yes please* regarding the *balian*. And then I did what any reforming left-brain person would do—I turned to the research.

I googled Cokorda Rai. There wasn't a lot to be found, which was refreshing in this day of "everyone must have an internet presence." Amidst a few blog posts and a spiritual guide's reference to visiting Cokorda Rai, what I did find left me feeling satisfied that I wanted to make an appointment. The tricky thing about Ubud is that there are few street addresses and phone numbers are apt to change as often as the moon circling around the sun.

I bookmarked a page on my phone that I found in my search and saved it to show our house manager when he came by the next day, which happened to be my birthday.

"Do you know this man?" I held my phone so Made could see.

"Yes," he whispered with reverence. "My father studied with him until he died three years ago." A tingle ran up my spine and I held my breath. "Would you like to see him?"

"Yes, please. Yes."

"I will make the arrangements for you."

"Thank you." Hands in namaste mudra, I nodded. "Thank you so much, Made."

Washed clean from our visit to Pura Tirta Empul (the holy water temple) near Tampaksiring village and brightened with Luwak coffee from a local plantation in the jungle, my daughter Janey, Sharon, and I giggle and glow in the back seat of our driver Wayan's car. Each of us is wrapped in a colorful sarong, a *selendang* (sash) at our waist, which Wayan says symbolizes the separation between higher and lower appetites, and our shoulders covered, all a sign of respect for the Holy Man, Cokorda Rai. Made had arranged a 10:00 a.m. appointment for the three of us. Wayan navigates the car in the narrow neighborhood alley, parks it, and leads us around the corner into the cluster of modest, open-air homes.

My research prepared me for the scene. Sessions are not private like Bill's was with Desak. Here, all was open, and half a dozen *bules* (white people, pronounced boo-lays) from Scotland, Australia, and the United States curl around the edge of the raised 20x20-foot area. Cokorda Rai sits on the far end of the covered porch in a carved wooden chair. He has smile crinkles around his eyes and skin the color of a caramel macchiato. His long fingers rest gently on the skull of a blond woman in her late thirties who sits in front of him on the floor, her legs outstretched. We settle in as quietly as possible to watch him work.

"Ouch!" she yelps. "Ouch! Ouch!"

The *balian* winces along with her and smiles at the same time, reminiscent of a compassionate friend who knows the pain is for your own benefit or a doctor who must re-break a bone before it can heal properly. Rai raises his gray, pony-tailed head skyward. "Many unhealed scars," he murmurs. The woman yelps when he presses again.

To watch Cokorda Rai with other people gave me a real sense of his process. I am last in this group of nine who wait together. Each session is unique. One man's pain is located in his lower back. The healer has him sit cross-legged and kiss each knee. A groan escapes, then laughter prevails. Others lay prone on the woven mat while Cokorda Rai pokes the pressure points in their toes with his stick that resembles a fat chopstick. Stifled screams erupt from most. They seem to lessen after Rai moves his stick over their energy centers. It is mesmerizing, like witnessing a wizard wave a magic wand on behalf of goodness.

An hour or so passes until it's our trio's turn. Sharon goes first. She sits with her back against the healer's knees, her sarong-covered legs stretched in front of her. Her eyes closed, dark curly hair framing her face. The healer moves his hands with intention across her crown. A golden beetle the size of a quarter lands on her nose. The healer keeps working. Sharon remains calm, because (as she tells us later) she can hear me laughing. She squeals when Cokorda Rai pokes her right ear. "You think too much," he declares. I chuckle from the sidelines, because I know my friend

well. Sharon moves to the mat. He prods her toes and elicits a yelp
or two. The two of them have a brief conversation and then it's
Janey's turn.

My daughter rises to her full height of five foot six and stands
in front of him in her blue-toned sarong and t-shirt.

"How old are you?" Cokorda Rai asks.

"Almost twenty-four."

"One so young," he continues. "So beautiful. So pure. Like
a blossoming flower." He motions for her to sit, then handles
her head with reverence and a serene look on his face. "You are
balanced for one so young. Be mindful in love. This is Mother
Earth's world, not Father Earth. A man works for three minutes to
make a child. A woman and her body work for nine months." He
offers kind words to Janey about remaining balanced in her body
and in love, offers her a blessing, and then sends the Little Flower
back to sit as I rise to stand.

"Why are you here?" He looks puzzled as if a healer is not what
I need. "What can I do for you?"

I tell him I've had a recent birthday and I want to check my
spiritual alignment for the coming year. He nods. I sit on the
mat next to him after he pats my head and throat, prods my ears,
and runs his fingers over my crown. I wonder if I've heard him
correctly, because it sounds like he was murmuring something
about happiness. Then his face turns solemn and he asks, "You
have a second child, yes? A son?"

It's like he can see the story and scars etched across my heart.
I know he knows it hasn't been an easy journey. Janey and Sharon
sense it too. A collective gasp flickers through the air. Is this a
parlor trick? Is he merely observant? But I get it. I understand
deep in my gut that when a question arises in one's intuition, a
need to ask it often ensues even if we don't understand why. This
time he says audibly, "You are a happy, happy woman and a very
good mother. A very good mother." His words wash over me as he

offers healing and a blessing that I didn't understand I needed or desired.

I am a happy woman. I am a good mother. I am here now. Free like the swallows. Silky as water. Happy like the chickadees. Glowing like the hibiscus.

As we part, he asks what I do in the world. "I help people." It is the simplest thing to say in the moment.

"Yes!" His smile broadens and he nods. "This makes you very, very happy. It makes the world happy. Happy you. Happy world."

CHAPTER 36

Rain Dance

"Don't let your dreams fade away. Write them down!"

—Unknown

September 2016

Writing down dreams is akin to the saying, "Be careful what you wish for because the Universe might deliver." In December 2015, I wrote down the single word "Bali" in my journal and then I was there. On our arrival, my desires whispered a longing to strip off my clothes and roll into the pool, to dance naked in the rain, to allow myself to become one with the water. It wasn't exactly a new desire. This longing to be one with the watery element and dance unfettered in the rain had surfaced more than once over the years. My first recollection was around 2007 when I was facilitating a workshop in the arid Texas panhandle. One morning, a swarm of dragonflies swooped across the dried grass near the house with their luminescent wings shining in the sun. They reminded me of mermaids glistening in water. They seemed out of place in that land of dried red dirt, and so did I. I'm not sure whether it was the dragonflies or the thunderstorm that rolled in later that evening, but in my mind's eye I recall the image of dancing in the rain, stripped of my cares and clothing.

I've often thought that God played a cruel joke on me when he planted me in a landlocked state at birth, far away from the rolling seas and crystalline sand that whisper to my happiest nature. Some of my fondest childhood memories are of visiting local lakes and floating on an air mattress for hours on end without a care in the world. Bobbing around in my aunt's swimming pool and running along the silky beaches in San Diego were my rewards after our odyssey drives across the lower western states. Now I live in a locale where the rain is often frigid and the beaches are best enjoyed with a bonfire. Still, there have been times when I wondered what it would be like to inhabit the spirit of a sprite and dance in the raindrops wherever I might be.

Be mindful what you wish for . . .

It's our last morning in Bali. 6:00 a.m. Sleep eludes me while a deep sense of stillness mingles with restlessness. I wander from spot to spot looking for a place to journal until I finally land in my corner—the place with that Goldilocks love seat and assorted blue pillows. Faded carvings sit over my shoulder and a white-washed table is by my side. It's the same table where the black ant introduced herself on our first day. The morning sky is blue and spotted with a few lacy clouds. It was pink an hour ago. Change is in the air.

The sun peeks through the waving palm trees and I hear a lone scooter on the road behind us. Even the roosters and the bugs are quiet this morning. A Balinese dog barks in the distance. According to our driver Wayan, this mongrel-like species is revered for guarding the family compounds and catching evil spirits that try to enter. We didn't have a dog at our AirBnb, but we had Clarence, our resident gecko. We much prefer him to Amelio the rat who hid in the refrigerator coils and startled us with his scurrying about in the dark. A tiny lizard in the corner says, "Don't forget about me!" How could I forget a single iota of the magic this place offers?

Yesterday Janey and I walked to the local juice bar for breakfast. I don't think I could ever tire of watching the scooter traffic go by on that road. Scenes play across the movie screen of my mind. Our landowner and his two-year-old grandson touring back and forth in front of the café. Workmen loading black rocks the size of small boulders into makeshift baskets. Wobbly tourists puttering by, their pale skin glinting in the sun. Families of four heading to town on single motorbikes. A Portuguese water dog splayed across his master's lap, resembling a slaughtered deer, though still very much alive.

A stunning rooster on a blue rope crows from across the road, his teal tail feathers sparkle in the morning light. The scene recedes to the background and I pick up my pen and begin to write.

Later that day as the sun began to lower, I sat on the veranda with my two best friends—Janey and Sharon, daughter and pal. I had felt safer and more vibrant since the morning we were dipped in holy water at Pura Tirta Empul and blessed by Cokorda Rai. The water temple had been the holy of the holiest until one more exquisite moment arrived and unfiltered holiness fell from the sky.

It was the last full day of our adventure, the birthday trip that marked my sixty circles around the sun. The Virgo girl turned woman. I, the woman of earth, the one with fire in my belly and love in my heart. My feet ached in the best possible way from a long, slow stroll into Ubud with Janey. I could still feel the air blowing through my hair from the return ride home on the motorbike taxi. My nose twitched with the earthy scent of the driver's body and caffeine breath. Both felt right, not repulsive.

Why? I didn't know. Maybe it was my father again, memories of riding through the Oklahoma backroads on his Harley, my arms wrapped tight around his waist. I felt safe there. Alive. Like I had on the motorbike taxi back to Villa Kolibri.

And now we were home at the villa, the one where I'd chatted with Clarence the tokay gecko, chased Amelio the rat with an open umbrella, and watched the ancestral black butterfly flit by at every mention of my father or any statement that deserved a *hell yes!* affirmation.

The three of us were stretched out on wicker lounges, soaking up the last sun rays of the day, Bintang beer in hand, tortilla chips nearby. Then came the late afternoon clap of thunder, tailed by raindrops that soon turned into a shimmering waterfall from the sky. We pushed our chairs back under the eaves and felt the spray that swirled with the gentle breeze.

I was happy like Cokorda Rai said. Content. Fulfilled. So much so that I nearly missed the grand gesture Mother Nature was offering to me. *Care to dance, my love?* The palm trees waved. The sky beckoned.

I had woken up that morning thinking about the dance. The one that had been so long in coming, the one I'd envisioned while standing in the arid West Texas land at Brazos de Dios, the arms of God. The dance that was too cold and impersonal to do in urban Seattle with its packed-in houses and open backyards, not to mention temperatures that could put goose bumps on the devil. It was the dance that snuck up on me even when I could see it arriving.

With a giggle and a gasp, I bolted upright from the lounge and dropped my skirt to the patio. My t-shirt was next, then my sports bra until finally I stepped out of my panties. In less than thirty seconds, I was bare ass naked and dancing in the rain.

Around the pool I went, skipping like my five-year-old self. Giggles turned into belly laughs. My human form blended into the rain as I threw my arms wide open and my head back until I tasted life on my tongue.

From the patio, the others . . . well, I didn't know what they were doing. I'd forgotten they were there. This was my dance of freedom and the world was my partner. It had taken me sixty years, but I finally knew the unfettered feeling of not giving a shit about what others thought. Rain tickled my naked breasts and bottom. Warmth, sky, air. No boundaries. No edges. I'd crossed another border into wholeness, into humanity, into my power and voice.

A modern-day Botticelli painting. No airbrushing. No Photoshop. Just shining, shimmering, sixty-year-old Me!

I remembered sitting with Cokorda Rai on his front porch, feeling his strong hands on my head and body. So many hands had touched me deeply that week, like the healing waters of the rain and holy water temple. Janey playfully slapping my bare butt after I got out of the shower; making love with my husband in the afternoon sun; curling into an outdoor petal-filled bath while watching ivory birds land in emerald rice fields; each soothing massage on the back deck; stripping down to dance naked in the rain. Layers peeling away with each reverent motion.

Teary and tender, I wondered how I could carry this dream-like existence home with me.

CHAPTER 37

Like a Ton of Bricks

"Intuition functions in a quantum leap. It has no methodological procedure, it simply sees things."

—Osho

October 2016

Back home in Seattle, curled up with my journal and reflecting on my time in Bali, my paternal grandfather, the first of three John David Stevens, arrives in my thoughts in a quantum leap. Even though I never met him, he is with me in the moment. I wonder if he was (or is) the spirit hanging around my son. Is he asking to be freed or forgiven for something? Does he want to make amends or does he simply ask that I remember him?

I know him only as the man who was killed by a sign in 1936, two decades before I was born. Killed by a sign, literally. The obituary read:

Man Hurt by Falling Sign Dies in Hospital

J.D. Stevens, 46 years old, died early Thursday in Oklahoma

City General hospital of head injuries suffered Sunday when he fell putting up a sign on a building in the 1100 block North Broadway.

The sign fell and struck Stevens on the head. A fellow worker said Stevens also was showered with falling bricks. Stevens's home is in Putnam City. The body was taken to the Street & Draper funeral home.

The newspaper account made it sound as if he'd been feted with gifts instead of fatal bricks. "Showered with falling bricks." Nowhere did it say what the sign said. I wonder if anyone bothered to ask.

He spent four days in the General Hospital in Oklahoma City. The Superior Neon Company was one year old when the accident happened; eighty years later, they're still in business providing neon signs for companies like Target and Mercy Hospital.

Lord, have mercy on us.

I wonder what kind of sign my grandfather was hanging when the stones gave way. Something for a diner or maybe the movie theater that's now been turned into a coffee shop? Could it have been at the same spot where Bill and I had coffee two years before I saw the obituary for the first time? Was the accident caused by negligence? Could John David have been drinking that day the bricks gave way and the sign struck him on the head? Was that the cause for his remorse? Did he have an argument with my grandmother Anne that morning? Or was it just an accident? He was doing his job. The bricks gave way and fell. He was struck on the head. He died.

The signs are everywhere, literally and metaphorically. Neon. Flashing. Subtle. Absurd.

SoulStrollers see signs everywhere and pay them heed.

I want to turn their wattage down . . . and I don't. There is so much more I long to know, like who sat vigil with my grandfather at the hospital. Did the doctors know he would die? Did my grandmother know? Could she sense that death was near? The first article made it sound as if he had a few lacerations that could be mended with stitches and a Band-Aid.

Was he frightened? Did he suffer? Without question I know the greatest grievance is that he was forgotten. Only a single photo of him in a light-colored suit with his two small sons, John David Junior and Paul, remains. The photo, a Xerox copy of three newspaper announcements in seventy-five words or less, and a statement announcing the memorial services: 10:00 a.m. Friday morning at the Street & Draper Mortuary. Even the date is absent.

I wonder if Street & Draper had one of those horrible grievers' rooms. At the funerals of my maternal grandparents, my father, and others, held at Merrill Funeral Home, I remember the grievers' room was off to one side of a chapel-like area and had a one-way glass partition to wall off the grieving family from the rest of the world. Archaic. Barbaric. Cruelty disguised as kindness. It was like being inside a police interrogation room in reverse. We could see the casket and the other mourners, but they could neither see nor hear us. Remembering all the times my family sat silenced inside that box makes rage boil inside me. I want to take my own brick and throw it through that damned partition, to allow our voices and tears to be heard by all.

Bricks and mortar. The world sees them as building blocks, but in my grandfather's story, they symbolize death. Like in Edgar Allan Poe's *The Tell-Tale Heart*, the voices of our ancestral line were walled in and forgotten, but our hearts continued to weep.

Did no one ever complain about being shut off behind glass? Why were the photographs thrown away and our stories left unspoken? Why did no one tend the ancestral fire or feed the ghosts? How *does* a hungry ghost demand to be remembered? What if he cries out through his great grandson's nightmares or his granddaughter's fragile psyche? What if he offers signs across our pilgrim's pathways like crumbs leading back to our beginning?

Few people in my lifetime referred to my grandfather, John David Stevens, by his name. He was simply the man killed by a sign.

Sitting in my Seattle bedroom pondering my grandfather's life, his death, and what it means to follow our own signs, a dream recorded in my Ireland journal leaped into my mind, a new thread in my ancestral connections.

Journal entry: October 19, 2009

Building a building in my dreams. Brick by brick. Inside an attic. Denzel Washington is there. Barack and Michelle Obama, too. Their daughter Sasha is a secretary who informs me that I lost out on an exam. Even though I was the most qualified, they still passed over me. In the dream, I was in charge (i.e., I knew the most), but no one could see that. Everyone came to me for help and answers, but I didn't have the appropriate credentials. In the dream, I was likened to an overqualified bricklayer— putting in windows and layering bricks with skill. I was doing the work with my mind instead of physical labor. Brick by brick. I was and wasn't the bricklayer. The laborers lost their jobs when the building was complete. My home, but not my home.

Eight years after I dreamed that dream in Ireland and recorded it in my journal, I wrestle with the signs of the bricklayer that I'd forgotten. I pondered the meaning of bricks and bricklayers. Was this dream a message from my grandfather?

Sitting in my local coffee shop in Seattle, I pull out my notes on what an attic represents from *The Book of Symbols: Reflections on*

Archetypal Images, as Dire Straits plays on the stereo and a man talks loudly on video conference beside me.

"Attic, the part just under the roof, evokes stored memories of childhood, bits of our personality still alive, which cling round us and suffuse us with the feeling of earlier times. It is accumulated treasures and trash, the residues of faded life and clues to family skeletons."

I've tugged on a new thread, and one more stitch falls into the makeup of my tapestry. Before I go any further, I recall a dream analysis tool from my Jungian studies. I tune out the loud talker next to me, grab my fountain pen, and jot down the primary elements of the dream along with what they represent to me. This is tricky, because it's essential to rely on the first words that pop into my mind, even though part of me desperately wants to edit and shape the story like a master artist working with clay.

Element	Attribute	Association with Attribute
Building	Structure, solid, solace	Faith
Bricks	Solid, death, red clay	Childhood, life stories
Attic	Dusty, remote, scary	The unknown
Washington/Obamas (African Americans)	Powerful, enslaved, wise, soulful	Me
Me	Qualified, unseen, forgotten	Ancestors

The next step in the dream analysis is to rewrite the dream and replace the elements with their associated meanings. Again, I'm challenged to rely on my intuition and remain true to the process. Here are the results:

Building solid faith and solace in my dreams. Childhood story by childhood story. Inside the Unknown. Powerful, enslaved, wise, soulful Me. Both/and. Even though the ancestors are the most qualified to help me, I pass over them. The ancestors know the most, but I cannot see that. Others come to the ancestors for help and answers, but in my mind, the ancestors don't have the appropriate credentials. One ancestor was literally an overqualified bricklayer (my grandfather)—putting in windows and layering stories. The ancestors do the work inside my mind and through physical realms. They lay feathers and stones in my pathway, but I must piece it together. Story by story. I am and am not my childhood stories. The stories lose their power for destruction when faith is complete. This world is my home, and not my home.

I sit and swirl in the soup of what this all means. I open up Facebook, go to the bathroom, come back to the table, and check my email. A dear friend has sent a message stating she will undergo surgery for a mass in her spine. She wants me with her as a "wise and strong" woman. I feel strong and weak at the same time.

Images of the ancestors dancing up my spine flash through my mind, stories of past and present intertwining. My chiropractor once said that our spinal cord is like a computer chip filled with memories of our lifetime. So many memories, some remembered, others lost or hidden away. I don't quite know how to adequately retrieve them. This world is my home and not my home. The ancestors are alive and well. My stories are not me, and of course they are.

Four days after making the connection between my grandfather Stevens' obituary and the Ireland dream, I drove through our Seattle neighborhood on the way to get the emission test for my VW Beetle. Such an ordinary thing. Driving north on the narrow street, I stopped behind a car pulled alongside a workman's ragged truck that, in hindsight, reminded me of something out of my childhood. A rusty sky-blue Chevy, maybe a Ford. A man's torso was leaning into the passenger side window to speak to the driver. The vehicles blocked my passage, but I tried to enjoy the crisp fall day rather than letting impatience win.

When the chatting duo noticed my presence, the workman patted the open car window, waved goodbye to the driver, then turned toward me. His face was weathered from working outside, hair steel gray, a youthful grin. His frame, slender, neither tall nor short, familiar. He waved his hand my way as if to say, "Thank you. Go on." A simple, everyday gesture. Still, my breath caught. It was as if I was watching the man in my Tuscan dream wave to me from across the bridge. Grandfather. Father. Son. The Stevens masculine line, there on my street.

When he turned to step out of the way, I noticed the tumble of bricks by the side of the house where he'd been working.

Stevens was showered with falling bricks.

The signs are everywhere.

The ancestors and I have remained silent for too long with statements like *I don't know where we're from. She's the shy one. You could never be a writer, sell a book, speak in public, travel the world. He's the (nameless) man killed by bricks.*

Is the story of my grandfather being buried beneath bricks really so different from my own story of being buried beneath lies? In her article, *Healing the Wounds of Your Ancestors*, Dr. Judith Rich, a pioneering teacher in the field of transformation and consciousness as well as a Jungian and archetypal psychologist, explains, "As you step to the front of the line in your ancestry, the energy they embodied has been passed on and is now expressing as you and those of your current generation in the lineage. As you transform, the energy of the entire lineage preceding you is transformed."

This is a premise that I became intrigued with in my early studies of family dynamics and counseling psychology. I've helped hundreds of individuals (myself included) wrestle with childhood stories in a quest for transformation and renewed freedom from the ties that bind us to past ways of being.

Yes indeed, we carry our history forward with us. It's easier to understand this scientifically by turning to DNA results that can be dissected and quantified beneath a microscope. The spiritual inheritance is harder to understand, especially in a Western culture that relies on physical proof. *Not all truths are explicable.* The whispered words come to me as audibly as the music wafting through the coffee shop sound system where I'm writing.

Sometimes the "carry-forward" is a welcome inheritance transmitted by enlightened or passionate forbearers. Other times the struggle to uncover a healthy path forward is more intense. It took me years to digest how my childhood stories of being silenced were impacting my adult life, and it wasn't until I came to understand that my own mother had likely been silenced by her mother that I was able to soften my heart toward myself and my maternal ancestors. Therefore, it was the second part of Dr. Rich's statement that caught my attention. "As we transform, the energy of the entire lineage preceding us is transformed." I can be the one to heal old wounds for my entire lineage, forgive old enemies, shift conditioning and beliefs, release pain that has held preceding generations captive for centuries.

Even though a DNA test indicated that I have no Native American ancestry, my Oklahoma roots run deep and I continue to be drawn to earth medicine and ritual. Crazy Horse's words still offer solace and hope for my family and the world at large, "I see a time of Seven Generations when all the colors of mankind will gather under the Sacred Tree of Life and the whole earth will become One Circle again." I see this vision not only for my family, but for the world I've come to love and embrace through SoulStrolling.

What I've learned during these journeys is that I am called to be the healer of the pain legacy in my family line, not only my personal pain but the pain of those who went before me and those who will come after. *Happy me. Happy world.* Specifically, I am called to give voice to the forgotten ones in my lineage. This is not an easy task, because my family legacy has been one of silence and secrets. All of my elders are deceased and even while alive, they did not openly share their stories. In death, they left a scant trail of photos and obituaries like miniscule breadcrumbs leading into a dark forest.

While poking around on Ancestry.com in 2016, I found the obituary of my great paternal grandfather, Elisha A. Stevens. His cause of death was listed as "accidentally falling from trestle on Santa Fe Railroad." He was sixty-nine years old. His son and my grandfather, John David Stevens (aka the "Brick Man") died at age forty-six, twenty years before I was born. Like his father, my own father, John David Stevens, Jr. died at age fifty-six when he burned to death in a trucking accident the day after my nineteenth birthday. A wave of emotion ripples through my body when I type those words. Decades later, I still miss my father and wish we could have traveled the world together and shared more stories from our lives. Sometimes I curse the Universe at its irreverent timing. Other times I am grateful for bricks and butterflies that help me remember no one is ever gone, especially when they live on in our memories.

It is from this lineage of trucks and bricks and trestles that my son, Jonathon, named after his maternal and paternal grandfathers, emerged. I can't help but wonder about his personal struggles with addiction and depression and whether or not there is a DNA pattern that gravitates toward tragedy that flows from generation to generation. Then I read more words from Dr. Judith Rich that feel like a promise. "If we're healing and transforming the wounds we carry from those who came before, we're also changing the trajectory of those who come after."

CHAPTER 38

Generational Healing

"Ancestral longings rise like smoke,
filmy blue swirls curl toward my heart."

—Judith Prest

November 2016

It is a night saturated with dreams, an evening filled with letting
go and releasing, as Bill and I build a refiner's fire on Shilshole
Beach to honor my ancestors. We face the north sky, our feet
planted in shifting sand that promises solid ground far beneath.
Earth. Turning toward the east, a multi-colored kite flies in the sky
and leaves rustle in the aspen grove. The wind reminds us of her
presence. Bill and I rotate clockwise to face the south. The south
where I was raised, the place of red earth and heat. Only this night
instead of earth and heat, there is a harbor and a hill, both lit by the
glow of the setting sun. Fire.

One more rotation and we've drifted to the ocean, the sea, the
place that calls me to come for healing and restoration. The sea
has a vast ability to hold our tears and yearnings, like a cradle for

the soul. I am grateful to be on the West Coast where the sun drops into the sea each night, as it should in my romantic mind. West and water. Weight and wings. All of the elements are here.

The breeze is strong enough to carry the small kite into evensong, but calm enough for us to light a fire in the open pit without struggle. We lay our tools on the grainy sand. Rolled up pages of a Barron's newspaper. A pack of kindling from the local grocery store. A curated bag of leaves and sticks for the offering. A burnt Budweiser can left in the common pit seems appropriate—the only thing better would be a can of Coors from my Oklahoma days.

Shilshole Bay is quiet and calm. I create the ritual as I go, or perhaps it is the ritual that creates me.

SoulStrollers create ritual and find ritual creating them.

Before we left home, I texted my brother and sister to let them know of my intention to honor our ancestors in this way. They reply with their support and offer blessings of prayers and candles from their homes in Bellville, Texas, and Walla Walla, Washington.

Together, we remember. We see you, dear ancestors.

I turn to the words from my journal that formed a few mornings ago.

Journal entry: October 29, 2016

The ancestors call, dressed in ash cloth, draped in grief. It is the men who call to me this time.

What is this thing called grief? The dust that does not shine. The soundless nod that wakes me and whispers to my broken heart. The thing I did not know existed until I spread my wings, until I opened myself up and fell into the past, the past where men died tragic deaths—showered by bricks, burned by fire, swallowed by bitterness and despair. Where lungs can't breathe and dreams are drowned in alcohol and drugs.

What is this thing called grief? The stranger I know by name. The one who beckons me to light a fire and honor it in ritual.

To say I'm sorry, dear grandfather. I'm sorry that you died. I'm sorry that we forgot to say your name.

To say goodbye, my father. I miss you so much and wish that we had cried. I'm sorry to the Wee Ones and grateful for your lives. I see you. I know you. I feel you.

I wish I could grieve today for my mother and that female line, but somehow, some way, I know it's not time. I see your strength in Trudy, in Grace, Arcylla, and Sallye. Anne, too.

It is the girls, the women, who meet me laughing in the labyrinth. They sit in the field stringing daisies . . . but the men, the Johns, stand at the edge of the cliff, on the other side of the bridge. They nudge me forward. They ask for my hand to guide them back to the other side on wings of owls, on wings of eagles and bees and butterflies. I am their wings. They are my weight. It's time to set them free.

I read the words and my throat catches at the phrase "they nudge me forward." Their presence is tangible. Can Bill feel it? What about the log beneath my legs? The sky? The fire? Do they feel the nudge toward healing, too? Are we all sentient beings?

It is a stretch for me to let anyone else in on this sacred ritual, but the elements are here to hold me. Earth. Wind. Fire. Water. With each small step, my voice—our ancestral voices—are becoming stronger. We cannot rush through the grief to grab the blessing. Yes, of course, I know the blessings are there, like new growth in an ancient forest that has burned to the ground. It takes time to strengthen and emerge.

I feel the longing to rush toward complete healing, the desire for all the past pain to evaporate into the night air and be gone. I want to rush toward the blessings. Instead, I slow down and pick a grief leaf out of my paper bag. This leaf is one that has sat on my altar for the past few days as a symbol of this healing work. It jumps into the fire and disappears.

The next leaf, the one that represents journey, does not go so easily. It is the one that holds infinite stories, numerous as grains of sand on the beach. This leaf blows away from the fire and I reach in to help it. Yes, I reach into the fire, this refiner's fire of my journey. The grief from when I was nineteen flickers in the night—a glimpse of my father dead in a blaze of diesel and crumpled metal. Time flashes forward and I wonder if this is what it was like when my son reached for a fix. Painful, harsh, necessary? But this time I'm not burned. Grace is with me. *I see you. I feel you. I remember.*

Next, I reach for a block of ragged, dense wood the size of my palm, a found treasure from another beach. This is for my grandfather, John David Stevens. It is shaped like a small brick. I offer it in remembrance of him and pray for the release of his pain. *I see you. I remember.*

More driftwood for my father and his brother, Uncle Paul. *May you be free from bitterness and pain. I see you. I remember.*

The last piece of wood, the size of a silver dollar, smooth and curved, is for our son, Jonathon. For dreams lost, the pain of childhood and adolescence, and adulthood. *May you be free. I see you. I remember. We remember.*

I toss in pine cones for the Wee Ones, my tiny sister who never breathed a breath and my unborn daughter. Bill asks if I know they were girls. *Yes. No. Does it matter?* They came to me as girls who showed me the way to laugh and skip and string daisies in an open field.

I add the obituary of my grandfather to the fire. Pieces of our story. The bag that held the treasures goes in too, for all the stories, spoken and unspoken, remembered and forgotten. I make this offering in honor of them.

Finally, I add the letter that has become a love poem to my loved ones. *I am your wings. You are my weight.* Together we fly into the night sky, lifted by fire, carried to the sea on the wind, cradled by the Mother Love that holds us all. Yes, the Mother Love. Those stern-faced women that *do* know how to love and dance and string their own daisy crowns in the field. They are still learning. As am I.

A newborn baby breaks the silence on the beach with his cry. A toddler comes down the path reaching for the warmth of our fire. His father gently guides him away. New life is rising. A young Eastern man with a motorcycle helmet sits by our fire at the curve of the log. He stares into the light but does not look our way. *I see you*, I silently say. He walks away in his own silence.

A small group of five or six about fifteen feet away from us have built their own fire. They munch on burritos and talk quietly among themselves. Life is all around us. A train rolls across the track to the east. A glimpse of my great-great-grandfather. I hear the clanking of wheels on the track. Our fire dies down. Bill and I are famished. The sun has set, evensong past. We gather our remaining things, say goodnight to the sea, walk back through the grove of white birch trees and head home. Tomorrow is a new moon. A new day.

It's the middle of the night at home, and I can't tell if it's this book project, my wacky dreams, or the whispering ancestors who have woken me up. One thing I know for sure is that I have to write. This book's end is forming.

I think once again of Cokorda Rai, the *balian*, and his words to me. "You are a happy, happy woman." If I were to die today, I would die a happy woman. Daily healing is taking place for our family, particularly for my son who set me on this journey of discovery. Jonathon is making his own way in the world, supporting himself as a tattoo artist, raising his daughter, working the Twelve Steps, writing inventories, attending meetings, and making amends. It is deep work. I wonder if he will always remain a bit distant, like the lone man standing on the far side of the bridge in my dream. Or will he come closer as my father has in recent years? Will we be blessed with continued healing and connection?

I continue to feel the strong thread between my father and son even though they never met in this earthly realm. It makes sense, therefore, that the man who helped raise me and his journeying spirit have made their way back to this story. While in Bali, I not only celebrated my sixtieth birthday, but also the forty-first anniversary of my father's physical death. I feel his absence in my life alongside his ethereal presence as I witness him in the whimsical black butterfly wings.

Weight and wings. My story carries it all. I imagine yours does, too. Weight and wings. Bees and stones. Boulders and butterflies. The weight of my story has given me wings to fly around the world.

My father was a rambling man. I'm not sure if he was ever truly happy. Apparently he enjoyed small spaces like the inside of a World War II submarine and the cabin of his eighteen-wheeler truck. But he liked large spaces, too—the open road and open sea. He was a sailor and a truck driver who, as long as I knew him, lived landlocked in the middle of the United States right off of Route 66. I hope he lives more freely now.

In Bali, hanging on the wall of a tiny café on Jalan Tirta Tawar is an original sign for Route 66. The Universe showing off yet again with her signs. They are everywhere, if we only open our eyes to see. Can I doubt that my father was there in Bali with me? Am I an authentic lightworker or am I merely open to possibility that time and space are not linear?

When I saw Cokorda Rai, I felt like he was reading my mind. Of course, he did and he didn't. It's not like he crawled inside my head and read a script scrolling past on a teleprompter, but still I knew that he could sense something more significant than could be logically named. We humans are travelers. We journey inside our minds and bodies every day.

I grew up in Oklahoma where the summers were blistering hot and humid. I've always wondered what produced so much humidity in that interior state. At my core, I am a tropical girl who doesn't complain when the temperatures rise in Seattle, my hometown of nearly thirty years. The tropics, however, kept beckoning. I was going back to Bali.

Three days after I arrived home in mid-September, the nudge to return to Ubud whispered its wisdom. There was more learning for me there. December is a hard month for me in the States with the fa-la-la-la-la of the holiday season and the darkness leading up to the Winter Solstice. I would travel to Bali shortly after Thanksgiving and return home to Seattle when the days began to lengthen again.

CHAPTER 39

Lonely Liquid Time

"Come with me, where dreams are born, and time is never planned."

—Peter Pan

December 2016

Time is liquid, especially while traveling. While at the writers' residency in Tuscany, my mind turned backward to Ireland, the Wee Ones, and lost childhood dreams. In Ireland, I saw myself in the future riding a camel in Egypt. In Egypt, I journeyed with Moses and the Sinai Christ. Paris had its own rhythm, and while in Bali, my words and essence blended back to the Tuscan hillside and the wise ones who travel forward and backward with me through this timeless, nameless wonderland.

It's morning in the pedestrian artist's village of Penestanan, where I've come to write for a month. I rest on the balcony of my tiny apartment, curled up on the chaise lounge. Loneliness seeps in. How can that be when I'm here in paradise? Loneliness is the bailiwick that shadows me regardless of place or season. Its arrival is often a precursor to a lesson I need to explore. Such is the way of the SoulStroller.

On this day, the weather is gray, gray, gray . . . *and* it is green with the lush richness of the countryside. I sit writing and whining to Nihdi, the house cat, about the darkness and my loneliness.

SoulStrollers may find loneliness as a precursor to a needed lesson.

Finally, I open an online lesson focusing on the season of darkness surrounding the Christmas holidays and the Winter Solstice. It is my own season of struggle. This doesn't change just because I've left the Pacific Northwest for a few weeks. Funny how I imagined I was heading toward the light.

A black ant, like the one who greeted me on my first Bali trip, journeys beside me on the balcony railing and disappears into a crack in the wood. Am I willing to disappear into the darkness and go deep? Am I avoiding my work here and blaming it on the weather? The Yule lesson asks how I will endure the darkness and then shows an image of a woman draped in fog, holding a bowl in her hand.

My inner wisdom responds: *Cup the darkness in your hands like a fragile gift. Sink into your feelings. Don't try to turn them into something they're not. Be okay with being alone. This is an inward time. This is why you're here. There is a boat that holds your stories. Turn it over and let them pour out like tears trailing down your face.*

The follow-up question: What is the potential here? The corresponding image is of six women dancing around a fire.

My internal response comes: *Dance in this darkness. Awaken the fire in my belly. Dance as if no one is watching. Write as if no one is reading. Light my own fire in this darkness. That is why I am here!*

Time melts. The stories of Tuscany beckon—Maiden, Mother, and Crone, the women who dance around me in the field, my tribe of ancestors and allies who call out in the darkness. I am led back to these stories that are timeless. May they dance in me until I feel the heat. It is safe here.

A white flag blows in the open rice field outside my tiny Balinese apartment. *Surrender*, it waves. *Surrender*. Open field. Fronds blow. Women dance. Tuscany blends with Bali, dancing forward and backward in time. *Surrender to the moment. Be who you are.* Maiden. Mother. Crone. Princess. Crag. Frog. Ant. Bee. Butterfly. We are all one.

The banana leaves and palm fronds wave hallelujah. *Yes! Yes! Yes!* The flag floats higher. Rooster crows. Hens cackle. The bridge story comes back into focus. *Yes*, the wind answers. A crossing. A pasture. A rice field. They are the same. Open spaces made for open hearts. The sun peeks through the heavy clouds, reminiscent of a sun break in Seattle. *Be here now.* The black butterfly is here with me again. It lands two feet away, then swoops off, chased by a red dragonfly. Wings. Weight. Magic is stirring. Deep breaths. Hanging on and letting go. I stand at this threshold, trembling.

It's Sunday in Ubud and I'm feeling rather wobbly. Lack of sleep? Too much rain? This isn't the Ubud I left in September, or perhaps I am not the same me. My head aches and the man next door pounds something with a hammer. A round *bule* walks by on the path below without his shirt. A rooster crows. Always a rooster crows. And when I begin to think I'm on this journey unaccompanied, the black butterfly wings by. My father is here.

Cicadas rise in song. Birds twitter. Roosters crow more. I need something, but I can't articulate what. I want to walk and I don't want to. I think about lying down to read, but then it feels like wasting the sunshine. *I'm on a threshold.* I need to find more ways to put my voice into the world. I don't want disciples. I don't want fame, but I do need to be heard. It's like my voice is playing hide and seek. When I travel, it rises to the surface like incense on the temple altar. It's there and then it's not.

This day I feel discombobulated. I think the shoulds are form-ing an army to take over my peaceful mind. They march through with phrases like *you should write* or *you should walk* or *you should take an aspirin to stop that incessant pounding*, but the pounding is both inside and outside. Life feels relentless. The only end game is death and even that I'm not so sure about anymore. I've been here before. How do I know? What do I see? Does it matter? I am here now. A voice on the path calls, "Come." Is that for me? Am I to come? A whistle pierces the air.

The ancestors are calling again. The signs are here. The black butterfly. The conversation I had last night with new friends, Melissa and Christine, traveling their own road. The article that showed up on my feed early this morning about ancestry. Another friend's Instagram post dittos the signs. I am immersed in the ineffable. I need incense and offerings and altars, the simple pieces of ritual that create meaning where words cannot suffice. I think about the class on healing the ancestral wound. I hear the ancient drums beating inside my chest. I long to sit in a temple and feel the touch of Cokorda Rai on my crown. I see the dragonfly. I want to walk. I need to fly. I am like the passion fruit swinging from the vine, not quite ripe.

I feel ripe and then I don't. I blossom and then fade. I reach and fall. I meditate like a yogi and then snicker like a school girl, all in the same moment. Last night in meditation, all I could hear were the frogs. The instructor using her most somber meditation voice. The voice. The one that can only be heard through the crown of my head or my third eye, if then. It is barely audible.

The theme of voice speaks even in the softest whispers. Black butterfly swoops across the balcony and nearly hits me in the head when I begin to write about voice. I must be on the right path. At least I'm on the journey. My eyes travel downward, away from the green passion fruit on the vine until I see another fruit, nearly ripe. Is that me?

Blessings on the ripening of us all. Blessings on this house. Blessings on me. Blessings on this day. Again, my mind goes back to offerings and tiny packets of holiness. I place flowers in my hair. I buy incense, but don't find the one I want. My thoughts jump like the tailless squirrel leaping across the power lines. Where is my power? How shall I bless? What shall I write? I am here now, watching the clouds roll in and the sun vanish, feeling my chest tighten, my throat close, my voice waver and grow stronger.

Yesterday, I was exhausted by mid-afternoon. My eyes drooped and my sanity begged for a nap that never came. Then, when it was time to sleep, I was wide awake after making two trips to the cash machine. One was for cash. The second was an unsuccessful attempt to retrieve the debit card that I left in the machine in my jet-lagged haze.

Today, I awoke early, around 5:00 a.m. Before the roosters began their earnest business, my mind was buzzing.

Find your rhythm. Remember it. It's the moment-by-moment one. Go take a dip in the pool. Really? It's 7:00 a.m. Why not? Check the temperature. Does it matter? Is the pool clean and fresh? Maybe. I need to swim then shower then eat then write and/or walk to the bank in town for that damned ATM card. Or simply be . . .

A bee stares at me from the page of my journal. *Weight and wings. Be kind to yourself. Go take a swim.*

And so I do. I step over all the reasons that swimming didn't make sense, like the sun wasn't out or I might wake my hostess or . . .

Walking through the still house, I push open the sliding door that I hadn't seen closed until now. The air is warm, but not hot. A bird makes a cat call. *Is he talking to me?* The quiet garden wraps around my spirit. Palm leaves the size of a full-grown elephant's ear wave in the breeze. Red bamboo-like stalks flash amidst the green Eden. I step into the pool and the cool water swallows my calves. I stand like a shivering statue and allow my body to adjust. The tailless squirrel leaps across the electric wires overhead and chatters. *Do it. Do it. Do it.* I suck in my breath, lift my arms over my head, and dive into the bracing water.

My chest clinches until I begin to move my arms in a crawl toward the other end of the pool. It's barely twenty feet in length, hardly long enough for lap swimming, so it's convenient that I'm not a lap swimmer. *You don't even swim.* One more argument for not getting into the water.

Whose voice is that? I ask as I propel myself back and forth, back and forth. Clearly, she doesn't know what she's talking about.

The morning air and water swallow me whole. I feel my body relax. The restless night washes away and I am restored. I hear the latch on the outside entrance loosen, and a striking Balinese woman dressed in ceremonial attire, lace top and sarong, comes through the wooden gate near the top of the pool.

"Hello," I say from my watery world.

"Hello." I notice her body shift. I've startled her.

"Are you Wayan?" I ask.

She nods.

"I'm Kayce." She nods again, smiles, then goes about her task.

She's come to make the house offerings. First, she removes the old offerings from the altar on the wall at the far end of the pool. Then she lifts the fresh gift to its place, lights the stick of incense, and waves her hand to send the fragrance toward the sky. I watch in rapt attention. This is my ceremony, too. Wayan seems to understand this.

She finishes at the altar opposite me, then comes over to the shallow end of the pool where I float in awe. What is happening? It's like my edges have softened and now blend into the aqua water. Tears shimmer like holy water as Wayan bends her knees and places another offering on the ground barely two feet from me. We are all in this together. The packets. Wayan. Me. Holy. Holy. Holy.

Three small bundles of greenery and twisted banana leaves are folded together and hold marigold, fuchsia, and pale blue blossoms. Wayan places them on the paneled deck, lights the single stick of incense, then sprinkles a water blessing over the trio. The aroma is heady as it fills my nostrils and I watch it waft into the heavens. I linger in the pool (*or does the pool linger in me?*) and allow the sweet scent to wash over my face and tickle my nose. Now I am air. Rising, rising, rising. The curtain lifts and it's like all the elements have gathered and conspired to carry me into this new day. Earthy flowers. Baptismal water. Fiery incense. Wisps of floating air. We have become one. Magic has arrived. Simple and pure.

CHAPTER 40

Mile High Prayers

*"Wherever you are, if you are close to God, you are close.
If you are far away, you are far away. It doesn't matter
where you live. It matters what you feel."*

—Anastasis, *Walking the Bible* by Bruce Feiler

December 2016

There was wildlife revelry in my room last night. This time a
catfight between Nidhi, the house cat, and a neighborhood stray.
They shattered the silence at around 1:00 a.m. and I got up this
morning to discover balls of black and white fur scattered across the
teak floor. Two nights ago, a large gecko—or perhaps the stray—
slid down my tile roof creating a racket. A few nights before that,
an army of tiny black ants invaded my bed. Sleeping in open-air
apartments is not without challenge. I wouldn't have it any other
way.

My alarm goes off at 5:30 a.m. I wash my face, brush my teeth,
dress in loose pants and a cotton top, and throw a bottle of water
into my daypack. I have a 6:00 a.m. date with a driver I've never
met to go to a site I just heard of, arranged by a meditation teacher
that I took a class from one evening. All feels right with the world

as I make my way to the bottom of the Campuan Stairs in the morning light and keep my eyes open for Mudiana, the driver.

Today is the ceremony for the full moon. Manis, the meditation instructor, usually takes a small group to celebrate *la bella luna* (my words, not hers) each month. She's unable to do so this month, but since she could see the disappointment and ache in my eyes, she arranged for her cousin, Mudiana, to drive me. Her "spiritual sister," Ning, is going to meet us at Puncak Penulisan, the site of Pura Tegeh Kahuripan, the oldest and highest temple in Bali. She will accompany me in a prayer ceremony. Somehow this temple treasure has stayed off the tour bus circuit and no one seems to know why. After visiting, I feel like the gods have protected it for visitors who show due reverence for this holy space. Dating back to the megalithic era (think Stonehenge 300 BC), little is known about the temple's history, which contributes to its magical ambience.

One and a half hours outside of Penestanan, through rice fields and curving mountain roads, I'm glad I took my motion sickness medicine. Even though I've been traveling for more than half a century now, my tummy still sours under such conditions. As we pull into the village of Sukawana, Mudiana tells me that the dense traffic we are experiencing is nothing compared to what will begin around 3:30 p.m. Villagers from all over the mountain will arrive to participate in the traditional ceremonies.

Near the bottom of the steps, a woman, barely five feet tall, wearing a maroon puffy coat over a white cotton top, sarong, and sash, waves us toward a parking space. This is Ning. She welcomes me with a nod, eyes my clothing, and says something in Indonesian to Mudiana. He hands her the blue canvas bag that he's carrying and opens it to reveal my official ceremonial attire. Ning ushers me into an open-air shed and nods again. I pull off my pants and she adeptly wraps me in the sarong.

"You want to wear that top or this one?" She holds up a white lace blouse, a *kebaya*, the formal ceremonial attire.

"That one," I gesture.

"Yes. This is more beautiful." She nods one more time. I pull off my own embroidered top and pull on the *kebaya*. Ning wraps a sash around my waist and my outfit is complete.

Welcome the stranger. Inwardly, I hear the words I've so often spoken. Today, I am the stranger. We climb up thirty steep stairs to where two statues draped in golden cloth stand. Ning asks me to wait. Before we can continue—before *I* can continue—she must offer a gift and a prayer to welcome me, the visitor/stranger. It is good to be welcomed. Being the stranger can be hard. I didn't see another *bule* that day except at the restaurant in Kintamani. I think for some of the children we saw, I was the first *bule* they'd ever seen.

Intrepid climbers, Ning and I make our way to the top of Pura Tegeh Kahuripan, one step after another. Ning stops to catch her breath at each flat segment and for that, I'm grateful. While I don't know at exactly what elevation we began, Puncuk Penulisan is 5,725 feet, basically one mile, above sea level. I'm thankful for the hills I climb at home in Seattle.

Three people are praying at the temple when Ning and I arrive at the top. I walk around the perimeter and take some photos of the surrounding area and different altars. Ning joins me and shares the meaning of various gods and symbols, then we sit together on a multi-colored mat to pray and meditate.

It's hard for me to slow my mind and settle in at first, partially because I've removed my shoes and am sitting on my feet. Today, this feels very uncomfortable. Nevertheless, it is peaceful sitting next to her. Ning emanates goodwill, humility, and a deep reverence for this space. Her manner is contagious.

To begin the ceremonial prayer, Ning shows me how to

symbolically cleanse my hands with herb grass and incense
from the small offerings we have carried to the temple. It is my
introduction into the deeper meaning of these tiny packets that
have mesmerized me since I first arrived in Bali.

The first flower we hold in our hands is yellow. The prayer
is to the sun, for welcoming the light into our lives. Next come
white, red, and yellow to acknowledge and pray for our neighbors.
We take the blossoms and tuck them behind our ears and into the
plaits of our braids. Finally, we select more white, red, and yellow
in honor of the world. We sit side by side, our palms together at
our hearts. Ning chants her prayers in Hindi and my lips move
along with her.

Oh Lord, hear our prayers.
The brokenness of the world. May the light come in.
May we be healed in the broken places.
May we all come to be neighbors, everywhere around the world.
May the ravaging of our forests, land, and seas cease.
May we all be protected.
Oh, Lord, hear our prayers.

East meets west and west joins east. No longer are we strangers.
My sweet friend, who is at least six inches shorter than I and twenty
years my junior, and I are locked in a soulful dance. We speak
through our hearts, not our heads. This is why I travel. This is
why I write. To heal the broken places in my heart and the heart
of the world. To meet a stranger who alchemically transforms into
a soul friend.

The incense carries our prayers to God. Ning offers me holy
water, first sprinkled like a baptism and then with three sips to
drink. Holy. Holy. Holy. Finally, she places moistened rice on my
forehead, temples, and upper chest as a symbol that I have prayed

today. To show that I have entered the temple with this sister and made offerings to the gods.

Ning apologizes in her broken English for not being able to teach me more. I am overwhelmed and grateful for her presence. We walked up the stairs as strangers, but we came back down as friends and neighbors. After we have descended the infinity of stairs, she gives me a milk-banana (indigenous to Bali) and two sun cakes. We hug each other, take a few photos together, and say goodbye. I hope to see her again.

Mudiana takes the wheel and drives us down and around and back up to Kintamani where I have a view of Mt. Batur, the lava fields that destroyed a village in one eruption, and Lake Batur, the largest lake in Bali. It's a cloudy morning, but clear enough to see the vast beauty.

In the restaurant that Manis selected, I dine on a breakfast buffet of noodles, spicy rice, crepe-like pancakes and little tempeh sandwiches, plus coffee and fruit. Bali magic surrounds me. I am a princess, but this is not my kingdom. I will always be a *bule*, but my spirit is here thanking God—the God who does not care what name we use. This power greater than us throws beauty at my feet. Green, blue, gray. These are the shades of the world today.

I take a couple of selfies, then Mudiana snaps a panorama for me. I smile at the rice on my face and wonder when all those wise wrinkles appeared. Then we start off for Mudiana's village far, far below Kintamani. Down we go, winding through narrow, pot-holed roads. There are hot springs near his village, heated by the volcano. He tells me that atop Mt. Batur, the steam is so hot you can cook an egg or a banana in the ground. There is a purple elephant (Ganesha perhaps) guarding the springs. It seems garish and out of place in this simple site that Mudiana calls "the real Bali."

An onion and tomato farmer, he has lived here his whole life, traveling only throughout Indonesia with no desire to go elsewhere. He is happy with his village and family; his wife Made, a boy aged eleven, a girl who is seven, and a baby on the way. Made speaks no English and seems to dislike me at first, but I realize she is shy. Yes, we have that in common. She is missing a few teeth, but her smile is warm and welcoming when she lets it out.

I wait in their modest home while Made and Mudiana dress for the village temple ceremony. Today we will welcome the full moon and if I understand correctly, we will visit a temple that is only used for full moon ceremonies. I am honored, grateful, and a bit intimidated to participate with all their neighbors. For the most part, I am welcomed with nods and handshakes. Ning has prepared me well for the ceremonies.

I truly miss ritual in our Western culture. It has been bastardized in many ways and the joy and beauty have been squeezed out with requirements and shoulds. Perhaps that has happened here too, but I don't think so. This is a celebration of community and gratitude.

Once we arrive at the village temple, I go with Mudiana into the open-air temple after a large group leaves. Made is not allowed to enter because she is pregnant and her husband tells me that she "honors the old ways." I follow Mudiana's lead and offer my prayers for sun, neighbors, and world in the same way Ning and I did at Puncak Penulisan. Incense, flowers, prayer, holy water, rice. We repeat the ritual together.

There is one more temple to visit. This one is larger with more of the village in attendance. The atmosphere is festive with balloons and people grilling food. Traffic police dressed in black are lined up and waiting for things to get busy, all the while smoking cigarettes. It's like a football game tailgate party. Later in the afternoon, the volunteer police will need to direct all of the traffic that is expected to come.

Mudiana and I enter the open air temple. We repeat the prayers. Made waits. I feel braver and ask to take more photos with the villagers. The police volunteers say yes. A shy little girl teases me and turns away. I see dyed birds, smaller than sparrows, in cages next to huge Mylar balloons and plastic toys for children. The people here are stunning in their beauty and warmth. I am grateful, so grateful.

Made and I ride in the backseat together. She offers ripe, sweet passion fruit to share and oranges the size of a baby's big toe. Best oranges ever! We arrive back at their home where I change out of my ceremonial attire, bow goodbye to Made, and offer thanks for the hospitality. My day in the village comes to an end and Mudiana and I begin the long drive back. I am templed up and tuckered out. The skies open up and rain pours down on the road. I later learn that this is an auspicious sign in Bali. My day has been sealed with good luck.

Our outing ends in the Bintang Supermarket parking lot. We say our goodbyes and I put on my pink rain poncho to walk the remainder of the way home. I'm soaked by the time I arrive, washed clean by more holy water from the sky. What a day! I'm exhausted and filled with gratitude.

Throughout the day, I watched myself from the outside and silently asked, "Who is this woman? The one who climbs mile high steps and makes offerings to the world?" She is I. I am she. A citizen of the world. An accidental pilgrim turned intentional. A SoulStroller. The one who says yes to follow my heart and see more of the world. The world that is my family now.

Take Your Soul for a Stroll

SOULST**RO**LL

I leave home and return. Following the seasons and the rhythms of my soul. The act of return and recede. It is ancient and new.

R is for remembrance, returning, receding. Opening more. Resounding with a wide-open *Oh My God!* as Louie Schwarzberg taught us. SoulStrolling® reminds us to rest and restore, because it is through rest and remembrance that our souls are rejuvenated. And yes, R is for rhythm—finding your own and living it in harmony with the world. Ritual. Risk. Reverence. Opening and offering ourselves to others.

At the time I traveled to Bali, it was the most exotic destination I'd ever visited. It was there that I found myself, a former Methodist girl born in Oklahoma, walking barefoot in Hindu temples and dancing naked in the rain. Of all the R's I've listed, I believe *reverence* is the one that resonates most loudly. Reverence for this amazing world that we live in. Reverence and respect for the individuals who welcomed me into their homes and shared their sacred rituals. Reverence that I opened myself to hear and listen to all that was offered to me during that time. It is my task to remember my stories of Bali, butterflies, bricks, and more.

Practice SoulStrolling®

- R is rife with possibilities. Make your own list. See what resonates. Then do the same for O. You've got this!

- Through SoulStrolling®, I've reignited my love for ritual. Consider which practices resonate with you. My way of experiencing ritual varies according to time or season, but one of the most beneficial is meditating first thing in the morning. I do it before getting out of bed. Writing in my journal while sipping a cup of tea or coffee sets my day up with a soulful beginning. Consider what rhythms or rituals support you best whether at home or away. Make it a priority.

- Remember that return and recede is a rhythm of the earth. Like the tides flow out and in, flowers blossom, die, and bloom, and the sun rises and sets followed by the moon. Such is the way of the SoulStroller. Notice how this rhythm flows in your own life.

PART EIGHT

Fini for Now

"There will come a time when you believe everything is finished. That will be the beginning."

—Louis L'Amour

CHAPTER 41

Following the Story

"Follow your story. It knows the way."

—Sarah Selecky

When a writer nears the end of a book project, there's always a question that looms: What have I forgotten or left out that still needs to be said? What do I want to write that I haven't tackled because it feels too scary or big? Have I said enough or perhaps too much? It's a sobering process. I've already shared the tale of the Wee Ones—my miscarried sister and aborted daughter who tracked me down to heal while I was on my Ireland pilgrimage. Theirs was a tough disclosure.

I spent hours, days, weeks, and months, considering how my story of growing up intermingled with that of my family—Bill, Jonathon, Janey, my parents and my siblings. I wondered how this narrative might impact them. Our stories intersect *and* they are unique. No two people grow up in the same family or share an identical experience. I would never dare to say that any one of the individuals in this book would mirror my description with their own. Yes, I changed a few names and places to protect anonymity, but I kept true to the telling and constructed scenes to describe the moments as best I recall.

From the beginning, I knew this was *my* story even though I was unaware how others would find their way into it. When I traveled to Ireland in 2009, I was finally beginning to deepen my personal practice of listening to my intuition. I began stepping into the realm of the ancestral mind that's associated with the area of our brain that makes meaning through feelings and images. The ancestral mind has the ability to connect with the world that lies below our consciousness. It is also associated with the attributes of wisdom and joy. It was a wildly different life approach from the fact-and-figure thinking mind I'd been raised to rely upon.

My connection with this intuitive way of being had been stirring inside me for I-don't-know-how-long. It was there when I heard the *yes* to that first trip to Paris and then again when I stared out my Seattle window on a gray March morning and the call to Ireland whispered my name. It was present for me as a child skipping around the block, waving a wand of ribbons and stars. When I begin to think of all the times and ways my intuition and the ancestral mind have showed up to support me, I must pause and take a deep breath, because I realize it's always been within me, waiting to be acknowledged.

It was on that first trip to Ireland that my dream of the brick-layers came to pass. While it's impossible to mete out all of that dream's messages, one thread is clear: the bricks. In the center of my core, I hear my grandfather's voice say, "Build your story and follow your dreams, brick by brick."

Brick by brick, I've been reconstructing my life and my ancestry. Stringing together stories like Great Aunt Trudy placing cinderblocks in her desert home. But me? I want a whole bloody cathedral, a fully formed story, to manifest like a bouquet of flowers out of a magician's sleeve. *Now!* I feel like I'm building the *Sagrada Familia* in Barcelona, Gaudi's masterpiece that has been in the works for over a hundred years and is still unfinished. Building is a process, writing and storytelling are mine. I'm learning in tangible ways that life is not about the destination, it is about the journey. Trite, but true.

Bricks and rocks. Symbols of Mother Earth. The stones of Ireland, those talismans for the heaviness in my life; the ones I held in my hand as I walked the trails of Glendalough and the boulder that smacked me down that crystallizing moment in 2003. The ancient whisper of bricks and rocks, weightiness and whimsy, and the lands where I've traveled rises upward in my soul. Feathers and stones. Streamers and sunshine. Weight and wings.

Weight and wings are the stuff of life. Being grounded in the earth, so we can lift our wings to fly. If we ignore the whispers to soar, we stay inert and immobile. We cease to love, and speak, and grow. Too little grounding and we lose connection, become flighty, and threaten to vaporize into thin air. When I began to recognize bricks and stones as paths and gateways to the eternal—instead of stumbling blocks—I sprouted wings from the keel of my sternum and raised them to the heavens along with my voice.

A part of me shrinks away from the telling because that part still worries about other people's criticism and judgment. What if this story is too wacky, worrisome, or weird? I hesitate, because I don't trust that you, dear reader, will fully understand or join me in this messy mystery. And then, in a moment of clarity, I realize that I don't care.

Of course, I care about you and what you love and believe and dream, *and* . . . The bounty of my heroine's journey is that I've come to trust myself, to trust my own voice in this process, and to know and believe deep within my soul that the stories strung together here are the necessary, misshapen pearls of my life that need to be told. They are formed from gnarly lessons not unlike granular nuggets inside an oyster's shell.

What else am I to do but write? To speak? To listen? I hear the ancestors whisper through the waves that crash outside my open door in Kauai, Hawaii, where I've come to finish this book.

Are they the same imps who jumped in my suitcase when I began this manuscript more than three years ago? Three years. Three aunts. Three (or more) pilgrimages. Three Marys. Three horses. Three magi. Six years old times ten. More threes. I am here now. My voice echoes at a higher vibration than it did when I was six or sixteen or fifty-six or last week. Numbers dance through my thoughts along with images. Six. Sixty. Dancing naked in the rain. Returning to nature like a skipping child. Once again, I'm wearing pigtails and my body is healthier than ever. Perhaps I could live to be 120. We never know when, how, where, or in what way our voice will find us. Perhaps in the glens of Ireland, or along the cobblestone streets of Paris, or tucked inside a cozy bed with a purring furry companion. Yes, it's possible I could have learned these lessons without ever leaving home. Of course, we have the opportunity of learning anywhere, at any time, but there is a power in stepping into new landscapes that are tinged with awe.

I don't believe I would have met my own Wee Ones in the same way I did if I had not sat with a pilgrim community in that fireside room in Glendalough and listened to the stories of the *cillín* and the unbaptized children. These children symbolize so many other forgotten ones. Tiny beings with no choice or voice to cry out in the world. Because I had set an intention of welcoming and offering hospitality during that pilgrimage, my spirit was open and God heard my cry in ways that had not happened in the United States in the forty-something preceding years.

Walking in the footsteps of Moses in the Sinai Desert where I heard the sun rise and rode Bella the camel, who punctuated the value of my own rhythm, could not have happened any other way than they did. Feeling the stones of Notre Dame beneath my feet, to know what it's like to stand on solid ground and hear Joan of Arc whisper words of solace from the heavens could only happen in Paris. Joan became a bit of an *anam cara* (soul friend) the day I prayed to her for my growing children and my young friend who had abruptly died from a brain aneurysm. Joan of Arc was burned at the stake for hearing voices. My hunch is that had she and I lived in the same era, I, too, might have been burned at the stake like the witches in Tuscany.

The voices and signs are everywhere. Ancient places have been storing them for centuries. The United States is a relatively new culture. I'm drawn to old treasures like Native American traditions, Celtic communities, and Balinese rituals that rely on spirit and the natural world. Like me, the world became voiceless when cultures began to rely only on thought. Our world is filled with opportunity and magic. At least my world is.

The cobblestones of Paris hold secrets not found in Seattle. Bali's air is infused with countless blessings like the *canang* (offerings) that line the pathways, homes, and temples there. Standing on the plains of the Burren in Ireland, I could hear the ancestors whisper through the breeze and feel their solidarity beneath my feet. Sailing through the Camargue on horseback, my body became one with the setting sun. It is impossible to describe the ineffable. This is why I tell a dear friend who recently acquired her first passport (even though we share a birth year), "Go someplace ancient. Pick a spot. Use your passport." I resisted adding, "Before it's too late."

Collecting stamps on my passport is not what I set out to do. This journey began by following my intuition and a desire to return to something I could not yet name. It surfaced on the road to Kino Bay in Mexico when I pulled over to witness the fingers of God rising out of the Saguaro cactus field into the heavens, and for that brief moment I knew I was never alone. The desire was with me when I skipped around the block to kindergarten. Was that when my journey began? Or did it begin before I was born with my great-grandfather J.C. Gilmore who planted seeds in Seattle after raising his girls in an Oklahoma City neighborhood that would ultimately become an artist's community? One of those girls was Great Aunt Trudy. Maybe my journey began when she headed to the Mojave Desert and placed that first cement stone and built her home with her own hands. Or did the story begin with my grandfather, John David Stevens, the man who was killed by bricks? Or seven generations before him? Or . . .

I ask myself one more time, what needs to be said? There are more threads I could tug and pull, stories left untold or undone. So what really matters? The journey matters, inner as much as outer. Voice matters. My voice. Your voice. The ancestors' voices. They wave their hands wildly from every corner of space and time. *Me. Me. Me. Don't forget me. Us. We matter. We may matter the most!*

I hear their message loud and clear. The ancestors are the threads of my journey toward wholeness and rewriting the story of what it means to be alone. The great aunties who hopped into my suitcase. My father on the hillside in a Tuscan dream. The patriarchal and matriarchal lines. The men who dance. The girls who giggle. They've showed up as butterflies and bricks. Met me in waking hours and dreams. Atop horses and hillsides. With drumbeats and washing waves. The ancestors matter. Their voices matter.

The places along the way are the containers, the cathedrals and deserts and cinderblock buildings. They hold moments in time. Travel opens up space in a different way than living in the quotidian. SoulStrolling invites us to take steps wisely and jump in wholeheartedly. The journey matters, no matter how you or I embark on or interpret it.

I said at the beginning of my tale that this telling is a labyrinth. Well, so is the living. It is not linear. It folds in and over itself, comes back to the beginning or near it, then veers out further and wider. I am drawn to places where the veil between here and the beyond barely exists—places like Ireland, Bali, barren deserts, as well as cultures where art and history abound like Paris and Italy. I am seduced by locales where symbols speak. The divine thing is that through my practice of SoulStrolling, paying attention, and deep listening, I am now able to hear the world's voice more clearly wherever I am, at home or away.

It's never too late to make a new ending. When people say to me things like, "I could never" or "I'm too old" or the myriad of other thoughts that get in the way of change, I ask: "Are you still breathing . . . even a little bit?" If the answer is yes, then isn't there room for one more yes, and perhaps another and another?

My *yes* is to travel in whatever method presents itself, to live freely and move unencumbered by fear and worry, and for my loved ones to do the same. That each of us— you and I—become and live as glowing free spirits. For my husband to be healthy and well; my daughter to be strong and calm and at peace; my son to find solace and happiness,

SoulStrollers know it's never too late to say yes to a new ending.

to be secure and love himself. For my ancestors to be remembered and me alongside them.

We see in others what we ourselves have. I look into the hearts of those who surround me. I see darkness, pain, and longing. I see the imprints of history, family, and society. I wonder about the seven generations that will come after me and those that have gone before. I see hurt, frailty, and fear, but mostly I see love and light.

Looking into each face around this circle, I am affirmed in the things I want to do and say in my lifetime that is both finite and infinite. My greatest desire is to bring more love and light into the world, to help illuminate the dark corners inside us, to reclaim lost voices (both living and ethereal), to invite wounded souls to take a stroll toward healing, to remember (for myself and others) the exuberance of skipping like a five-year-old and dancing naked in the rain at any age. I validate my own experience by feeling the solid earth beneath my feet as my toes curl around the stones. I experience the freedom of spreading my wings to soar through the heavens when a flock of parrots rushes by. And in this moment, I know that I am no longer voiceless. I trust that I am perfectly imperfect just as I am. I am an intentional pilgrim who is never alone. I am a SoulStroller.

In her book, *With Love for the Journey*, Lou Ann Granger says the stones didn't speak to her until she began to bring art into her process. We are each different. I see the signs everywhere now—in cups of coffee with hearts and leaves, in an owl painted on a local mural or graffitied on a grungy wall, in a four-year-old girl atop a horse in Sayulita. My life is infused with meaning and yours is too.

With sincere gratitude for reading and witnessing my journey, I issue this invitation to you: Please stop whatever you're doing. Pause. Pay attention. Follow *your* signs. Listen for the call. When it comes, *Go!* Pick up a pen and write. Purchase a plane ticket and fly. Take your beautiful soul for a stroll.

Take Your Soul for a Stroll

SOULSTRO**LL**

It's never too late to make a new ending. Are you still breathing . . . even a little bit? If the answer is yes, then isn't there room for one more yes, and perhaps another and another?

L is for letting go of limitations and limiting beliefs. Laughing until you cry. Crying until you laugh. It's for listening and learning.

And, of course, L is for Love. Love. Love.

S urrender

O pen

U nite

L inger

S tretch

T rust

R emember

O ffer

L et go

L ove

One more time I offer this invitation with sincere gratitude: Stop whatever you're doing. Pause. Pay attention. Follow *your* story. Listen for the call. When it comes, *Go!* Take your soul for a stroll.

Learn more at www.soulstrolling.com

With Gratitude

"If the only prayer you ever say in your entire life is thank you, it will be enough."

—Meister Eckhart

"How can you sleep when there is a river of gratitude flowing through your heart?" The pesky-yet-wise voice beckons me one final time in the hours before dawn. She begs me to write these words that will never feel like quite enough. I resist the call because I'm afraid I might forget someone or the words won't be perfect. Old patterns die hard.

If there's one thing I've learned on this journey, it's to simply begin. Take a step. Write a word. Trust the whisper and follow the story. I awaken with names and faces flowing and speaking through my dreamlike world. *Remember us. Remember me.* It is another labyrinth to navigate. Where do I begin? *At the beginning, of course.* Ah, but where is that?

The ancestors. I will begin by thanking the Wee Ones, the giggling girls, the women who string daisies in the field. Rooftop dancer. Kissing aunts. The brick man and his legacy. Seven generations before. Seven generations after. Those I cannot name and those I can who offer me their grace and say, "We know you know. We hear your thanks."

Please, dear reader, know that if you're following these words, I am grateful for you and offer thanks for being on this journey. You matter to me even if your name doesn't appear on these pages. Memory, like luck, is a fickle mistress. You matter. *Merci beaucoup.*

To Terri Leidich at BQB and WriteLife publishing for trusting me as an author and saying, "Please send us your manuscript. We want to read it." For my dream editor Olivia Swenson, who accepted this project in a messy state and formed the unshaped messages of my mind and heart into a story that others could follow. You made what might have been an excruciating project fresh and exciting. What a blessed journey!

To the readers of my early manuscripts—Sharon Richards, Dianna Woolley, Jan Fisher, Theo Nestor. To those who listened to me read aloud while this story wrote me and I found my voice— Shelby Duckworth, Betsey Beckman, Jen Louden, Julie Gardner, Sarah Selecky, Lemon Tree House, and all the writers who joined us at writing sessions and workshops around the world.

To my creature companions Curry and Aslan. The winged ones—bee, butterfly, hummingbird, dragonfly, flamingo, owl, raven, eagle. The four-leggeds—Bella, Furia, the pups and kittens.

To Terri Gaffney, Christine Valters Paintner, and Pixie Lighthorse—the spiritual mentors who taught me that grief can be a healing balm. To Mrs. Peck who opened her arms, wrapped me in unconditional love, and introduced me to my magical power of helping others awaken.

Karen Mace, who offered an invitation for the bridge stories to emerge. Charissa, who taught me what it means to cross over. Marylinda, who shared the definition of nefelibata and made my heart sing with truth. Pamela K, who reminded me of the strength in knowing that we never stay lost.

For the therapists, teachers, and mentors who came alongside my family and me. I couldn't have done this without you. The Seattle School of Theology and Psychology, Kay Hartzog, Carole Rosenberg, the Soltura Foundation, facilitators Alix, Pamela, Nancy, and dear Frank who now resides with angels. My island sisters—Lisa, Laura, Corky, B.J., and Sandi. Martha Beck and the Wayfinders 2011. The open-hearted women of Earth Medicine

School. Debra Smouse, who nudged me to set deadlines and write down my goals then shared with me her own symbol of becoming.

To my SoulCollage® sisters. The late Seena Frost. Judith Prest. MaryEllen, August, and Jenny—you ladies mean the world to me. Joanna Powell Colbert, who introduced me to her beautiful Gaian Tarot deck and helped break down my hesitancy to learn from things I'd been taught to fear. Carl Jung and Joseph Campbell, I give you a nod too.

For pilgrimage guides Regina, Marcus, and Rabia. Thank you for following your personal call and inviting me to come along. To all my fellow pilgrims, especially Donna, Christine, Arleen, and the Sisterhood of the One-eyed Camel. To Phil Cousineau for his inspiring work *The Art of Pilgrimage*. To all of the SoulStrollers around the world, especially Lisa, Erika, Leslie, Jody, and the Betsys. There will never be another "first" like you ladies! *Merci beaucoup*.

To Betsy P., who witnessed my blurt when I was asked the question "If you could do anything," then held me accountable. To Jaylene, who pressed *The Lightworker's Way* into my hand and said, "Take my copy. You need to read this." She was right. To Alix, who saw something in me, then spoke it and followed up with her gift of *The Artist's Way*. May you and yours experience deep peace, love, and beauty each day.

To the blogging community of the early 2000s. Kate Iredale, Abbey of the Arts, Sunrise Sister, Geezer Dude, and more. You welcomed me into a broader world and encouraged my voice that was beginning to emerge. To Tess who followed her own *yes* and joined me in Paris and Ireland. Thank you for trusting your quiet whispers. Your lilting voice is etched on my soul.

For all the authors, poets, scholars, musicians, and artists who offer up their works and words that grace the beginning of each chapter in *SoulStroller*. You inspire me. To my guides and hosts around the world who welcomed me into their homes and cultures.

Ruth, Wayan, Made, La Frazione, the Bedouins, Glendalough Inn, Chester and the mechanics. For luscious accommodations, AirBnbs around the world, and lumpy sleeping bags under star-filled skies. The drivers, cooks, waiters, shopkeepers, and all of the angels unaware!

To Wilson and Camplese—my September sisters—who swore they would have pulled me back down the aisle in 1976 like a runaway bride if only I'd spoken up. Big love to you for hanging in there with me across time and space, through stability and change. It takes a long time to make an old friend.

To Sharon Richards. What can I say? You taught me how to laugh and skip again and to embrace freedom and sing silly rhyming songs while dancing along foreign shores on mist-filled nights. We need another book for our soul-filled adventures. *Merci beaucoup, mon amie. Je t'aime.*

Last, but never least, my family. My parents John and Daisy Ernestine. Thank you for letting me share pieces of your story. May you be at peace wherever you are. To Dianna. For many years you led the way as big sis. Now you walk beside me, an *anam cara*. Who knew there was an artist and an author buried beneath all those good girl rules? Hurray for us! Brother David, I love you. Follow your story. It knows the way.

For my French son-in-law (yes, I have one) Max, who brings me wine and asks how my writing is going. Thank you for loving my daughter. For Brenna, who stood her ground when naysayers said circumstances weren't right to bring a child into the world. You are a great mom to our precious Violet Grace. Thanks for listening to your truest self.

Violet, you give this story a happy ending.

To Bill, my beloved, who has gone to hell and back with me. Sometimes together. Other times not so much. Your steadfast support means the world to me. I don't know of anyone else who would put up with my shenanigans for more than thirty years. May we continue to stroll, laugh, love, and travel for many more to come.

Maryjane, you are my heart walking around outside my body. It's an honor to be your mother and watch you blossom and grow into the beautiful woman that you are. Thanks for traveling to Bali with me and becoming my friend along the way.

Jonathon, this book is for us. You are a healer whether you know this truth or not. I hope one day you will find the perfect platform to share your story. The world needs to hear it.

To each and every person who has touched my life, I say thank you. The divine in me bows to the divine in you.

Namaste. Amen. Later y'all.

About the Author

Kayce Stevens Hughlett is a soulful and spirited woman. In her roles as author, spiritual guide, artist of being alive, and speaker, she invites groups and individuals to playfully and fearlessly cross the thresholds toward authentic living. A strong proponent of compassionate care in the world, Kayce's live and online work focuses on the principle that we must live it to give it. Her early career began with a multi-national accounting firm to be later refined as the path of an artist. She delights in walking alongside others as they explore and unearth their own pathways toward passionate living. Co-creator of SoulStrolling, Kayce holds a Masters in Counseling Psychology from The Seattle School of Theology and Psychology and is a Certified Martha Beck Life Coach. Kayce is a trained SoulCollage facilitator and colleague of Abbey of the Arts—facilitating the formation, nourishment, and deep inner work of soul care practitioners. Raised in the heartland of Oklahoma, she now resides in Seattle, Washington with her family and muse, Aslan the Cat. Discover more at www. kaycehughlett.com